CANDIDATES '88

Congressional Quarterly Inc.
1414 22nd Street N.W.
Washington, D.C. 20037

Photo Credits: p. 21—*Washington Post;* p. 39—Sue Klemens; pp. 55, 141, 247—UPI/Bettmann Newsphotos; pp. 71, 191, 205—Associated Press; p. 89—Marty Katz; pp. 109, 125—Frank Johnston/*Washington Post*; p. 159—Marty LaVor; p. 219—Nydia Leiby.

Copyright © 1988 Congressional Quarterly Inc.

All rights reserved. No part of this publication may be reproduced or transmitted in any form or by any means, electronic or mechanical, including photocopy, recording, or any information storage and retrieval system, without permission in writing from the publisher.

Printed in the United States of America

Library of Congress Cataloging-in-Publication Data

Candidates '88.

    Includes index.
    1. Presidents--United States--Election--1988.
2. Presidential candidates--United States. 3. United
States--Politics and government--1981-
I. Congressional Quarterly, inc.
E880.C365   1988   324.973'0927   88-3886
ISBN 0-87187-458-X

CANDIDATES '88

PREFACE

Four years ago there was a sudden surge of interest in Gary Hart, the surprise winner of the New Hampshire Democratic presidential primary. People wanted to know more about the man, his record, his political philosophy, his so-called "new ideas."

Newspaper subscribers to Congressional Quarterly were well prepared to supply that information. CQ, as it's commonly known, had profiled Hart and other major candidates several weeks before the primary. Many newspapers ran the Hart story intact; others used it as a framework for their own articles. Directly or indirectly, CQ had again provided important, straightforward information to the public.

That was not unusual. The great newspapers, television networks and other news media that keep you informed rely heavily on CQ for reliable, thorough, unbiased data about Congress, government and politics. So do libraries, colleges and businesses all across the country.

Congressional Quarterly Inc., a Washington-based editorial research and publishing company, is a subsidiary of Florida's *St. Petersburg Times*, a newspaper that confines its diversification to related journalistic or publishing enterprises, including the *Trend* magazines of Arizona, Florida and Georgia, and *Governing*, the new CQ magazine covering state and local government.

When *St. Petersburg Times* publisher Nelson Poynter (1903-78) and his wife, Henrietta, founded CQ in 1945, they set the high journalistic standards that still guide the company. They said, "Congressional Quarterly presents the facts in as complete, concise and unbiased form as we know how. The editorial comment on the acts and votes of Congress we leave to our subscribers."

The *Weekly Report* magazine was and still is CQ's basic publication. An electronic online information system, Washington Alert, provides immediate access to the full text of the *Weekly Report* as well as to CQ's databases of legislative action, votes, schedules, profiles and analyses.

Other CQ publications include the *Congressional Monitor*, a daily

Preface

report on congressional committees, and the newsletters *Congressional Insight*, a weekly analysis of congressional action, and *Campaign Practices Reports*, a semimonthly update on campaign laws. CQ's Editorial Research Reports covers current events in weekly and daily reports.

Congressional Quarterly also publishes college political science textbooks under the CQ Press imprint and timely paperbacks on current public affairs. CQ hardback reference books include *American Leaders 1789-1987*, the *Guide to Congress*, the *Guide to the U. S. Supreme Court*, the *Guide to U. S. Elections*, *Politics in America* and, soon, *Congress A to Z: CQ's Ready Reference Encyclopedia*.

The CQ *Almanac*, a compendium of legislation for one session of Congress, is published yearly. Other annual books include *Historic Documents* and the *Washington Information Directory*. *Congress and the Nation* is a record of government and politics for a presidential term.

In conjunction with other organizations Congressional Quarterly publishes reference books that have become staples of political science research. They include *America at the Polls* and the *America Votes* series (both with the Elections Research Center) and *Vital Statistics on Congress* (with the American Enterprise Institute).

In election years Congressional Quarterly publishes a variety of paperbacks about the candidates, the issues, the timetables and other aspects of the races coming up. For 1988 these books have included *Candidates '88*; *Elections '88*; the *Guide to the 1988 Presidential Election*; *National Party Conventions 1831-1984*; *Presidential Elections Since 1789, Fourth Edition*; and *Race for the Presidency: Winning the 1988 Nomination*.

All of the profiles in *Candidates '88* were carefully reviewed to ensure that they met CQ standards of quality. The editor and one of the writers, Philip D. Duncan, is the current political editor of the CQ *Weekly Report*. Other current or former staffers who wrote the profiles were Peter Bragdon, Ronald D. Elving, Dave Kaplan, Dirk Olin, Margaret C. Thompson and Thomas C. Watson. The other authors were Richard Marshall, a free-lance writer specializing in foreign and military affairs; Joel V. Nilsson, an *Arizona Republic* editorial writer who formerly covered Arizona state government and politics; and Ann Downing Schmidt, a veteran reporter formerly of the *Denver Post*.

One of the men profiled in this book almost certainly will be the next president of the United States. The writers and editors of *Candidates '88* have done their best to give you all the pertinent, unadorned information about that man.

Editor: Philip D. Duncan
Assistant Editors: Colleen McGuiness, Dirk Olin, Thomas C. Watson
Writers: Peter Bragdon, Philip D. Duncan, Ronald D. Elving, Dave Kaplan, Richard Marshall, Joel V. Nilsson, Dirk Olin, Ann Downing Schmidt, Margaret C. Thompson, Thomas C. Watson
Coordinator: John L. Moore
Production Assistant/Researcher: Richard Karno
Proofreaders: Jane S. Gilligan, Jodean Marks, Tracy W. Villano
Indexer: Bernice Eisen
Artist: Dan Sherbo
Cover Designer: Julie Booth

Congressional Quarterly Inc.

Eugene Patterson *Chairman*
Andrew Barnes *President*
Wayne P. Kelley *Publisher*
Neil Skene *Executive Editor*
John J. Coyle *General Manager, Electronic Information Services*
Robert E. Cuthriell *Director of Development, Electronic Information Services*
Jonathan C. Angier *Business Manager*
Robert C. Hur *General Counsel*

Book Division

Robert C. Hur *Director*

Book Editorial

David R. Tarr *Director, Book Department*
John L. Moore *Assistant Director*
Joanne D. Daniels *Director, CQ Press*
Mary W. Cohn *Associate Editor*
Nancy A. Lammers *Managing Editor*
Carolyn Goldinger *Senior Editor*
Margaret Seawell Benjaminson *Project Editor*
Ann Pelham Cullen *Project Editor*
Ann Davies *Project Editor*
Carolyn McGovern *Project Editor*
Colleen McGuiness *Project Editor*
Jane S. Gilligan *Production Editor*
Kerry V. Kern *Production Editor*
Noell H. Sottile *Production Editor*
Kimberly A. Davis *Editorial Assistant*
Richard Karno *Editorial Assistant*
Linda White *Secretary*

Book Marketing

Kathryn C. Suárez *Director, Book Marketing*
Jacqueline A. Davey *Sales Promotion Administrator*
Ellen Kresky *College Services Coordinator*

Production

I. D. Fuller *Production Manager*
Maceo Mayo *Assistant Production Manager*

TABLE OF CONTENTS

Introduction   1
   1988 Presidential Primary and Caucus Dates   4

Profiles
   Bruce Babbitt   17
   Bill Bradley   35
   George Bush   51
   Mario Cuomo   67
   Robert Dole   85
   Michael S. Dukakis   105
   Pierre S. "Pete" du Pont IV   121
   Richard A. Gephardt   137
   Albert Gore Jr.   155
   Alexander M. Haig Jr.   171
   Gary Hart   187
   Jesse Jackson   201
   Jack Kemp   215
   Pat Robertson   233
   Paul Simon   243

Other Candidates
   Lyndon H. LaRouche Jr.   261
   Harold Stassen   262
   James A. Traficant Jr.   263

Candidates' Previous Elections Results   267

Index   273

INTRODUCTION

Candidates, Spectators, Process and Expectations

In the movie "The Last Hurrah," aging mayor Frank Skeffington asks a sportswriter which American spectator sport is most popular. When the writer starts comparing ticket sales, the mayor smiles and answers his own question. "Politics," he says.

In politics, of course, spectators also participate. They choose the winners. In the big leagues of presidential politics, fans of all degrees of devotion get to watch a pre-season, an actual voting season, playoffs and a kind of World Series between the party champions—before determining who has won.

Approaching 1988 many spectators foresaw a season of historic importance. For the first time in two decades the voting would begin without an incumbent president in the race. This attracted big fields in both major parties—a rarity in our history. Because the contest seemed so wide open, both parties were expected to enter their heaviest hitters. It was widely presumed that any political figure of national or regional significance would find this presidential cycle irresistible.

Partly because of this increased pressure, and partly because of events in recent presidential elections, the nominating season (the primaries, caucuses and summer conventions) spawned a pre-season of unprecedented length and media interest. In this period, beginning even before the congressional elections of November 1986, the candidates stalked each other and staked out their territory—politically, intellectually and financially.

The candidates were also being scrutinized by the media, particularly by a small community of reporters for major newspapers and magazines. The heavy media coverage would not begin until the Iowa caucuses in February of 1988 (except for occasional bursts of notice surrounding candidate announcements and withdrawals). Yet a handful of full-time presidential reporters were crisscrossing the country in 1986 and 1987, in greater numbers and with more resources (including space in their publications) than had ever been marshaled so early. Their work would identify and characterize the "short list" candidates. And it would subtly inform the opinions of the far larger cast of image makers and opinion makers that would follow.

For some, the size of the early fields and the intensity of early interest meant that multiple, well-matched candidates would battle through to the final weeks of the 1988 primary season. There was even talk of nominating conventions that would really decide nominations, rather than merely rubber-stamp the products of the caucuses and primaries.

Structural interest was also added by the expansion of what had become known, in 1984, as "Super Tuesday." That year nine states had held primaries or caucuses on the second Tuesday of March. For 1988, 20 states were planning to express their Democratic presidential preference on March 8. Seventeen of these were also scheduling their Republican choice for that day. And while this was the closest thing yet to a national primary, 14 of the states involved were below the Mason-Dixon line.

Finally, some spectators eagerly awaited the election as a referendum—not so much on President Reagan's two terms in office as on the nation's future direction. Would the "Reagan revolution"—lower tax rates, higher defense and lower social spending, aggressive anti-communism abroad—be continued, intensified, modified or reversed?

The answer would not be determined by the November general election alone. Equally momentous choices might be made in the spring and summer decisions, as the parties winnowed the field in search of a winner. The champions of each party would then meet in a final test of themselves—and of the national mood. The results might even be construed as a political watershed, from which power and policy might flow in new directions.

The Republican Field

The most intriguing aspect of any pre-nominating season is the jockeying for position among individuals who think they may have a chance of being elected president. This includes those who know they cannot be the next president, but who think they may be president some day if they start running now. Others do not expect to be president but have another purpose in mind—personal, political or ideological.

Introduction

In the Republican Party, which voters have preferred in recent presidential politics, the overwhelming facts of the pre-season were the personage and stewardship of Ronald Reagan. The man had revitalized the party and redefined conservatism. At his popularity peak, some said he would also realign the electorate, installing the GOP as the majority party for the first time since Franklin D. Roosevelt established Democratic hegemony half a century earlier.

In one sense, this created a favorable context. Prospective heirs to the Reagan legacy had a clear sense of what that legacy was and of their subservience to it. Whatever mixed feelings the general electorate might have about Reaganism, no prospective heir could afford to denigrate the patriarch within the family.

The would-be inheritors began with the nation's number-two man, Vice President George Bush. Here was a former congressman, national party chairman, special envoy to China, director of the CIA—and a Reagan loyalist to the point of self-effacement. In turn, Bush enjoyed the loyalty of most GOP officeholders and traditional party players. His problem was his win-loss column as a candidate. Elected to a safe Republican seat in the House, he had twice run statewide and lost. Running for president in 1980 he had won a plurality in Iowa but had been badly embarrassed in New Hampshire (and thereafter) by Reagan.

Bush's main 1988 challenger was Robert J. Dole, who was thought to have handled the Senate well as majority leader in 1985 and 1986. A conservative but pragmatic politician, he was attractive to traditional Republicans appalled by the Reagan-era budget deficits. But Dole carried bruises from the party's loss of the White House in 1976, when he was the vice presidential running mate of President Gerald R. Ford. His own disorganized presidential bid in 1980 collapsed early. Once a political point man for President Richard Nixon, Dole had never shed his image as an ignoble infighter—too quick with quips that cut too close to the bone.

Next on most GOP lists was Jack Kemp, the Buffalo congressman and former professional quarterback who had adopted more of Reagan's upbeat style and rightist philosophy than either Bush or Dole. But despite his fine conservative credentials (especially on taxes) and a decade of working the country, Kemp remained frozen in the polls and without a clear path to a breakout in any early states.

The wild card was Marion G. "Pat" Robertson, known primarily as the TV evangelist who founded the Christian Broadcasting Network.

Party Primary, Caucus Dates ...

This updated calendar includes 1988 presidential primary and first-round caucus dates. The Republican contests select 2,277 delegates to the GOP convention. Democratic primaries and caucuses select 3,517 out of the 4,162 delegates to their national party convention. The Democrats'

Date	Primaries	Caucuses
Feb. 1		Kansas (begins) (R)
Feb. 4		Hawaii (R)
Feb. 8		Iowa
Feb. 9		Wyoming (begins) (R)
Feb. 16	New Hampshire	
Feb. 18		Nevada (R)
Feb. 23	South Dakota	Minnesota
Feb. 26		Maine (begins) (R)
Feb. 27		Alaska (begins) (R)
Feb. 28		Maine (D)
March 1	Vermont (non-binding)	
March 5	South Carolina (R)	Wyoming (D)
March 8	Alabama	Hawaii (D)
	Arkansas*	Idaho (D)
	Florida	Nevada (D)
	Georgia	Texas (D)
	Kentucky	Washington
	Louisiana	American Samoa (D)
	Maryland*	
	Massachusetts	
	Mississippi*	
	Missouri	
	North Carolina	
	Oklahoma	
	Rhode Island	
	Tennessee	
	Texas*	
	Virginia	
March 10		Alaska (D)
March 12		South Carolina (D)
March 13		North Dakota (begins) (D)
March 15	Illinois*	
March 19		Kansas (D)

... For Selection of Presidential Nominee

remaining 645 delegates are guaranteed slots by virtue of the party or elected positions that they hold ("superdelegates").

States in which presidential and congressional primary voting occurs on the same day are noted with an asterisk (*).

Date	Primaries	Caucuses
March 20	Puerto Rico	
March 22	Democrats Abroad (mail-in ballots due)	
March 26		Michigan (D)
March 29	Connecticut	
April 2		Virgin Islands (D)
April 4		Colorado
April 5	Wisconsin	
April 16		Arizona (D)
April 18		Delaware (D)
April 19	New York	Vermont
April 19-20	Democratic Senate and House superdelegates selected	
April 24		Guam (D)
April 25		Utah
April 26	Pennsylvania*	
May 3	District of Columbia* Indiana* Ohio*	
May 10	Nebraska* West Virginia*	
May 17	Oregon*	
May 24	Idaho*	
June 7	California* Montana* New Jersey* New Mexico*	
June 14	North Dakota*	
July 18-21	Democratic National Convention in Atlanta	
Aug. 15-18	Republican National Convention in New Orleans	

Robertson spent the pre-season raising money and lowering the profile of his religious career. He resigned his ordination and insisted he not be called a TV preacher or televangelist. But he also pitched his candidacy to fundamentalist-evangelical Christians turned off by the conventional political process. This "Invisible Army" of supporters served him well in early caucus states but showed relatively poorly in the bigger vote pools of the primaries—including in his presumed stronghold in the South.

Rounding out the GOP field were two horses as dark as any in recent memory. One was former Delaware governor Pierre S. du Pont IV, who preferred to be called Pete. Intelligent, patrician and often forceful, du Pont was arguably the most attractive gentleman in the early joint appearances of the candidates. He won the endorsement of the iconoclastic Nackey Loeb, publisher of the largest newspaper in New Hampshire. But his voter response was weak enough to force him out after that state's primary.

The only Republican striking his tent even earlier was retired Army general Alexander M. Haig Jr., who had been Nixon's last chief of staff and Reagan's first secretary of state. Haig seemed to be in the race to beard Bush and vent steam about the directions Reagan's presidency had taken after Haig resigned.

The Democratic Field

In 1986 and 1987 the departures from the lists of Democratic contestants generally drew more attention than the entrances. These included, in order of their demurral: Massachusetts Sen. Edward M. Kennedy, New Jersey Sen. Bill Bradley, New York Gov. Mario Cuomo, Arkansas Sen. Dale Bumpers, Arkansas Gov. Bill Clinton and Georgia Sen. Sam Nunn.

And, while a preponderance of big names opted out, two high-profile candidacies flamed out. The first and foremost of these was former Colorado senator Gary Hart's. The 1984 runner-up to nominee Walter F. Mondale, Hart had been so far ahead in the polls (preferred by more than 60 percent in Iowa) that most considered the nomination his to lose.

But lose it he did, when a newspaper reported he spent a May weekend alone with a Miami model. Hart denied impropriety, but the story unleashed a cavalcade of cheesecake pictures and a catalog of other accusations regarding Hart's private life. Hart left the race within a week of the initial newspaper exposé and spent several months in a kind of limbo. Finally, unable to stay on the sidelines, he re-entered seven months later as a low-budget dark horse. Briefly, he seemed to have shattered the field and taken the lead again in some polls. But the novelty of his return faded after his lackluster initial appearances with the other candidates. With his latest boomlet over, Hart's support dwindled to the point of being microscopic.

A major beneficiary of Hart's fall was presumed to be Delaware Sen. Joseph R. Biden Jr. Almost unknown nationally, Biden had gained attention as an uplifting orator and a bright new face. He assembled an impressive staff. But he also borrowed several lines from a speech by a British politician without attribution. The ensuing media scramble discovered inaccuracies in Biden's résumé and misstatements of his record. Shaken, he pulled out of the race.

The Biden fiasco was traced to a tape (later called an "attack video") provided to reporters by a staffer for another candidate, Massachusetts Gov. Michael S. Dukakis. For several days, the adverse publicity threatened the governor's candidacy. In the end, Dukakis sacrificed his campaign manager and political coordinator to the furor; but his rebuilt organization would still be the envy of his party rivals. An uninspiring campaigner, Dukakis made headway with a low-key pitch of managerial success and competence. And as other white candidates with appeal to liberal voters stayed away or fell by the wayside, Dukakis loomed ever larger.

Jesse L. Jackson, the only candidate from 1984 still playing a major role in presidential politics, reached the spring of 1988 in a state of new and special grace. While still tied closely to the black vote, he had begun to draw impressive numbers in states with few black voters (New Hampshire, Vermont, Maine, Minnesota). Moderating his earlier associations with militants of one stripe and another, he seemed increasingly focused on an insider's power in the party in 1988 and beyond. Ironically, he was the single candidate best positioned to prosper in the Southern regional primary on Super Tuesday.

The flip side of Jackson's Southern coin was that of Tennessee Sen. Albert Gore Jr. Tempted into the race by fund raisers seeking a moderate-conservative Democrat, Gore had withdrawn from the Iowa and New Hampshire contests to concentrate on his home region. The strategy of staking everything on the South was a risky one, but it paid enough dividends on Super Tuesday to keep Gore in the running.

In the pre-Super Tuesday voting, Dukakis' main competitor was Rep. Richard A. Gephardt of Missouri. A sixth-term congressman and chairman of the House Democratic Caucus, Gephardt mobilized scores of fellow House members to campaign for him. But with pre-Iowa polls showing him mired near the bottom, Gephardt recast his message. The new line was a hot brand of populism—relief for farmers and retaliation against trade competitors. Although badly mauled as a flip-flopper by TV interviewers, newspaper editorialists and Democratic competitors, Gephardt had found an audience and was threatening to go all the way.

Clinging to candidacy was Illinois Sen. Paul Simon, who took second in Iowa and third in New Hampshire but slipped in subsequent tests and saw his funding base shrink to zero. Although he almost had to stay in for the March 15 primary in his home state, his candidacy was de facto finished when he could not afford to compete in Super Tuesday states.

The first Democrat to drop out was former Arizona governor Bruce Babbitt, whose candor and humor had charmed much of the media. Like Gephardt, Babbitt focused on Iowa to the near-exclusion of the rest of the country. But his message did not find an audience—at least the kind that could act as a cohesive force. After another humble outing in New Hampshire, he withdrew.

The Profiles

This book profiles all the major pre-season candidates who remained in the running as 1988 began. Although some of these were winnowed out early in the primary and caucus process, their effect and significance were not necessarily retired along with their campaign apparatus.

Several may reappear as vice presidential possibilities at the conventions, or as power brokers who could deliver delegates to a candidate still in the running. Any of them may run for president again, and some almost certainly will.

More important, each had his effect during the preliminary phase of the campaign. Haig was the man who pushed Bush hardest on the latter's role in the Iran-contra affair. Babbitt was the one candidate to detail his complete plan for reducing the federal budget deficit, including an unpopular national sales tax. By so doing, he forced the other candidates to tell more of their plans. Du Pont was willing to take the even more

Introduction

perilous position that Social Security would not perform as promised for young people now entering the workforce.

Each of these candidates had his ideas extensively aired in the debates and forums that preceded the Iowa caucuses and the New Hampshire primary. And it is this full range of candidates—with their ideas and personalities—that defined the presidential debate of 1988.

Moreover, each of these candidates offers another interesting specimen of American politics—if not at its best, at least at its highest level. To study them together is to learn how a combination of personal drive and impersonal process elevates certain personalities to great power and responsibility.

Also profiled here are Cuomo and Bradley. Although Cuomo steadfastly refused to run, he nonetheless retained an air of mystery. On the weekend before Super Tuesday he drew overflow crowds when he visited Texas. And he was certainly the likeliest draftee should the Democratic convention find itself deadlocked in Atlanta in July.

Bradley's role as instigator of the 1986 tax code overhaul and his background as a Rhodes scholar and professional basketball player gave him a certain "star quality" lacking in the active Democratic candidates.

Precarious Expectations

To hope is always to risk disappointment. And as the long pre-season gave way to actual caucuses and primaries early in 1988, the expectations of some spectators looked as battered as those of some candidates.

The candidates themselves were the first source of disillusionment. In the Republican Party, Reagan's prospective successors had always known they would suffer somewhat in comparison with the incumbent. An argument may be made that most, if not all, of these claimants could grow into the presidency as well as Reagan did. After all, Reagan's own qualifications had been highly suspect when he sought the presidency in 1968, 1976 and 1980. But the perceived deficiency of the 1988 GOP candidates was not one of competence but of political magnetism. None of the six major contenders offered the winning personality—or commanded the personal loyalty—that powered Reagan's last three presidential campaigns.

But if no one had been expected to match Reagan's assets, no one had quite expected to shrink along with Reagan's own force and stature.

If no one in the field was considered the president's peer, it was no help to have the president appear as disengaged and decidedly mortal as he often did in 1987. And it did not help to have his administration besieged by the Iran-contra investigations, distracted by lesser scandals and stalemated by a Congress where Democrats had reclaimed control of the Senate.

The Republicans also felt a chill wind in October 1987 as the stock market dropped 500 points in a day. The economy did not come apart, but no one can read the political history of our century without noting that the GOP has yet to fully recover from the Crash of 1929.

The Democratic candidates had no successful patriarch to overshadow them. But their party seemed hobbled by the candidate blunders—and the epidemic of cold feet—that afflicted them in the preseason.

As a result, the remaining candidates seemed, at least for a time, inadequate. They were derided for months as "the seven dwarfs." These newer aspirants, some still little known nationally when the voting began, seemed inherently less newsworthy than their erstwhile competitors or their counterparts in the GOP.

In an era of divisive issues (civil rights, the Vietnam War, Watergate, recession, inflation, high taxes or a general perception of national weakness) candidates could augment their perceived importance by association with issue positions. But the 1988 Democratic field seemed to disagree on relatively few issues (trade policy being the major exception).

In general, the Democrats were forced to compete largely as personalities, as if participating in what one campaign staffer called "a national job interview." But, except for Jackson, the man who had carried black aspirations all the way to the convention in 1984, no one in the Democratic field was much good at exciting an audience—in person or on TV.

The Process

In the absence of galvanizing issues or charismatic personalities, the campaigns competed largely as organizations. Great weight was attached to such fundaments as filing delegate slates and identifying and turning out individual voters (the campaign trail term was "block and tackle").

Even in the final days of campaigning before Super Tuesday, much of the Democrats' energy seemed drained by the mechanics of airing commercials and moving the candidates rapidly from airport to airport. The "negative advertising" used by several campaigns to attack rivals often dwelt not on substantive differences but on procedure. Gephardt was criticized for taking money from corporate interests. Dukakis was scored as a dirty campaigner.

The campaign seemed caught in its own thicket. Some spectators began to wonder whether this election was about anything more than getting elected.

To some degree, the process would have loomed large in 1988 regardless of issues and personalities. Several reasons for this suggest themselves. But surely the first is that candidates in years past have manipulated the mechanism well enough to seize the nomination. This was once thought of as the McGovern scenario, in recognition of then-senator George McGovern of South Dakota, the nominee in 1972. It later became the Jimmy Carter scenario, following the Georgian's even more improbable march to the nomination in 1976. Today, some of the campaign's younger road warriors refer to it as the Hart scenario, referring to Hart's nearly successful ambush of Walter Mondale in 1984.

Poring over these recent histories, the candidates of 1988, especially on the Democratic side, envision themselves taking the same sort of quantum leap in the national consciousness. If a relatively minor senator can run so well on so little money and fame, and if a peanut farmer and former Southern governor who'd been out of office for years can not only win the nomination but move into the White House, then why not a first-term senator, or a boyish-faced congressman or the governor or ex-governor of a relatively small state?

The media contribute to this. Campaign mechanics, though often arcane, have become a major subject for news reporting, commentary and public debate (especially as pre-season political reporting has become a cottage industry). Of course these mechanics were widely perceived as susceptible of manipulation by the candidates. But despite this, or perhaps because of it, the early contests mesmerized national reporters and other political opinion makers.

It no longer seemed to matter whether Iowa, where the first large-scale caucuses are held, or New Hampshire, the first-primary state, really revealed anything that should be meaningful beyond the borders of those states. What mattered was that the nation had been programmed to believe that they did.

Everything may be different in 1992, but no one should count on it. First, the early states have realized such palpable benefits from their positions in the batting order that they will never willingly relinquish them. Second, the candidates themselves find it expedient, if not downright mandatory, to cater to these small states where a relatively modest amount of money can have a high yield.

And third, the media too have found these gatekeeper states an economical means of narrowing big fields of candidates. For a major network that must commit overkill for competitive commercial reasons, it is far easier to commit and manage resources to multiple candidates in Iowa or New Hampshire than it would be in a larger state or region.

The Perversity of Reform

For all these reasons, 1988 seemed bound to disappoint those spectators who craved a long campaign featuring many competitive candidates and many points of view. Instead, the early voting chopped the two fields as ruthlessly as in years past. Bush and Dukakis proved that superior organizations with strong financing can beat weaker and poorer organizations—even when the latter have arguably stronger candidates with distinctly sharper messages for the voters.

Money, organization and media have long been the watchwords of successful national campaigns. If 1988 proved anything, it proved that 20 years of tinkering with the nominating system (mostly by Democrats, although the GOP has been forced to hold more primaries) have only served to change the identity of the insiders who wield disproportionate power over the nomination.

For many generations, delegates to the nominating conventions were chosen by bosses from state and local political machines, by labor and business leaders, by elected officials and by wealthy contributors. Their choices pleased those they represented, and the general electorate took a "wake us when you've decided" attitude. As recently as 1968 Hubert H. Humphrey won the Democratic nomination without having participated in a single primary.

But Humphrey's victory destroyed the system, which was seen as having frustrated the party's peace wing. Ascendant following the debacle of that year, the anti-war activists designed a new system more conducive to nominating one of their own.

Since then, the rules that worked for McGovern in 1972 have been modified to restore some power to elected officials and party insiders. But the heavy lumber is swung by special-interest groups (including unions), community activists, candidate-oriented volunteers and hired consultants. The money comes not from a handful of big donors but from a handful of big "collectors" who bundle large, legal individual contributions (up to $1,000 per person) for delivery to cash-starved candidates.

In 1988 spectators will be treated to the ultimate example of unintended consequences—Super Tuesday. A change in the rules so pronounced as the 20-state delegate extravaganza of March 8 was bound to change the game. But opinion was divided as to whether selecting nearly a third of the convention delegates (31 percent among Democrats, 33 percent among Republicans) on one day would make the race a dash or a marathon. Given a date relatively early in the voting season, it might seem to shorten the process by enabling an early pacesetter to assume an insurmountable lead.

But the Southern originators of the strategy believed it would enable a Southern candidate, or one with strong appeal in the South, to survive weak showings in early tests (especially Iowa and New Hampshire). With relief ahead on the calendar, such a candidate could continue raising money and then leapfrog the pack in the Southern regional voting. This would enable him at least to extend his bid into the later rounds of primaries.

The Southerners also wanted to heighten interest in the Democratic side of things among moderate to conservative white males. This group had moved toward the GOP in national elections and sometimes taken their local and state votes with them.

As it happened, however, Super Tuesday got too big. The candidates could not spend concentrated time in any Super Tuesday state and instead campaigned on the airwaves and in the air between airport news conferences. The immense cost of such tactics meant only a few candidates could be competitive. Most ironic of all, Democrats in many Southern states had to watch their party defined on Super Tuesday by its two most liberal candidates—Dukakis and Jackson.

Watching for a Watershed

The ultimate disappointment for electoral spectators may be the failure of the 1988 election to fulfill its historic potential. The weakening of the Reagan legend and the rapid acceleration of changing circumstances seem to be moving the campaign away from the controversies of the 1980s, and perhaps away from the left-right dynamic. Ideologically inclined observers are already talking about 1992 as an election more likely to produce a decisive victory with far-reaching effects for the nation's political future.

The voting of 1988 is unlikely to do more than pick a person the nation prefers to its other options. Although that may seem a reductive description, it is generally all the presidential election process has ever done. Reagan was preferred to Carter, as Carter had been to Ford. Even the great divides in American politics have involved the choice of a personality, who then took the country in a direction he may or may not have signaled during the campaign. Even so pivotal a president as Franklin D. Roosevelt was a narrow choice at the convention. And he then ran on a platform that gave little hint of the New Deal that would follow.

Political caution—also called timidity—has kept most of the 1988 contenders from detailing real plans. The candidates who were most explicit (such as Babbitt and du Pont) were also the first to fold. Historically, where presidential candidates have proposed stark policy choices they have generally been rejected.

A Not-So-Distant Mirror

In 1988 the electorate is not driven by the distress of 1932 or 1968. Nor is it so dissatisfied with the status quo as it was in 1976 or 1980. Barring another collapse of stock prices, an economic disruption of equal magnitude or the outbreak of a war, the electorate may well enter the autumn with a great collective yawn.

The 1988 election seems more analagous to the last contest in which a personally popular, two-term Republican president was leaving office. His late years in office were marked by flagging momentum, Democratic gains in Congress, minor but bothersome scandal, a faltering space program, a communist takeover in Latin America and shaky prosperity at home.

That was in 1960, when the retiring incumbent was Dwight D. Eisenhower. The president's party nominated his vice president, who had never been especially close to the incumbent either personally or politically but who had been seen as slavishly loyal. The Democrats nominated a relatively little known liberal from Massachusetts.

Introduction

The Nixon-Kennedy race proved one of the closest in our history. Perhaps the chance to decide the outcome of a similar contest will make American political spectators forget their disappointments in 1988.

Ronald D. Elving

March 1988

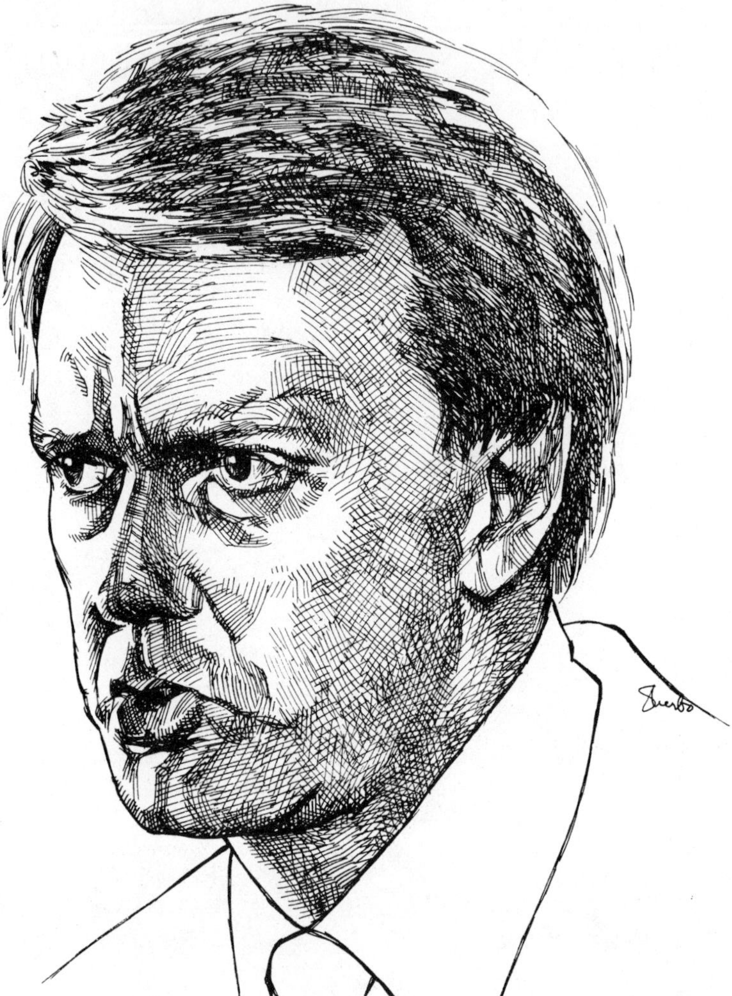

BRUCE BABBITT

Dark Horse Stands Up Alone for Raising Taxes

Former Arizona governor Bruce Babbitt was about as dark as a dark horse could be among contenders for the 1988 Democratic nomination. He was not just relatively unknown. He was arguably too candid for his own political good.

From the outset, Babbitt and his staff were accustomed to poking fun at what they called their "asterisk status" in national public opinion polls, wondering what it would take to rise above the 2 or 3 percent mark. Somehow, they remained quietly confident that the candidate's background, plus superb organization in Iowa and New Hampshire, would replicate Jimmy Carter's 1976 campaign.

However, the candidate faced an obstacle that was still taller than obscurity: his own plan to raise taxes. In the middle of 1987, Babbitt began telling audiences that federal budget deficits could not be brought under control by cutbacks alone. He castigated the inability of Congress to set priorities via the automatic, across-the-board cuts mandated by the Gramm-Rudman-Hollings deficit reduction law. He argued that infusions of revenue would be required.

Babbitt called for a national consumption tax—exempting food, medicine and housing. The candidate insisted that this was the proper and progressive complement to program cuts if the federal budget ever was to be balanced again. He also hoped to separate himself from the pack by pointing out the hypocrisy of the budget debate. His staff, meanwhile, hoped that the stance would help to paint this tall, lanky and cerebral Westerner as a man of vision, courage and substance.

"How much longer can 15 presidential candidates travel around the country and say we must get the budget deficit under control without speaking what everybody knows: taxes will have to be raised," asked Chris Hamel, the campaign's Iowa coordinator and a long-time confidant

Bruce Edward Babbitt

Profession: Lawyer.
Born: June 27, 1938, Los Angeles, Calif.
Home: Phoenix, Ariz.
Religion: Roman Catholic.
Education: University of Notre Dame, B.A., 1960; Marshall scholar, University of Newcastle, M.A., 1962; Harvard University, LL.B., 1965.
Career: Member, President's Commission on Accident at Three Mile Island, 1979-80; chairman, Nuclear Safety Oversight Commission, 1980-81; member, U.S. Advisory Commission on Intergovernmental Relations, 1980-84; Arizona attorney general, 1975-78; Arizona governor, 1978-87.
Family: Wife, Hattie Coons; two children.

of Babbitt's during his nine years as governor.

The answer to Hamel's question lay with the voters, of course. Would Babbitt's proposal suffer the same consequences as Walter Mondale's acceptance speech at the 1984 Democratic Convention in San Francisco—when his call for a tax increase gave Ronald Reagan all the campaign fodder he would need? Or was there a different mood in the hinterlands? Perhaps the electorate would applaud the courage and honesty of a fiscally conservative former governor who said, matter-of-factly: "Everybody knows you can't cut $200 billion out of the budget."

The tax proposal story appeared in the *Des Moines Register* the day Babbitt boarded a plane for Michigan's scenic Mackinac Island, where Democratic governors had invited all hopefuls to talk privately about how to win the White House in 1988. Babbitt was staking his chances upon a willingness to take such risks, and he said as much to a writer from the *Arizona Republic* who was traveling with him:

"Everybody's already saying, 'These guys all sound exactly alike. It's all rhetoric.' If you delay any longer you'll lose your claim to be the first who is talking the most directly about reality. It's going to create, I think, an interesting dilemma for the other candidates as they virtually denounce my proposal and try to explain where it is they're going to find $200 billion. I think, for the most part, they'll hope this will all just go away and that we can set back to the kind of polite evasion that has characterized this debate."

Babbitt's prescience was uncanny. Word of his plan seemed to disrupt the unifying aspects of the assembled Democratic contenders. They blanched when informed of his idea. His rivals either vented their opposition or diplomatically said they needed more information. All the while, Babbitt was telling everyone it was time to end this "conspiracy of silence." It was left to party chairman Paul Kirk to avow, "The Democratic Party shouldn't be running on a platform of taxes."

A Progressive from the 'Conservative' Southwest

Babbitt's proposal was but the latest in a series of innovative and eyebrow-raising plans he had unleashed: from a controversial "universal needs-testing" for all entitlement programs, to his belief that the world's major trading nations should scrap their current system and support one in which imports and exports were kept in balance under the threat of tariffs.

Anybody who thought Babbitt would be a candidate like the rest of the 1988 field had not been paying attention. In 1985, sensing that the party was ripe for internal change after Mondale's crushing defeat, Babbitt had used his position as chairman of the Democratic Governors Association (DGA) to speak directly to party regulars attending a meeting of the Democratic National Committee in Washington. It wasn't a long speech, but it was direct. "We must reject a lazy orthodoxy which tends to view the future as a linear projection of the past," said Babbitt. He then called for fiscal sanity and argued that the time had come to stop bowing to typical constituencies.

It was only a prelude. Using his position at DGA, and aligning himself with the putatively moderate-to-conservative Democratic Leadership Council, Babbitt spent most of the next two years criss-crossing the country. He criticized his party's direction, and peddled his own ideas.

In finally launching his long-shot campaign for the presidency, Babbitt's announcement speech on March 10, 1987, in Manchester, N.H.—and again in Des Moines—carried the same themes that he had unleashed earlier before the DNC.

"The next president of the United States must dare to be different, willing to cast aside the tired orthodoxies that hold back our leaders," Babbitt said. "The next president must chart a course that lets America take charge of its future. He must say and do what other politicians dare not even think. He must risk offending some potential supporters. He must risk breaching the etiquette of Washington. He must lead."

Babbitt was to assume the recently proven political mantle of an outsider running against Washington's politics as usual. However, he hoped to demonstrate that he was both electable and competent to govern—by citing his image as a progressive Democrat from a heavily conservative Southwestern state.

Arizona's reputation as a sleepy and rural bastion of conservatives had followed its rapid growth after World War II. Easier air travel had made the hot, dry climate accessible to the elderly. And an urbanized boom caused the population to reach one million by the early 1960s. Yet the metropolitan centers of Phoenix and Tucson were not just the promised land for retirees; younger Americans began finding jobs there. Today, more than 80 percent of the state's three million people are urban dwellers. And, notwithstanding the state's conservative traditions, only the last few years have seen Republicans edge ahead of Democrats in voter registration.

Barry Goldwater's special brand of conservatism enjoyed widespread appeal among both Arizona's old-timers and its new immigrants during the 1950s and 1960s. The Arizona Legislature was dominated by rural interests and was firmly in the hands of Democrats until the U.S. Supreme Court's landmark "one-person, one-vote" decisions shifted control of the legislature to the GOP. Statewide, this was clearly a time of Republican dominance. Arizona was the only state to vote for the GOP presidential nominee every time since 1948, and Republicans had occupied the governor's office virtually uninterrupted from 1958 to 1974.

Enter one Bruce Babbitt, man of contrasts: a graduate of Harvard Law School, schooled in the Democratic conservatism of his elders, yet possessed of a social conscience that took him to the turbulent civil rights marches in Selma, Ala. A student of history, Babbitt would sport button-down shirts and pin-stripe suits but would be just as eager to hike the Grand Canyon, pointing out geological formations and identifying wild flowers. He would seek out forums and publicity for his ideas but retreat to a cabin in the mountains to be alone with his family. He would charm the socks off anyone with his insightfulness, intellect and fecund sense of humor, but at other times he could be cool and aloof. Some even sensed an uncaring or ungrateful politician.

"Bruce, I consider a warm and fuzzy fellow," says Alfred Outierrez, the Arizona Senate's former Democratic leader and a Babbitt ally during much of his tenure as attorney general and governor. "And that offends some people." Adds a frequent GOP adversary, House Majority Whip Jane Kull, "I guess he did drag us kicking and screaming into the 20th century."

Raising Arizona, Going Nationwide

The descendant of a pioneer family, Babbitt redefined the office of governor in Arizona: from one in which occupants would defer to powerful legislators and ceremonial trappings, to one with an active chief executive no longer content to passively preside over a bureaucracy.

Babbitt never was afraid to exercise the veto. Only six weeks in office, he surprised legislators with two vetoes in one day. By the time he left office he had recorded a record 114 vetoes—messages that partly intimidated a once-powerful legislative majority.

Despite his proclivity for throwing bills back in the laps of

Bruce Babbitt addressing supporters in Manchester, Iowa.

lawmakers, on critical and far reaching proposals Babbitt worked cooperatively with Republicans. Together, they forged a landmark water conservation law, a plan for the management of state-owned urban lands, a prison building program and a health care program for the poor.

Those who know him well view Babbitt as a consensus builder and compromiser. As Paul Eckstein, an adviser and former law school classmate says, "Bruce is a lot less confrontational than people give him credit. But he will stand behind principles and veto legislation."

To many, Babbitt was a cool technocrat, absorbed by the details of complex legislation. Much of that reputation came in 1980 from his total immersion for eight months with competing and vested interests who sought to draft a water management plan—legislation that now stands as Babbitt's shining achievement.

In many ways, the characterization of a detail-man is accurate. Babbitt was truly fascinated by the intricacies of the arcane water law, whether they were surface rights or Indian water rights. But he also proved an astute enough politician to know that in tough bargaining the individual with the most information usually controls the discourse. Still, as Babbitt's intentions for national office became more publicized out of state, the analogy to detail-oriented Jimmy Carter was inevitable.

Early in Babbitt's political career he approached his job "like any lawyer who doesn't trust others," says Eckstein. As attorney general, Babbitt constantly was rewriting legal opinions, which helped explain why legislators carped about inordinate time delays in receiving answers to their questions.

In the governor's chair, Babbitt gradually became more comfortable with those around him. He also hired his alter-ego as chief of staff, Andrew Hurwitz. And he became confident in delegating detail work. That left him more time to use what Babbitt more so than any other Arizona chief executive realized was the office's chief weapon: the bully pulpit.

Critical to carrying out this function of Babbitt's was a receptive Capitol press corps that generally respected him. He kept an open-door policy to the media from his days as attorney general. Additionally, well-placed leaks did wonders for his legislative agenda—whether to release a trial balloon, threaten a veto or cajole a reluctant legislator.

Outside the boundaries of Arizona, principally through his work in the National Governors' Association (NGA), Babbitt quickly began receiving notice for his developed and provocative ideas. A couple of years before Ronald Reagan made New Federalism a cornerstone of a

State of the Union address, Babbitt had pressured NGA to make it a priority. Convinced that states and local governments could do a better job if they were solely responsible for education and transportation, Babbitt simply argued that the federal government should pick up the full tab for welfare programs.

As word of Babbitt's expertise on the water issue spread, other governors deferred to him on the subject. At annual NGA work sessions in Washington each February, the governor frequently and eloquently castigated Reagan budget and tax cuts as unduly helpful to the rich at the expense of the poor.

Like other centrist governors, Babbitt also articulated the need to achieve equity with fairness. He criticized what he saw as the party's old dogma of spending more on programs, coupled with an inability to make cuts based on priorities.

On the presidential stump, Babbitt has likewise decried the indiscriminate, across-the-board cuts mandated by Gramm-Rudman-Hollings as indicative of "everything that is rotten in Washington." Again, his critique would lie with the system's lack of priorities, as he complained that federal buildings were being treated with the same emphasis as sick children.

As the first caucus and primary approached, however, Babbitt's own solution—in conjunction with his national sales tax—had not generated much enthusiasm from the Democratic mainstream. They viewed universal needs-testing not only as heretical, but as a bit ignorant of political reality.

"I am more liberal than the liberals on entitlements," he told syndicated columnist George Will. "Entitlements, like taxes, ought to be progressive."

Babbitt's Robin Hood approach would tax the benefits of those who do not need governmental largesse, with the revenues dedicated to reducing the deficit. Social Security benefits for those earning more than $32,000 a year, for example, would be fully taxed. As he said in his announcement speech, "Do the Vanderbilts and the Mellons really need just the same tax exempt Social Security benefit as a widow in a cold water flat?"

Former Colorado governor Dick Lamm is one who thinks Babbitt is one of the most creative thinkers in American politics today. "I think he is the one person running for president," Lamm said in 1987, "who is willing to take on some of the hard issues like means-testing entitlements," and look at Medicare, farm subsidies, Social Security, veterans' benefits. "But the Democratic Party is neither smart nor creative enough to turn to Bruce Babbitt. I think it is quixotic, but I am sure glad he is doing it."

Early Days

The second oldest of Paul and Frances Babbitt's six children, Bruce was born in Los Angeles on June 27, 1938. From age 7, he was raised in Flagstaff, Ariz., a logging and ranching town south of the Grand Canyon where his forebears had settled in 1886.

Babbitt's grandfather and four great uncles made the trek westward from Cincinnati. They hoped to turn a small grubstake from the sale of a grocery store into a decent living; Arizona land and cattle were cheap, and the opportunities seemed endless.

What began as a cattle ranch and general store was parlayed into a vast mercantile empire that included retail stores, Indian trading posts, a bank, a slaughterhouse and meat-packing plant, an ice house and even an opera house. Although smaller today, the holdings still are valued at roughly $30 million. Babbitt's share is put at about $500,000, which is in a trust for his two sons.

As a youngster growing up in a dusty Western town of 7,000 people, Babbitt early developed an appreciation for the mountains and forests. An amateur geologist and anthropologist, his father inspired an interest in geology, which eventually led to an undergraduate degree in geology from Notre Dame University.

Babbitt's mother, a former violinist and cellist with the Los Angeles Philharmonic Orchestra, was no less an influence. She required all five sons and one daughter to become proficient at a musical instrument. The future governor played trumpet.

Babbitt's skinny frame was not cut out for the more traditional high school sports of football and basketball, but he is an acomplished skier and hiker. The closest he got to the gridiron was as team manager for the Flagstaff High School Eagles—a point he jokingly raises when anyone has the temerity to suggest, as some have, that Babbitt is probably the only Notre Dame alum who never saw a football game at South Bend.

Despite gawkiness and his academic prowess, Babbitt befriended everyone from tough Chicanos to youthful rednecks to classmates struggling with homework lessons. A straight "A" student, Babbitt was valedictorian of his senior class and student body president, and he was voted "most courteous." Not that he was averse to a good party now and then. As former classmate Richard Anderson, later named by Babbitt to the Yavapai County Superior Court bench, once recalled: "He was as wild as the next one. We'd bend an occasional elbow."

Although the Babbitts had money, Babbitt's father put him to work summers in the family's business enterprises. One miserable year is etched in his memory. He was on the graveyard shift of the ice plant, from 10 p.m. to 7 a.m., hauling 300-pound ice blocks to the crusher. "It was sort of like my father telling me I should never take anything for granted," Babbitt has said of the experience.

Instead of returning home after graduating from Notre Dame, Babbitt's quest for more education took him to England. He studied geophysics at the University of Newcastle as a Marshall scholar. He seemed well on his way to a career in science.

It was in the summer of 1961, on a field trip to Bolivia where he and his classmates joined oil company crews looking for oil, that Babbitt came face to face with abject poverty. With lots of time on his hands, he came to the realization that helping people would be far more to his liking than studying rocks.

Thinking ahead, he thought it might be wise to get a law degree as an insurance policy before embarking on his social agenda. Meanwhile, he worked summers in Latin America, became fluent in Spanish and developed a warm affinity, very evident today, for Hispanics.

It was in Cambridge that Babbitt met a trio of classmates—Ron Warnicke, Robert Allen and Eckstein—each of whom would play a major role in Babbitt's political fortunes. Indeed, they later would be known in Arizona alternately as the Founding Fathers or the Harvard Mafia. Allen, who played squash with Babbitt, one day confided to Warnicke: "Babbitt's an important name in Arizona. Some day he's definitely going to be in politics, perhaps in the Congress or the U.S. Senate. He has a social conscience."

In 1963 Babbitt took his law degree in a satchel to join the antipoverty forces of the federal Office of Economic Opportunity. He worked in Texas, and then later moved to Washington as a special assistant in VISTA. The two-year tenure gave Babbitt a taste of field work and managerial experience, but it also made him skeptical about forcing social change.

Back in Arizona, Babbitt threw himself into law. He was a

workaholic, and shrewd when it came to case strategies. Still, in a few years, he seemed to lose interest in daily practice.

He says his epiphany came while challenging the Arizona Legislature on behalf of the Navajo Indians. The battle was joined over a redistricting plan that sought to divide the reservation into three legislative and two congressional districts. In federal court, confronting a lawyer from the state attorney general's office, Babbitt realized that the state's top prosecutor's office was defending racial discrimination.

The Turn to Politics: Attorney General

In 1974 Watergate dominated the headlines nationally. In Arizona land swindlers were making their own scandalous headlines by ripping off unsuspecting buyers from across the nation. Babbitt and his Harvard friends would meet frequently to brainstorm about current affairs. Conversation inevitably drifted to state politics, the dynamics of which were changing as fast as new homes were built.

The group turned its attention to the state attorney general's office. "It was a very propitious time for a bright, thoughtful candidate, and while Democratic fortunes had been fairly bleak, the time was ripe for a good Democratic candidate," recalled Allen, a former national president of Young Democrats and former vice-chairman of the Democratic National Committee. Given Babbitt's family name and money, his government experience and his commitment to change, he was clearly the choice of the group. But, as Eckstein recalls, Babbitt "was a reluctant dragon."

His first political campaign was a model effort despite Babbitt's uneasiness before groups. His uninspiring, halting speech pattern—punctuated with innumerable "uhs"—was not conducive to snappy 30-second sound bites for radio and television. But the candidate was able to capitalize on land fraud and crime. He ran a "law and order" campaign that solidified his image as a tough prosecutor who would put the crooks away. He also learned early the importance of timing a news release to coincide with the day's breaking story, often getting his statements quoted on the evening news. Babbitt won 13 of 14 counties in the primary, then eased past his GOP opponent with almost 56 percent of the vote.

The new attorney general quickly set about to reorganize the office. His agenda was to pursue white-collar crime, organized crime and complex conspiracy cases. Until that point, the office had been exceedingly weak, doing little but serving up legal opinions and advising state agencies on legal matters.

Babbitt immediately befriended influential Republican lawmakers and convinced them to broaden the attorney general's powers so that he could bring criminal charges previously limited to county attorneys. The results were impressive for Babbitt, who charmed legislators with an explicit emphasis on bipartisanship. Over time, laws made their way into the statute books that repealed blind trusts and provided for a state Racketeering-Influenced and Corrupt Organizations Act patterned after the federal RICO law. Babbitt had obtained enormous civil and criminal powers to go after organized crime.

Receptive lawmakers, weary of adverse national publicity, went along with Babbitt's proposals despite a feeling in some GOP quarters that the aggressive attorney general's barrage of antitrust suits was anti-business. Most gladly went along with the anti-crime legislative parade, while Babbitt reactivated the dormant antitrust division and filed price-fixing lawsuits against asphalt suppliers, bakeries, dairies, cement manufacturers, school material suppliers and medical doctors.

The attorney general seemed to be everywhere. He smooth-talked and bantered freely with reporters, who were located just down the hall from his Capitol office and were encouraged to drop in unannounced. The accessibility endeared him to journalists.

For all of Babbitt's efforts, the news that a car bomb had killed *Arizona Republic* reporter Don Bolles revealed a criminal element undeterred by tough talk and tough laws. As the investigation began foundering, Babbitt persuaded Gov. Raul Castro to take the case away from the county prosecutor and give it to him. Although one man was subsequently sent to death row, some felt that the failure to uncover the ultimate sponsor behind Bolles' murder took the sheen off Babbitt's record.

Governor by Fate

His prowess as a prosecutor started people talking about what lay ahead in Babbitt's rosy future. Gov. Castro had resigned his position in October 1977 to take an ambassadorial post in the Carter administration, elevating Secretary of State Wesley Bolin to the governor's office. Babbitt felt he needed three more years as attorney general, and contemplated a run for Goldwater's U.S. Senate seat in 1980.

Then, in 1978, the spring rains came early. Floodwaters created havoc in many parts of the state. Bolin tried to stay on top of things, but the strain was too much. He succumbed to a heart attack in the early morning hours of March 4. Because Bolin's replacement as secretary of state was not an elected officeholder, Babbitt found himself next in the line of gubernatorial succession.

Ironically, it was not exactly the place Babbitt wanted to be. He thought fate had dealt him a cruel blow. The governor's office was weak, he thought, subservient to the powers at the Legislature. He didn't want to waste his time or his boundless energy in a ceremonial post.

Another reason for Babbitt's reticence was purely political. His re-election campaign for attorney general was starting to gear up, and two Democrats already had announced for governor.

But Babbitt was unaware that over the preceding decade lawmakers surreptitiously had been adding new powers to the governor's office, a fact also apparently lost on his ceremonial predecessors. It took Babbitt only 48 hours to figure out the real state of things. In turn, it took the Legislature but six weeks to realize that a different sort of man occupied the chief executive's chair, a shrewd and astute political thinker unafraid to use the veto.

In almost nine years as governor, Babbitt vetoed a record 114 bills, modernized state government by exerting control over myriad state agencies operating as fiefdoms, installed the best and brightest agency directors he could find and put his imprimatur on key pieces of legislation to keep Arizona and its services in sync with the state's rapid growth rate. He enjoyed broad based bipartisan support, in part because he reached out early to the well-established business community. He also practiced the politics of inclusion and consensus-building on major issues such as groundwater conservation and transportation finance.

On strictly partisan bills, however, Babbitt could be as petty as any chief executive beholden to constituent groups. Once, he vetoed GOP Majority Leader Burton Barr's bill to subject federal funds to legislative appropriation, despite Barr's being his chief ally among Republicans during his entire career in public office. On the other hand, no piece of legislation exemplified Babbitt's strengths as a decision maker, consensus builder and detail man quite like the 1980 Groundwater Management Act. The bill passed the Legislature in one day, without a single amendment. It became a model for the nation.

Nothing in arid Arizona is more precious than water, supplies of which were rapidly diminishing owing to burgeoning growth. Babbitt was successful in framing the debate by characterizing water conservation goals as being in the economic interest of the state. The linkage brought major water users, copper mines, agri-business, utilities and municipalities to the bargaining table for eight months of deliberate discussions punctuated by occasional head-knocking.

Critical to Babbitt's scheme was a charade he hatched with Interior Secretary Cecil Andrus. Together, they convinced the federal government to threaten a cutoff of funding for the all-important Central Arizona Project, a multibillion-dollar reclamation project approved by Congress in 1968; the project was to use aqueducts to transport Colorado River water to central and southern parts of the state unless competing water users succeeded in fashioning their own water management plan.

The ruse worked. Discussions got back on track. Often, the groups would meet until midnight on weekdays, and even over weekends. Frustrations ran high. It was, Babbitt says, "a process of searching for a way of defining people's rights that took something away from everybody and gave enough in return that they came to the next meeting."

Bill Stephens, one of the participants and a lawyer representing the Municipal Water Users Association, says Babbitt kept the group together. "He was the driving force. Bruce was patient and it took the patience of Job. He's a quick learner. He grasped the issues very quickly and probably understood the ramifications faster than most of us."

Far less successful, by contrast, was Babbitt's handling of the state's alternative to Medicaid, the Arizona Health Care Cost Containment System. The pre-paid and capitated program for 170,000 indigents was set up in 1982. From its inception, cost overruns and allegations of mismanagement plagued AHCCCS, which quickly became a nasty six-letter acronym for legislators and the administration.

In February 1984, 13 months into the three-year experiment, the roof started to cave in on the administration. The magic in Babbitt's wand was gone. Republicans had been sniping at him for months, and now fellow Democrats were critical of his inattention to the program's growing administrative and financial problems. Both sides charged Babbitt with judgmental errors.

For several months Babbitt had received status reports warning about AHCCCS woes. A legislative oversight committee requested the memos, but Babbitt refused. Only notification that the media would take him to court to gain access to the papers caused Babbitt to relent.

On several rare appearances before legislative committees, Babbitt subjected himself to intense grilling. He put his political career on the line with his acceptance of putting AHCCCS under state control instead of a private contractor. "I recognize that this infant is being delivered into my arms," he said at the time.

Babbitt cleared his calendar for 90 days to deal only with the foundering program. He put trusted aide Bill Jamieson in charge of the transition; within three months AHCCCS was back on its feet operating smoothly. The governor called for changes in eligibility as a cost-saving move, a tactic that prompted liberal Democratic leaders to publicly declare the governor's plan punitive and to warn of an all-out intraparty war. Ultimately, the Legislature pumped millions into the program, and no one was cut off the rolls. Babbitt had weathered much more than a squall at sea.

"AHCCCS is the perfect example of the best and worst of Bruce Babbitt," says Hurwitz, his former chief of staff. "It got into trouble because of his hands-off style of management ... delegating to capable, professional people. It works because it's an incredible idea that makes sense ... and once he became aware his hands were needed, he went in and personally fixed it."

Of all Babbitt's decisions, however, none generated so much national publicity, nor caused so much enmity from organized labor, as his controversial decision to send the National Guard to quell strike-related violence at the Phelps-Dodge Corp.'s copper mines in the eastern Arizona mining community of Clifton-Morenci during 1983 and 1984. Babbitt has said he has no regrets about his decision—even though it gave him the moniker of "Gov. Scabbitt"—because it was his duty as chief executive to maintain the peace. "It was an unhappy event in the history of this state," Babbitt says, but "the bottom line [is] nobody got hurt."

Although the presence of the National Guard had nothing to do with the eventual result of the strike, scabs and replacements were hired who later voted to decertify the union. Subsequently, in the strike's aftermath, Babbitt was in Detroit and was refused a breakfast meeting with union leaders.

Time has helped to heal the division, as did Babbitt's success in mediating 1986 contract talks between copper companies and unions. Although he walked away from the negotiations with praise from both management and labor, he also came away with a belief that workers toil in an atmosphere in which they are viewed as commodities. That experience strongly has influenced his "workplace democracy" ideas, which have since taken their place in his standard stump speech along side the national consumption tax, needs-testing of entitlements and various children's issues.

Unconventional Ideas for a Conventional Campaign

Babbitt's proposals, aimed at restoring America's competitive edge, are pretty revolutionary coming from a man who was raised in a right-to-work state. His basic idea is to spur productivity through equitable treatment of employees in the workplace. Babbitt would ban golden parachutes for executives, or restrict them to companies that also give multiple salaries to departing workers; executive bonuses would not be tax deductible unless workers also received them; company ownership would be restructured to permit partial company ownership by workers if firms receive government loans or guarantees; bonuses would be given to employees of federal contractors if contracts are completed on time and under budget; and a uniform national child care voucher system would be instituted for the workplace.

In a calculated ploy in Iowa a month before the caucus vote, Babbitt injected himself into a local issue to dramatize his workplace-democracy proposals and to make headway with unionists, a constituency that had not rallied behind his candidacy. IBP, the state's meatpacking giant, which is anti-union and has a poor safety record, wanted to build a plant in Manchester. Babbitt earned headlines when he labeled the plant a "corporate outlaw." Like his unrelenting advocacy of a national sales tax, his outburst against IBP was but another example of the Babbitt prescience in framing the debate. Babbitt was being Babbitt.

With virtually no base outside of Arizona—and a candidate generally unknown among the nation's electorate at large—the Babbitt campaign strategy evolved early and quickly. In March 1985, when Babbitt opted not to seek a third term as governor and ruled out a 1986 run for the U.S. Senate, close advisers began talking about Jimmy Carter's race in 1976. They recalled how he parlayed a win in the Iowa caucuses to a string of primary wins, to the nomination and the presidency.

The strategy was simple: survive the cut in Iowa and New Hampshire, then ride the wave of "free media" to the South, where a "moderate centrist" like Babbitt just might catch fire. Capitalizing on an eager and loyal staff that had served him well as governor, Babbitt was quick to set up a Washington-based political action committee to raise funds, along with a tax-exempt educational foundation and a think tank to set several of his issues before the public. He stepped up his speaking timetable, careful to make several profile-raising appearances in Iowa and New Hampshire.

Throughout 1986, organizational wizard Chris Hamel divided his time between Phoenix and Iowa, spinning together a network of support. By the eve of the Iowa caucuses, the organization was considered top-notch in the Hawkeye state—though it still had failed to garner significant support according to opinion polls.

Babbitt's first extended visit to Iowa was on the seat of a 10-speed Schwinn bicycle, a grueling week's ride in July with his wife, Hattie, sons Christopher and T.J. and nearly 10,000 other cycling enthusiasts in RAGBRAI, the *Des Moines Register*'s Annual Great Bicycle Ride Across Iowa. For 17-hour days, Babbitt pedaled and politicked. Every 10 miles, he would stop and chat with Iowans, listening and introducing himself. Evenings featured outdoor barbecues at private homes.

As Hamel would explain the rationale for participating in RAGBRAI to a *Wall Street Journal* reporter: "We've gotta be different. If we walk around saying, 'Me too,' we're dead meat."

Yet whatever gains Babbitt may have made in Iowa were lost in Houston, the site of the campaign's first nationally televised debate among Democratic candidates. Critics singled out Babbitt for harsh comment, not so much for what he said as how he said it. His head bobbed; he hemmed and hawed. Past references to his Donald Sutherland good looks were replaced with comments that he looked like Carter and sounded like Richard Nixon. Columnist Jeff Greenfield suggested Babbitt get a voice transplant. *Time* magazine thought Babbitt "lost long yardage."

The national press, Babbitt since said, "whopped me over the head with a dead fish." Although publicly he thought the press criticism fair, privately he likened the scribes to a school of sharks in a feeding frenzy.

Not that television ever was a Babbitt strength. Swallowing words, smacking lips and twitching jowls tended to convey his awkwardness to viewers, which in turn raised questions about Babbitt's ability to lead and inspire a nation. This was particularly true in the wake of Ronald Reagan's presidency, which perhaps more than any other has underscored the use of television as a vital component of executive leadership.

Babbitt's poor Houston performance immediately raised concerns over his electability. It fueled rumors that his two-state campaign, in debt, was on the verge of collapse. National polls still showed him in single digits. And for all his efforts in Iowa, little upward movement could be discerned.

Babbitt set about to improve his television image. Hours of videotapes were studied. "I'm nothing if not a learner," he said. "I understand what went wrong and why."

Perhaps the study worked. During an NBC-TV debate televised nationwide with Tom Brokaw, Richard Gephardt was admonishing Paul Simon, labeling the Illinois senator's economic policies as "Reaganomics with a bow tie." Added Gephardt: "And I think it's time to stand up and say to people what it is we're going to do to get this budget balanced."

Babbitt saw an opening. In fact, his campaign staff had told the show's producer that Babbitt would stand up during the debate, and the cameramen had better be prepared.

"I've just heard a lot of flimflam from Senator Simon and from Representative Gephardt," said Babbitt. He suddenly got to his feet, challenging his opponents also to stand and admit that the budget would only be balanced through a mix of program cuts, needs-testing *and* raised taxes. An uncomfortable silence followed. Babbitt's opponents stayed put.

"See?" he said peering into the camera. "I kind of expected that. There aren't a lot of profiles in courage here tonight. There really aren't."

The gimmick produced its intended result, focusing the spotlight on Babbitt. Within weeks, a spate of positive publicity descended from newspapers, magazines and television. Almost overnight Babbitt had become the darling of the national press corps. Just six months earlier, his campaign had been written off.

In the end, Babbitt's 1988 campaign may be judged for its growth, rather than its success. The candidate clearly had learned some valuable lessons in the art of presidential campaigning. And, while his poll numbers remained low, many commentators acknowledged that his presentation had marked Babbitt as a new national figure. If his candidacy was doomed in 1988, some foresaw his political re-emergence in the not-too-distant future.

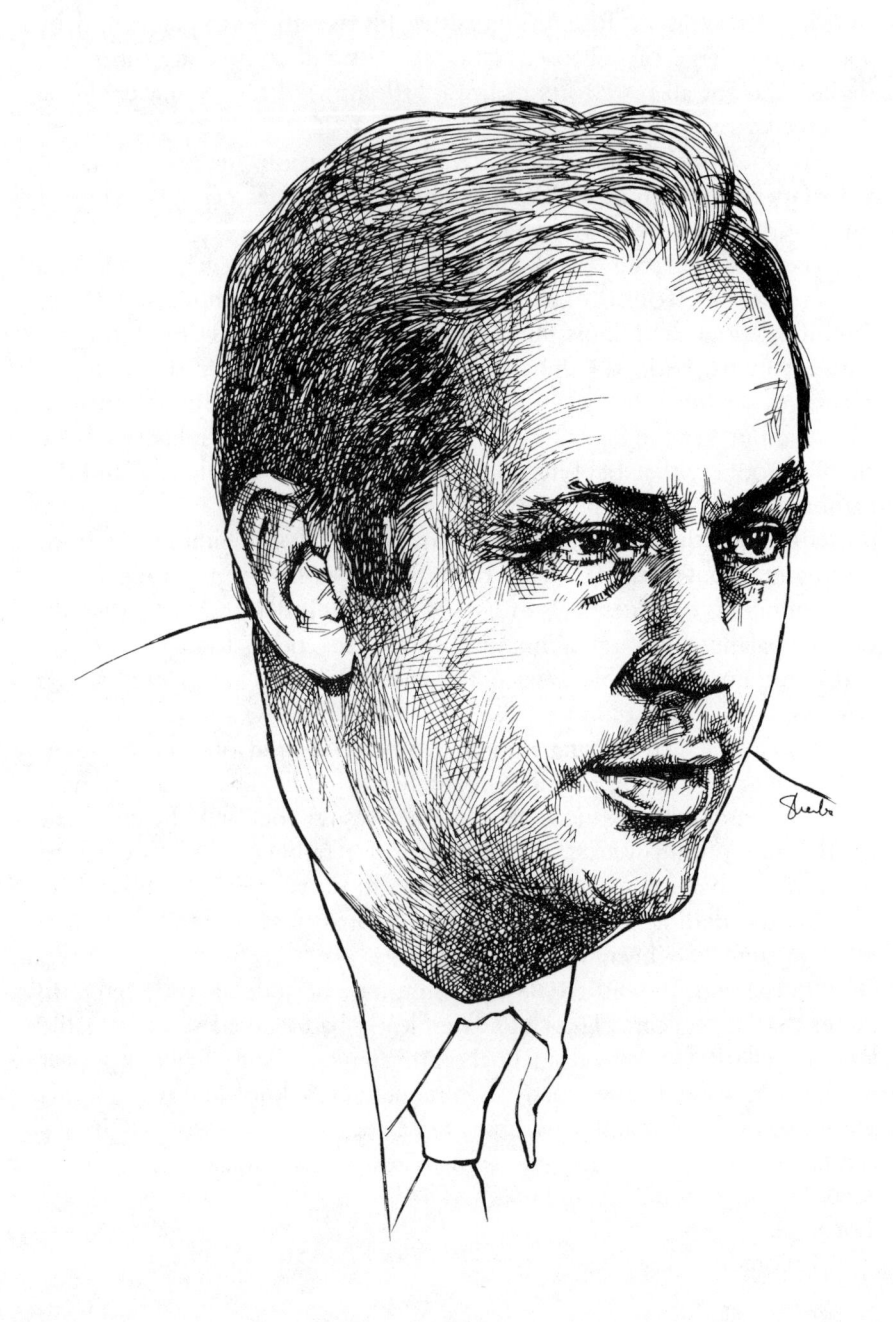

BILL BRADLEY

A Senate Celebrity Waits in the Wings

The anteroom of Bill Bradley's Senate office is dominated by a pair of campaign posters. In one, the six-foot-five-inch former professional basketball player is depicted against an abstract map of New Jersey. It reads "Bill Bradley—Senate 1978." The second, emblazoned "Senator Bill Bradley—1984," shows the lawmaker with the U.S. Capitol looming over his shoulder. Bradley has so far been able to resist the pressure for a third poster—in what many think should be a natural progression: the Senate, the White House and the words "President 1988."

Although he has indicated he might be interested in the presidency at some time, the 44-year-old Bradley has steadfastly maintained he is not a candidate for the 1988 nomination. "I will know when the time is ready," he answers repeated entreaties to run for the nation's highest office. "I'll know it when I'm there."

A colleague, Timothy E. Wirth, D-Colo., says that Bradley "apparently has developed some very clear criteria as to why he's not running for the U.S. presidency." Wirth, who serves with Bradley on the Senate Energy and Natural Resources Committee, adds, "It's refreshing that there's somebody around who believes that you have to be qualified for the United States presidency to run, not just that you want to be president."

Bradley is, by anyone's definition, an unusual politician. Not only does he self-effacingly refuse to bite off a job he doesn't feel he is ready for, he pays an inordinate amount of attention to the job he already has. The phrases most often mentioned to describe the senior senator from New Jersey are not ones used to describe the bulk of his colleagues: intelligent, thoughtful, always prepared, does his homework, low key, thorough.

Colorado's other senator, Republican William L. Armstrong, also

William Warren 'Bill' Bradley

Profession: Professional basketball player; author.
Born: July 28, 1943, Crystal City, Mo.
Home: Denville, N.J.
Religion: Protestant.
Education: Princeton University, B.A., 1965; Oxford University (Rhodes scholar), M.A., 1968.
Political Career: U.S. Senate, 1979-present.
Military: Air Force Reserve, 1967-78.
Family: Wife, Ernestine Schlant; one child.
Senate Committees: Finance, 1979-present; Energy and Natural Resources, 1979-present; Special Committee on Aging, 1979-present; Select Committee on Intelligence, 1985-present.

cited Bradley's quiet diligence: "He is very hard working and he has a lot of the kind of personal habits that are not only attractive, but are in some ways very unusual in presidential candidates—most of whom seem to be at least mildly egomaniacal."

The senators from Colorado, one a conservative Republican and the other a "Neo-liberal" Democrat, provide an apt illustration of the esteem in which the former basketball player is held by members from both sides of the political aisle.

"He is very impressive the way he does his homework," said Wirth. "He sticks to a few things and does them very, very well. He doesn't allow himself to get carried away with all the media hype that surrounds him."

Armstrong, who serves with Bradley on the Finance Committee, adds, "He was out front on tax reform for a long time before it became a serious possibility. He was the intellectual leader, along with Jack Kemp, long before anyone else."

A staff aide who works for a Republican senator on the Senate Finance Committee commented on the New Jersey senator's ability to "think in the long term and see things in the future."

"Another thing stands out," the aide added. "Bradley works on issues whose value and importance are not readily apparent, but that are critical issues. And there's something else. It's kind of subjective—but his size. He's a big man and his presence just dominates a meeting."

Making a Name as Legislator

To date, passage of the Tax Reform Act of 1986 is Bradley's crowning achievement in the Senate. It also is a testament to the dedication and thoughtful approach he brings to the legislative process. While he is neither an arm twister nor a legislative tactician, he can be tireless at promoting the ideas he is pushing and at helping his colleagues make up their minds to invest in them.

For four years he pushed the notion of a tax overhaul that would lower individual rates, simplify the tax rate structure and close loopholes for both individuals and corporations. "Tax reform has been my obsession for the last several years," Bradley told fellow Princetonians as he accepted the 1987 Woodrow Wilson Alumni Award.

Even his young daughter would confirm that, he laughed. She refused to watch him on a taped television show one Sunday afternoon, telling a playmate, "Let's go—all he's going to talk about are loopholes."

Bradley even wrote a book, *The Fair Tax*, in an effort to build public support for his tax reform idea. Likewise, he spent a good deal of his time making speeches and writing articles about it. In 1984 he urged Democratic presidential nominee Walter F. Mondale to make tax reform a key part of his platform. But Mondale was enmeshed in his conviction that he would have to raise taxes, while Bradley's colleagues were having a hard time taking the idea seriously.

By 1985, however, President Reagan had made tax reform the top domestic priority of his second term, and Congress began to pay heed. In an unusual move, Bradley struck up a close alliance with Rep. Dan Rostenkowski of Illinois, the burly Democratic chairman of the House Ways and Means Committee. Bradley sought the powerful House veteran's help to pass the companion tax bill that had been introduced in the House by Rep. Richard A. Gephardt, D-Mo.

Putting senatorial ego aside, Bradley worked closely with Rostenkowski and would cross the Capitol to call in person on reluctant House members—something few senators have ever done. For the sake of passage, he once even agreed to a basketball game in the House gym with members of the committee—the only time he has played the game in public since his retirement from the New York Knicks in 1977.

Bradley's collaborative approach with the House leadership worked. Spurred by House passage in 1985, the Senate Finance Committee took up tax overhaul in 1986. Bradley was reform's beacon on the committee. But his colleagues loaded their plan with one special-interest benefit after another—oil and gas breaks, advantages for the timber industry, help for farmers and miners, favors for businesses investing in new equipment.

With each committee session, the list grew longer. Bradley made a few stabs at stemming the tide but spent most of his time reminding his colleagues that an alternative was available. Their measure would topple under its own weight, he warned them. At the end of each day of markup, he would stick around to talk to reporters, making sure that his side of the argument got prominent mention the next day.

As it turned out, Finance Committee Chairman Robert Packwood, R-Ore., came around. He suspended markups after the committee had cobbled together a tax bill that, at a time of soaring deficits, would have cost the government $29 billion in lost revenue.

Then Packwood started over. He huddled with Bradley and five other committee activists. A week later they came back with the skeleton of what eventually became the Tax Reform Act of 1986: a proposal that, in many of its basics, was the plan Bradley had been pushing all along.

In the weeks that followed, Bradley played a key role in convincing liberal Senate Democrats, arguing the intellectual merits of major sections of the measure and dealing with the press. When the bill eventually passed, Packwood and Rostenkowski gave Bradley considerable credit for its success.

The Golden Days of 'Dollar Bill'

There have been remarkably few disappointments in the golden career of "Dollar Bill," a nickname Bradley acquired for his frugality during the high-paying pro-basketball days. He purportedly still has the first dollar he'd ever been paid.

The only child of a well-to-do Presbyterian banker and a mother who was active in community affairs, Bradley grew up in Crystal City, Mo., where he enjoyed an uneventful but highly disciplined childhood. His mother and father still live there. Except for brief visits, he has not gone home again.

Bradley's career path has been characterized by major decisions made after much thought, but against seasoned advice, that have turned out well. After achieving some success as a high school basketball player—he was not a natural at basketball, but he honed his skill with more than three hours of practice after school every day and eight hours on Saturdays—Bradley resisted advice that he go to a "jock" college where his talent would stand out. He chose instead Princeton University, where sports are second to academic pursuits.

As a member of the basketball team, Bradley was named an All-American. He led the team to a conference championship. During the summer before his senior year, he captained the U.S. Olympic team, which won a gold medal.

It was at Princeton, and later at Oxford, that Bradley's social consciousness was roused, never again to be dormant. "The day I listened to H. H. Wilson's first lecture on American government, I was stunned. The day Alan Downer lectured on 'Death of a Salesman,' I cried," he recalled during the lecture to the Princeton alumni.

Another college experience had a profound effect. He spent a summer on Capitol Hill in Washington as an intern. He was in the gallery the night the 1964 Civil Rights Act was passed. He was to say later that

Bill Bradley's supporters hope he will join the race for president.

due to the summer's experience he knew his "life's direction had changed."

After graduating with honors in history from Princeton in 1965, Bradley again acted against the conventional wisdom, which counseled that he immediately accept an offer to play professional basketball. He opted instead for two years at Oxford University in England as a Rhodes scholar. At the end of that stint, however, he once more countered his advisers. Rather than enter law school at the end of the English tour, he joined the National Basketball Association's New York Knickerbockers.

Bradley played with the Knicks for 10 years, criss-crossing the country while leading the team to two NBA championships. In the overall scheme of his political career, however, they were not wasted years. The *New York Times* commented later that the years Bradley spent "running up and down basketball courts from coast to coast with men fundamentally unlike himself have lent him the image of a truly national man ... a man rooted in a sort of classless egalitarianism."

Basketball also gave him the time, money and freedom to follow his nose for politics. Another plus was something that politicans will do almost anything short of murder to obtain—name recognition. His fame as a player made Bradley, if not a household word, at least a familiar one in all corners of the country. Likewise he was able to make invaluable contacts with a wide network of people.

During the off seasons, Bradley used his time to good advantage. He worked with college-bound, minority inner-city kids. He conducted basketball workshops around the country, working on prison and welfare reform, campaigning for the environmental movement, writing and studying.

Indeed, one piece of legislation he introduced in 1987 stems from those days on the road. His colleagues were bemused when the senator from New Jersey introduced a bill to return part of the Black Hills in South Dakota to the Sioux Indians. But Bradley's old friends from the days he had conducted workshops on the reservation had roused his interest in the issue.

Taking an Outside Shot at Politics

Although it is doubtful that he ever again will be enticed into a friendly game with House members—even in the interest of passing a bill—Bradley's basketball experience is in many ways an integral part of the way he operates. Winning the game has always been more important than hogging the limelight for him. Indeed, despite a deadeye jumpshot, Bradley the NBA star was always known as one who would sacrifice a scoring role to help the team.

"In my previous profession, I always got as big a kick out of giving an assist as making a basket," he told the *Wall Street Journal*.

"In my case as a player the whole thing was recognizing that you were part of a team, realizing that your success would be determined by the success of that team," he said in an interview with *Life* magazine. "The legislative process and sport are similar because both are about getting people with different personal agendas and styles to work together to achieve a common goal."

Bradley's experience as an athlete has also given him the power to "see the whole court," observers believe, which is one of his strengths. It contributed to his sense of discipline, the ability to do the manageable and not take on more than he can handle.

"The essence of the game is selectivity, knowing one's limitations and abiding by them," he said in another interview.

After retiring from professional basketball in 1977, Bradley was ready to enter the political arena. Characteristically, he listened to his own instincts and went against advice of the pros. As he was married to Ernestine Schlant, a professor of German literature at Montclair State College in New Jersey, he decided to make the Garden State his home base.

As early as 1974 Bradley had refused an offer to leave basketball for a run at the House of Representatives. Now, however, he was not content with starting at that lower level and working his way up through the ranks. He announced in 1978 that he was going to run against popular senator Clifford Case, a liberal Republican who was finishing his fourth term.

His decision was not greeted with hurrahs of enthusiasm from the Democratic organization, which was—from the governor on down—supporting the candidacy of Richard Leone, a former state treasurer.

Bradley was not the only young Turk in New Jersey to tweak the nose of the establishment that year. Jeffrey Bell, a conservative ideologue who, like Bradley, was only 34 years old, challenged Case in the Republican primary.

As things turned out, the old incumbent war-horse had fallen prey to overconfidence born of great personal popularity and long years in office. It was a fatal miscalculation. Case failed to campaign vigorously and Bell won the primary.

On the Democratic side, Bradley was also successful. He won handily, despite the fact that he was a relative newcomer to the state, had a speaking ability that was charitably characterized as one "capable of turning a friendly gathering of fellow Democrats stone silent" and had no support within the party organization. He carried 20 of New Jersey's 21 districts and won 60 percent of the Democratic vote.

The superior organization that Bradley had put together, the name recognition he had earned in the NBA and his ability to raise large sums of campaign funds were generally credited with his victory over Bell. Bradley won 56 percent of the vote in the general election, a healthy margin for a basketball player in his first try at elective politics. New Jersey now had two Democratic senators for the first time in 40 years.

Six years later in an election that carried Ronald Reagan to victory on a crest of overwhelming personal popularity, Bradley won re-election with an unprecedented 65 percent of the vote. He carried all 21 counties.

Although his opponent, Mary Mochary, was a well-financed Republican mayor of Montclair who strongly supported Reagan, Bradley easily dealt with her challenge. She accused Bradley of having "a second agenda" and charged he would use the Senate as a springboard to the White House while neglecting the needs of New Jersey. Bradley deftly responded that he was "flattered" by her suggestion he might run for president, but intended only to be a "good senator."

Learning Political Ropes: The Amateur Turns Pro

When he arrived in Washington in January 1979, Bradley was the Senate's youngest member. He was preceded by his fame, of course, and the way he had successfully challenged the establishment. Yet, once esconced in office, he reverted to type and became a team player again.

For a man who had been a celebrity ever since he was in college, Bradley's ability to shun the limelight has been remarkable. It is just as if all the attention he got while playing basketball had never happened. He was content to lie low, to learn the system, to build his bridges within the Senate hierarchy. He assembled a top-notch staff of young aides, many of whom are still with him.

One of his priorities was becoming a member of the Senate Finance Committee, which was then chaired by the consummate Senate politi-

Bradley's Interest Group Ratings

Vote ratings by interest groups help to give a picture of Bill Bradley's orientation during his Senate career. This table shows how often Bradley voted on key legislative issues in accordance with the positions of groups chosen to represent liberal, labor, business and conservative viewpoints. They are the Americans for Democratic Action (ADA), AFL-CIO, Chamber of Commerce of the United States (CCUS) and Americans for Constitutional Action (ACA) or American Conservative Union (ACU).

	ADA	AFL-CIO	CCUS	ACA	ACU
1979	68	95	38/25 [1]	4	—
1980	72	100	38	0	—
1981	90	82	13	20	—
1982	100	85	29	24	—
1983	85	82	32	20	—
1984	85	64	29	35	—
1985	85	81	28	—	9 [2]
1986	85	87	31	—	23
1987	80	100	28	—	21

[1] In 1979 there were two Chamber of Commerce scores for members of the Senate. The CCUS originally calculated scores based on 11 votes and excluded several procedural votes. Subsequently, the chamber revised its ratings, using 16 votes instead of 11. Revised score follows original score.

[2] Congressional Quarterly began publishing ACU ratings in 1985.

cian, Russell Long. Bradley admired the Louisiana Democrat and felt he could learn a lot from him.

Bradley chose to observe the by-then-often-violated rule that freshmen senators should be seen but never heard on the floor in their first few months on the job. In another unusual move, he volunteered for duty to preside over the Senate, a job most senators consider distasteful and a waste of time. He used the opportunity to study the system and soak up the ins and outs of parliamentary rules.

While other members of his class were gathering news stories on some of the sexier issues or making speeches on the Senate floor, Bradley was steeping himself in the complicated issues confronting his committees—Finance, plus Energy and Natural Resources. He quietly did his homework and learned his new craft. He has since added the Special Committee on Aging and the Select Committee on Intelligence to his assignments.

Bradley says that his success with the tax bill illustrates the validity of the way he has approached his job: "If you do your homework, if you think through an idea, if you figure out how to communicate it and focus on the big picture and what it means to people's lives, you can persuade your colleagues against all odds."

With the passage of the 1986 tax bill, Bradley turned his attention to another issue—the huge debt burden carried by Third World nations, particularly those in Latin America. It is an incredibly complex issue, one difficult to articulate, not "sexy," and far from the mind of the average voter.

It is also a topic that brought him into even sharper conflict with the Reagan White House. Bradley accused the administration of failing to develop a policy to alleviate debt pressures, which he warns could cause explosive social unrest within Latin nations.

In addition, Bradley argues, the fiscal austerity policies employed by debtor nations to meet their obligations have forced them to cut back on purchases of U.S. goods, thus contributing to the trade deficit and costing the United States an estimated $1.4 billion in 1986. Bradley has proposed his own debt plan, calling for interest-rate reduction and selective forgiveness of loans combined with new policies aimed at promoting economic growth within debtor nations.

In the Energy and Natural Resources Committee, Bradley has not been so successful in pushing legislation. He lays claim, however, to a passionate interest in environmental issues, perhaps stemming from the basketball tournament days that took him to remote corners of the country. He is working on fulfilling a vow to visit all the national parks, and he has taken an active part in pushing clean-up legislation on toxic waste sites.

The Intelligence Committee has provided Bradley with the opportunity to gain expertise in foreign affairs. And he has been making the most of it, according to an interview with the *Newark Star Ledger*, by spending many hours receiving national security briefings and scouring international intelligence data.

Another issue he has been focusing on is the shape and future of U.S.-Soviet relations. He characteristically started at the beginning by analyzing Russian and American history in some depth.

On a recent trip to the Soviet Union he concentrated on meeting with Russian people, not leaders, and even held an impromptu seminar on democracy at an American exhibit in Tvilisi in the province of Georgia. When a Soviet citizen asked Bradley if he thought it had been fair to force former Colorado senator Gary Hart out of the race for the Democratic nomination based on personal reasons, Bradley suggested the question be put to a democratic vote of the Russians who had surrounded him:

"In my country we vote on many issues. Let's put it to a vote here. How many of you think Gary Hart should *not* be forced out because of his personal conduct?" Bradley asked. Nineteen of those in the group raised their hands. But 24 thought Hart's conduct should be a factor when Bradley asked the reverse question.

Inklings of Independence

A middle-of-the-road Democrat, Bradley, much to the dismay of the regulars, parted company with his party and initially supported giving limited aid to the anti-government "contras" in Nicaragua. In his usual method of approaching an issue, he avoided jumping on the band wagon of popular public opinion but instead studied the situation thoroughly. He concluded that the pressure exerted by the contras would help keep the Sandinista government from exporting its revolution to neighboring nations. "We have to give some time for fledgling democracies in Latin America to develop," he told the *Wall Street Journal*.

After Nicaraguan President Daniel Ortega's peace overtures at the end of 1987, however, Bradley adopted a wait-and-see attitude to Reagan's call for immediate aid to the contras. The peace talks, which he said are testimony to the growing strength of democracy in the region, should be given a chance.

Although he raises few negative feelings, Dollar Bill Bradley is not without his detractors. Despite his down-to-earth, low-keyed manner, many find him aloof and remote. He is perceived as harboring an intellectual intolerance in his approach to issues. Some also see a degree of naivete and singlemindedness in his reliance on instincts. In a world of extroverts, Bradley is a very private person. He is an anomaly in the rough and tumble, hail-fellow-well-met sphere of politics.

His image is perhaps Lincolnesque, which may or may not play well through the medium of television. No Beau Brummell, Bradley hardly sets a sartorial example. Crumpled suits do little more than hang on his big frame. His former teammates on the Knicks used to say he was never in any danger of being mugged on the streets of New York City—because he always looked as if he just had been.

If Bradley has an Achilles heel in this day of mandatory communication via the electronic medium, it is his speaking ability. His style is most often described as "wooden." His ability to mangle a punch line is legendary.

"Where can you go from the bottom, but up," his press aide Nick Donatiello says when asked if Bradley is getting any better on the stump. "In nine years in the Senate he has done a lot of speaking and he's made some marginal improvement. But no one would tout him as an outstanding orator."

Another factor contributes to Bradley's problems as a speaker, Donatiello points out. The issues on which he is most knowledgable are ones hardest to communicate. "He likes to talk about ideas—complex ideas like tax reform and Third World debt. You can't boil them down to a 10-second sound bite on the evening news."

It may be that the New Jersey senator is getting a bum rap, however. When he is emotionally involved in the subject, or is speaking off the cuff, Bradley has been known to wow audiences.

"I went to this luncheon where he was scheduled to be the speaker, expecting to be bored out of my mind," confessed former ambassador Nick Veliotes, president of the Association of American Publishers. "But he was sensational."

The occasion was a meeting with business leaders put together by *Washington Post* editorial writers. Bradley spoke extemporaneously and answered questions for almost an hour. Recalled Veliotes: "He was witty, projected well, and was absolutely enthralling—and he made more sense in that 45 minutes than anyone I've heard in a long time."

On other occasions Bradley has delivered unexpectedly eloquent speeches in the Senate. Once, while sitting in his office, he was watching the televised floor debate on establishing a holiday in honor of Martin Luther King Jr. He was so upset by the speech of North Carolina Republican Sen. Jesse Helms, who was leading the campaign against the measure, that he hurried over to the floor and spoke from the heart.

"I want to give the senators from North Carolina the due respect of a colleague," he said. "But, I must say it's just not possible in this case. They speak for a past that the vast majority of Americans have overcome."

Beyond the bedrock of his beliefs, Bradley has other assets going for him. He has been described as a "rare politician who continues to grow." He has an unassailable reputation for honesty, he never stops studying and he has stepped up his foreign travel. The trip to the Soviet Union is a good example. He toured factories in Tvilisi and Azerbaidzhan and talked with ordinary citizens.

"He wanted to see for himself what effect the early stages of Perestroika [Restructuring] were having. He was surprised at the extent to which he was recognized," said Nick Donatiello. "He had appeared on television there on a telebridge program. People kept coming up to shake his hand and tell him they'd seen him on TV."

Bradley's marriage to Ernestine Schlant, who maintains a full teaching schedule in New Jersey, is a happy one. He is as proud of her accomplishments, including the writing of several books, as he is of his own. Indeed, for three days a week he is the primary parent for their 11-year-old daughter, Theresa Anne, while his wife commutes to her teaching job.

"He goes home at a reasonable hour in the evening so he can be with his daughter," Donatiello says. "But he takes his work home with him to do after she's gone to bed. It means we have staff meetings sometimes at 9:30 at night in his house."

Even during his pro-basketball days, Bradley was scrupulous. He refused to trade on his fame and endorse products. He brought and has maintained a new air of uncorruptability and respectability to New Jersey politics, which has suffered from a sometimes unsavory reputation. Three years after his arrival in Congress, Bradley, painfully, spoke on the Senate floor in favor of expelling his fellow New Jersey Democrat, Harrison A. Williams Jr., who had been convicted of taking a bribe in the Abscam scandals.

"Williams' misconduct has gone to the core of democratic government and the faith people extend to political institutions," Bradley said in explaining his vote. He described that ballot as the "toughest decision I've had to make."

Such an image makes Bill Bradley some observers' answer to the country's prayers for leadership. He has, wrote the *Wall Street Journal's*

Washington bureau chief Albert Hunt, "demonstrated a remarkable ability not only to seize on but to take the lead on important issues."

Many political pundits, including analyst Alan Baron, think Bradley is the most electable Democrat in the country today. His advisers worry that his time to run for the presidency may come and go before his vaunted self-instinct flashes the go-ahead signal.

"Timing is everything in politics, and few elections have offered as wide-open opportunities for both parties and many politicians," Hunt pointed out. A former campaign manager commented, "He doesn't sense that this is the only time the door may be open."

Some believe that Bradley's unwillingness may stem from his reluctance to be the Herbert Hoover of his generation. "He doesn't want to be a president sitting over a God-awful mess and be tagged with it," a Democratic fund-raiser told the *Newark Star-Ledger*.

Others think he wants to wait and see how the tax reform works out before he tosses his hat in the ring. Still, although he is ambitious and has demonstrated that he feels a sense of his own destiny to reach high places, Bradley may never get the "fire in the belly" deemed necessary to make the campaign for the nation's top prize.

His speech to the Princeton alumni may have been a prophetic statement of his future. "Elective office is one of democracy's marvelous abstractions," he told them. "You exercise power but you must not claim it. You work, you create, you affect people's lives, but you do so with a sense of your own frailty and your own place in time, which always passes."

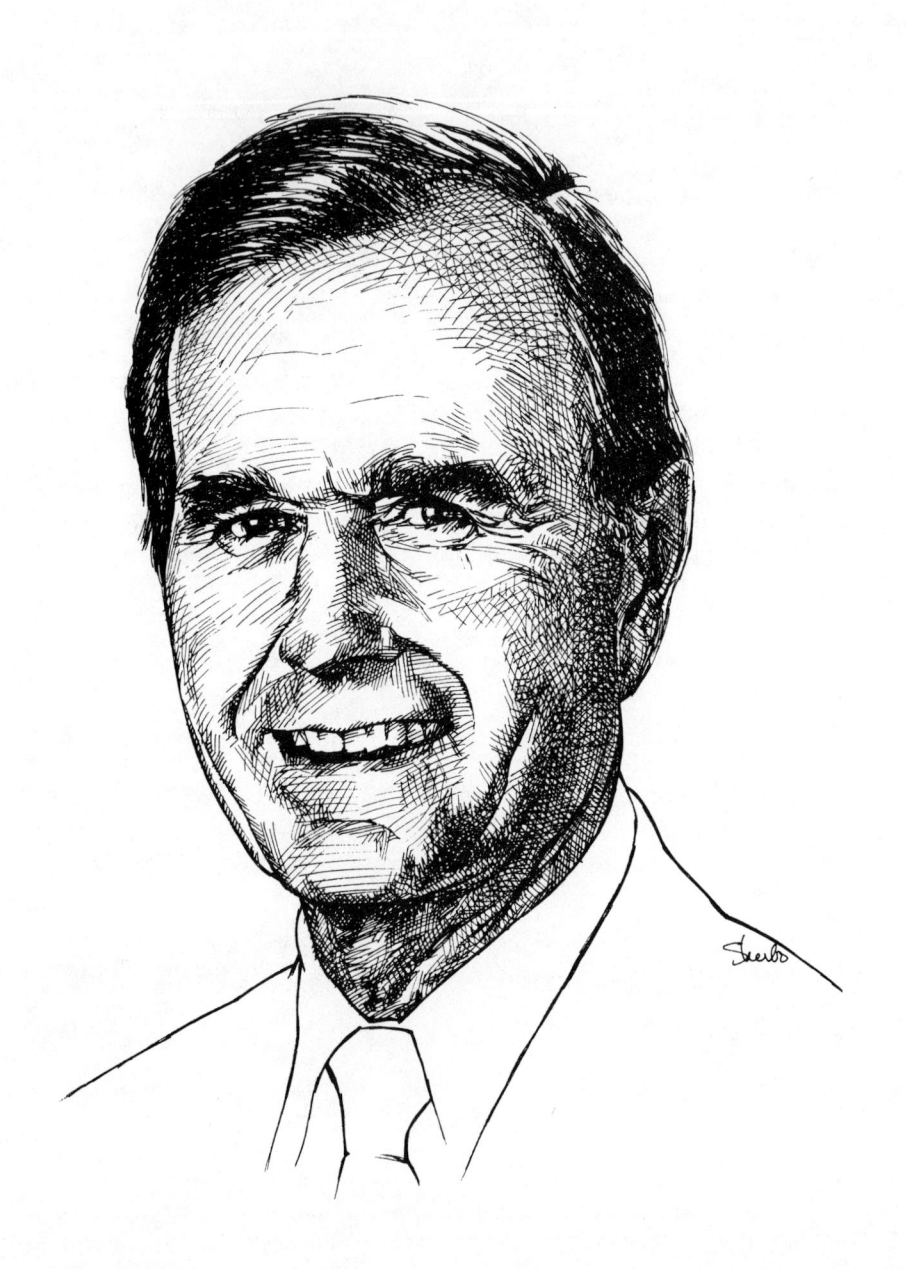

GEORGE BUSH

Wall Street Bows to Main Street As Route to Avoid Old GOP Pitfall

In his quest for the GOP presidential nomination, Vice President George Bush faced two major obstacles as he entered 1988. First, questions lingered regarding his participation, or lack of it, in the Iran-contra affair. Second, some observers mused that the vice president's broad résumé belied an electoral lightweight who might not have an appropriate character to win the presidency. Despite his impressive array of high-level appointments, he had not won election for public office on his own since a 1968 House race. Certain commentators had even called Bush a wimp.

Then, when he appeared on the "CBS Evening News with Dan Rather" in late January, Bush abruptly confronted both of these problems. Following a six-minute taped segment reviewing the Iran-contra affair, Rather, in a live interview with Bush, heatedly asked when and if Bush had voiced objections to the appearance of an arms-for-hostages deal. Halfway through the interview, the vice president suddenly lashed out at the anchorman for misleading him about the nature of the interview.

"It's not fair to judge my whole career by a rehash on Iran," he said. "How would you like it if I judged your career by those seven minutes when you walked off the set in New York? Would you like that?" Bush was referring to an earlier controversy when Rather had left the CBS News set, temporarily forcing the network to black out its transmission. Rather was visibly flustered by the reference. But irrespective of the particular squabble between Rather and Bush, it was the vice president's very display of rhetorical offense that impressed many observers.

During the 1980 campaign, Ronald Reagan had seemed to intimidate the more rarefied Bush. In his 1984 vice presidential debate against the less experienced Geraldine A. Ferraro, Bush had appeared far

Candidates '88

> ## George Herbert Walker Bush
>
> **Profession:** Public official; former oil drilling company executive.
> **Born:** June 12, 1924, Milton, Mass.
> **Home:** Houston, Texas.
> **Religion:** Episcopalian.
> **Education:** Yale University, B.A., 1948.
> **Career:** U.S. House of Representatives, 1967-71; ambassador to the United Nations, 1971-73; chairman, Republican National Committee, 1973-74; head, U.S. liaison office, Peking, 1974-75; director, Central Intelligence Agency, 1976-77; sought Republican nomination for president, 1980; U.S. vice president, 1981-89.
> **Military:** U.S. Navy, 1942-45.
> **Family:** Wife, Barbara Pierce; five children.
> **House Committees:** Ways and Means, 1967-71.

more peppy than combative. Not until his first four debates with contenders for the 1988 GOP presidential nomination had Bush used quips with aggressive poise. And not until his encounter with Rather had he exposed that disposition to a prime-time television audience. "Who'd have suspected," wrote the *New Republic*'s Fred Barnes, "that Bush would be funny, assertive, confrontational, succinct, and very, very quotable?"

Indeed, as putative front-runner in the Republican pack, Bush had substantially avoided such confrontation or debate until the late 1987 candidate forums. Then, in the first nationally televised debate, the vice president parried a thrust from former Delaware governor Pierre S. "Pete" du Pont IV. "My friend, Pierre, let me help you on some of this," he had said, gently chiding du Pont about his name. Bush went on to ridicule du Pont's idea of Social Security reform. "It may be a new idea," he said, "but it's a dumb one." Later still, during the January debate sponsored by the *Des Moines Register*, Bush was to go on the offensive against the newspaper's editor.

The verve and flair were new. Yet if Bush had partly overcome an image of timidity among political observers, he was still struggling in the first caucus among Republican voters. Bob Dole, the Senate minority leader who hailed from neighboring Kansas, was leading in the Iowa polls.

With a farm community that had not shared all the bounty of the economic recovery during the Reagan administration, Iowa was ripe for Dole's campaign. The senator invoked regional pride and sympathy; he had no connection to the Iran-contra affair; and he claimed to be a self-made man, portraying Bush as a privileged member of the blue-blood Eastern establishment.

Dole had opened the old Republican rift between Main Street and Wall Street. It was the chasm that had separated Thomas Dewey from Robert Taft, Nelson Rockefeller from Barry Goldwater and even George Bush from Ronald Reagan.

Yet in 1988 the contours would be different. The conservative resurgence ushered in by Reagan had left GOP contenders with few differences in an increasingly doctrinaire philosophy: opposition to big government and support of military strength. Tom Rath, a Dole adviser, explained before the Iowa caucuses that the battle for Republicans' hearts and minds already had been settled by recent history. So the 1988 nomination, he said, would be decided by voters conducting "a national job interview," which was a double-edged sword for Bush. While Bush ostensibly lead the second most important job in the land, no sitting vice president since Martin Van Buren had won election to the White House. Consequently, notwithstanding his newfound assertiveness, Bush was to campaign more on résumé than personality. The son of a senator, a war hero and Yale graduate who could point to private riches and public service, Bush simply argued that he was the best applicant for the job.

Moderate Conservative, Conservative Moderate

If nothing else, George Herbert Walker Bush could indeed lay claim to extensive experience. After an early adulthood making his fortune in the oil development business, he went on to become a veritable handyman of American politics.

Beginning in 1967 Bush served four years in the U.S. House from Texas. Although he failed in two runs for the U.S. Senate from Texas in 1964 and 1970, the result of the second loss was that Bush became a politician by appointment, rather than election. He followed his Senate defeat with stints over the next six years as U.S. ambassador to the United Nations, chairman of the Republican National Committee (RNC), head of the U.S. liaison office in Peking and director of the Central Intelligence Agency.

The appointments undoubtedly shaped his philosophy, yet Bush's appreciation of centrist politics was most evident in his brief career in the House. There he avoided extremes, shunned shrill pronouncements and often put something in his speeches that appealed to almost everybody.

Beneath the rhetoric, his voting record basically was conservative. His affluent constituents in suburban Houston's 7th District would not have it any other way. It is still the most Republican congressional district in Texas.

Through his four-year House tenure, Bush generally scored high in the ratings of the conservative Americans for Constitutional Action and low on the scoreboard of the liberal Americans for Democratic Action. In Congressional Quarterly's conservative coalition support studies, Bush generally earned a higher score than the average Republican in the House.

But there was flickering evidence of more moderate leanings in Bush's congressional record. The most notable was his vote for the Civil Rights Act of 1968 and the open housing requirements it contained. It was not a popular position with many of the voters in his home district. Indeed, in an interview with the *Christian Science Monitor* in late 1987, the vice president recalled just how much opposition he had faced on the issue at home.

During one meeting with constituents at Memorial High School, the young member of Congress heard jeers and catcalls from a crowd of angry white voters. They saw the open-housing law as a radical, governmental intrusion into the realm of private property. Bush had no choice but to confront the issue, and he did so with a deftness that would mark him as more than another run-of-the-mill GOP moderate.

Bush touched on civic responsibility. He mentioned black Vietnam veterans. The jeers began to wane. "Somehow it seems fundamental," Bush told the audience, "that a man should not have a door slammed in his face because he is a Negro or speaks with a Latin American accent." His conclusion brought a standing ovation.

Bush used the same touchstones on the House floor: "I do not want it on my conscience," he said, "that I have voted against legislation that would permit a Negro, say a Negro serviceman returning from Vietnam, where he has been fighting for the ideals of his country, to buy or rent a home of his choosing if he has the money."

At the same time, Bush qualified his support, saying that he would like to amend the bill and "remedy some of the inequities in the open-housing section." He soon distanced himself from any image of dyed-in-the-wool civil rights advocacy. Despite his backing for the 1968 civil rights bill, Bush expressed dismay at what he saw during the Poor People's March on Washington. Bush said that the march had rapidly deteriorated "into a power struggle at the expense of those honest poor people who made this long and often arduous trip to petition their government."

"This Congress will not buy threats," Bush wrote to civil rights leader Ralph Abernathy. "It will not condone violence. It will not accept legislative goals which are financially impossible and which lack inventiveness and stifle the initiative of the individual."

In 1970 when he was a Senate candidate, Bush bluntly told Congressional Quarterly: "Civil Rights legislation has caught up with the conscience of the country. No more major legislation [is] needed now."

A campaigning George Bush prepares to move an 18-wheeler in Greenland, N.H.

Also in 1970 Bush signed an anti-busing brief, prepared by Rep. William C. Cramer, R-Fla., that was filed with the U.S. Supreme Court.

Bush's ability to balance progressive and conservative agendas also was seen in his reaction to the civil disorders of the late 1960s, as well as in his proposals for environmental protection and political reform.

In 1967 he supported legislation that would have made interstate travel to incite a riot a federal crime. "There is no place for professional agitators who incite or take part in rioting, no matter what the cause," Bush said. On the other hand, in 1969 Bush opposed legislation that would have withheld federal funds from higher educational institutions that did not curb campus disorders. "I do not feel that we should pass legislation that will penalize the innocent to get the guilty," Bush told the House.

Concerning urban disorders, Bush advocated creation of a Neighborhood Action Crusade, volunteer organizations working to ease tensions in urban communities. It was another example of reaching for the center from conservative bedrock.

On environmental and consumer issues, Bush typically called for "responsible" action in both areas. He also supported world population control. In late 1969, as chairman of the House Republican earth resources task force, Bush noted that environmental problems were becoming a top priority among young voters. Still, he warned that little progress could be made from looking for scapegoats.

"Inherent in this concern for the environment, however, is the danger that some will place an unrealistic overemphasis on problems to the detriment of the interests of the consumer and our national economy," Bush once said. His idea of proportional response included support for creation of the Environmental Protection Agency in 1970 and for legislation proposed in 1969 by President Nixon to establish a consumer protection division in the Justice Department.

Bush also was in the forefront of the movement for procedural reform in politics. He called for full disclosure by public officials of assets, liabilities and sources of income. He disclosed his own finances, including the expenses of his House office. He likewise advocated banning foreign travel by House members after they were defeated for re-election.

Beyond political finance, Bush also advocated certain alterations in the systems of governance. In 1969 he voted for a proposed constitutional amendment, passed by the House, that would have abolished the Electoral College and provided for direct election of the president.

The next year Bush spoke in favor of extending the Voting Rights Act of 1965, but he objected to a provision that extended the franchise in all elections to 18-year-olds. Bush said he believed it was improper to attempt such a change by legislation. He preferred instead to see 18-year-olds receive the right to vote through a constitutional amendment, of which he was a cosponsor. Still later, he was a cosponsor of the Equal Rights Amendment.

Such positions did not infringe upon a consistent conservative tendency in Bush's approach to federal government and fiscal policy. A CQ study of 1967 House votes showed that out of 11 key votes, Bush was near the middle of House Republicans. He voted four times for expanding the federal government, seven times against.

The fiscal outlook was orthodox Republican. As a member of the House Ways and Means Committee in 1967, Bush cosponsored the ultimately unsuccessful Human Investment Act, which was designed to combat poverty through tax incentives instead of through categorical grant programs. He also opposed tax reform of the progressive variety.

Bush abandoned such delicate philosophizing, however, when it came to his old bailiwick, the domestic oil industry. While he had divested himself of his oil holdings upon election to the House in 1966, he continued to fight hard for those interests. He promoted curbs on the amount of oil that could be imported to the United States. He favored higher natural gas prices as a means of stimulating exploration. And he opposed reductions in the oil depletion allowance.

"I do not consider the oil depletion a tax break," Bush said during House debate on the Tax Reform Act of 1969. "It is not a gimmick; it is not a loophole." Although he admitted that the act would provide meaningful tax relief, Bush ultimately voted against the measure and its reduction in the oil depletion allowance.

In June 1970 Bush opposed President Nixon's plan to have all nations renounce their claims over seabed resources beyond a depth of 200 meters. Bush said such a renunciation would give up access to natural gas and oil reserves. "He unloaded his oil stock," said Jack Anderson in 1969, "but could not unload a heart that remained with oil."

And the same was true a decade later, when a far more broadly experienced Bush appeared on NBC's "Meet the Press" as a presidential candidate. Asked whether his oil background would make it difficult for him to deal with energy problems as president, Bush replied: "I have never accepted the Washington thesis that if you know something about a problem that should automatically disqualify you.... I sold out of a drilling contract business ... in 1966, just so cynical people couldn't make the charge against me that I was in it to feather my own nest."

Up From Finery

Texas oil man though he had become after college, Bush's bouts of intermittent moderation revealed him to be more New England Yankee than cowboy businessman. He still resembles the suave Ivy Leaguer, not the Sun Belt merchant. The son of Connecticut Sen. Prescott Bush (R-Conn., 1952-63), he was born in Milton, Mass., and graduated from Phillips Academy in Andover, Mass.

Bush did not always pursue the special dispensations of a silver spoon upbringing, however. On his 18th birthday he enlisted to become a Navy pilot, considered the youngest at the time. And, as detailed in the *Christian Science Monitor*, the years that followed in the air war against Japan forced Bush into a number of harrowing situations.

A mechanical problem once forced the young pilot down in the Pacific, with a full load of 500-pound bombs aboard. The payload exploded just moments after Bush and his crew escaped in a life raft. On another occasion, Bush won the Navy's Distinguished Flying Cross for completing an attack after his plane was hit by flak. His two crewmates died when the plane was ditched at sea.

Bush returned to New England a war hero. He attended Yale University in New Haven, Conn., captaining the baseball team and completing his degree in two and a half years. Following graduation in 1948 he moved to Texas to enter the oil business. He had $3,000 in savings from his Navy days, and he had a wife and child.

To be sure, with his father having moved into a prestigious investment banking firm, Bush could have chosen an easier path. But he wanted to make his own mark and his own fortune, by learning the oil business from the ground up. He did accept a foot in the door, however. He first took a job as warehouse sweeper and then supply salesman with the Odessa, Texas, firm of Dresser Industries—an oil field supply company of which his father was director.

In 1951 he helped start the Bush-Overbey Development Co., which traded oil leases and royalties. Two years later he co-founded Zapata Petroleum Corp., and in 1954 he became president of the Zapata Off-Shore Co., first based in Midland and then Houston.

In Houston Bush became active in Republican affairs and eventually became chairman of the GOP organization in Harris County. In 1964 he sought the Republican Senate nomination. Against three other contenders, Bush was forced to overcome the stigma of being from the East and the handicap of not being well-known.

Avoiding the party's far-right wing, he finished first in the initial GOP primary with 44 percent of the vote. A month later he won the nomination in a runoff with 61.6 percent over the better-known Jack Cox, who had come within 132,000 votes of upsetting John Connally for governor in 1962. Against Democratic Sen. Ralph Yarborough, Bush won a respectable 43.6 percent of the vote, losing by 333,000 votes while Lyndon B. Johnson was carrying his native state by 704,000 votes in the presidential election.

So the loss hardly stigmatized the young Bush, given the state's longstanding predilection for the Democratic Party. And in 1966, with his rising name recognition, Bush won a newly created House seat in the Houston suburbs, defeating a conservative Democrat, with 57.1 percent of the vote.

By 1968 Bush was being mentioned as a vice presidential possibility. But Nixon bypassed the one-term representative, and Bush instead won re-election to his House seat without opposition.

Two years later Bush made another bid for the Senate. He was preparing to run against the liberal Yarborough, but his plans were upset when the incumbent was defeated in the Democratic primary by Lloyd Bentsen. The equation had changed, as the *Texas Observer* put it in November 1970: "The main question seems to be whether the next conservative senator from Texas should be a Republican or a Democrat."

Ironically, Bush received indirect aid from the liberal wing of the Texas Democratic Party, which found Bentsen unacceptable. Liberal economist John Kenneth Galbraith and former senator Ernest Gruening, a liberal Democrat from Alaska, wrote letters in behalf of Bush. On the other side of the fence, the conservative Americans for Constitutional Action also endorsed Bush over Bentsen. It seemed that the young transplant had successfully charted his conservative-centrist course.

But the endorsements and campaign appearances by Nixon and Vice President Spiro Agnew were not enough for Bush. Nor was his sophisticated television advertising campaign. He lost by nearly 160,000 votes, receiving 46 percent of the vote. Again, though, Bush had made more of a name for himself.

Power by Appointment

In December 1970 Bush entered the second phase of his political career when Nixon announced he would appoint the Texan as ambassador to the United Nations. The selection drew praise from Democrats as well as Republicans in the House, though the appointment was criticized in other quarters because of Bush's lack of foreign policy experience. The Senate confirmed his appointment by a voice vote in February 1971.

At the U.N. Bush pushed unsuccessfully for keeping Taiwan in the United Nations while seating the People's Republic of China. By advocating the U.S. policy of representation for both Chinese governments, Bush displayed a shift from his 1964 campaign statement that the United States should leave the U.N. if the Peking government were admitted. Yet the reversal went unnoticed, and his efforts in behalf of the Taiwan government silenced most complaints that he knew nothing about diplomacy.

In December 1972 Nixon selected Bush to be the Republican national chairman. His tenure in that post covered the turbulent last year and a half of Nixon's presidency. Bush faced the difficult task of defending the interests of the party while Nixon was under fire in the Watergate scandal. "We've struggled mightily to make it clear that the party is separate from Watergate, but I don't know that I've been overly successful," Bush said at the end of 1973.

Bush attempted to be loyal to Nixon while criticizing Watergate. "You don't see pictures of Gordon Liddy [on the walls of the party headquarters]; you see them of Nixon...," Bush told Congressional Quarterly in early 1974. "I don't feel inhibited from criticizing Watergate. I do believe in supporting the president. I don't think that's contradictory."

That approach did not satisfy everyone. Columnist George Will wrote in November 1975 that "in spite of all the available evidence, he [Bush] never expressed independent judgments inconvenient to Richard Nixon." On the other hand, when Bush's appointment as CIA director was pending, Sen. Barry Goldwater, R-Ariz., defended Bush, saying "I think Bush was the first man ... who let the president know he should go." It had been at the height of the Watergate crisis, in fact, when Bush wrote to Nixon, "It is my considered judgment that you should resign."

Even as late as October 1979, Bush continued to chart a middle course between independence and loyalty to Nixon. "In some ways, Nixon was a good president," he said. "In some ways he was flawed."

Keeping his eye on tact, loyalty and opportunity all at once kept Bush in high Republican esteem throughout the 1970s. In August 1974, after Gerald R. Ford succeeded Nixon as president, Bush was mentioned as a possible choice as Ford looked to fill the vacant vice president's post. Instead, Ford picked Bush as the U.S. envoy to Peking. The appointment did not require Senate confirmation.

Bush received little public attention in Peking and had served slightly more than a year when President Ford fired William E. Colby as director of central intelligence and named Bush.

Bush's selection to head the CIA met with opposition from Frank Church, D-Idaho, chairman of the Senate Intelligence Committee. Critics objected to his past political roles, particularly as RNC chairman, and the possibility he would be Ford's vice presidential running mate in 1976. Bush told the Senate Armed Services Committee in December 1975 that he would not forswear acceptance of the number-two spot on the 1976 GOP national ticket. But he promised to actively discourage any campaign on his behalf. On Jan. 27, 1976, the Senate confirmed Bush by a 63-27 vote after Ford gave assurances that he would not propose Bush as his 1976 running mate. And by the end of Bush's tenure as CIA director in early 1977, several of his Democratic detractors praised his stewardship of the intelligence agency.

Pursuit of the Presidency

Shortly after the end of the Ford administration, Bush began preparing for his own shot at the presidency. His first vehicle was the Fund for a Limited Government, which he formed to pay for his travel expenses while he was campaigning for Republican congressional candidates and which contributed money to those candidates. In early January 1979 he formed the George Bush for President committee.

That month, Bush publicly outlined his plans for pursuing the GOP presidential nomination. In an interview on ABC's "Issues and Answers," Bush displayed a keen awareness of the nomination game: "The strategy is going to be to go up into New Hampshire and other early primary states. Right after that is Massachusetts, Vermont, Connecticut and Alabama. Go in there, work my heart out, not with a large entourage, not with a lot of public attention, going one on one in small towns, in counties and at the same time trying to peel away from what now is a strong Reagan in-cadre up there."

Bush also said he was "trying to get people that were for President Ford for me." That statement described the essentials of a strategy that was designed to make Bush, rather than Tennessee Sen. Howard H. Baker, Jr., the more moderate alternative to Reagan.

It was a strategy that faced considerable obstacles. A Gallup Poll in December 1978 showed that Bush was less well known among Republicans than either Reagan or Baker and trailed both of them as the presidential preference. In January 1979 Bush said: "I am back where Jimmy Carter was at this time in 1975."

By September 1979 Bush still had a low standing in the polls. A Gallup Poll released Sept. 23 showed he was the choice of 3 percent of the Republicans and independents interviewed. But he had increased his recognition to 38 percent from the 33 percent standing in 1978.

At the end of the third quarter of 1979, the Bush committee had raised about $2.4 million. Among Republicans, that put him behind Reagan, John Connally and Rep. Philip M. Crane in total funds raised. But, in line with his efforts to appeal to politically disparate elements, he had succeeded in assembling a campaign staff that was diverse in its background.

His campaign chairman had run Ford's general election campaign in 1976. Bush's political operations director was a key leader in Reagan's 1976 campaign. His campaign press secretary was a former communications director for the Republican National Committee, and the deputy press secretary had been the Democratic National Committee's communications director. What's more, several aides of former Alabama governor George C. Wallace, a Democrat, were working the field for Bush.

Again and again, Bush hewed to the moderate conservative line. He proposed a $20 billion tax cut, of which half would go to individuals to encourage increased personal savings and to provide tax incentives for home purchases. The other half would go to the business sector for investment tax credits and incentives to hire and train young workers.

As president, Bush said he would not allow federal spending to grow by more than 7 percent a year. The candidate did say he would propose a balanced budget by 1982, but he opposed a mandatory balanced budget through constitutional amendment.

On energy issues, Bush supported decontrol of oil prices, but with a windfall profits tax. He favored expansion of nuclear power, after taking steps to improve weaknesses in the Nuclear Regulatory Commission.

On defense, Bush advocated restoration of new weapons systems canceled or delayed by the Carter administration, including the neutron bomb. He opposed the Strategic Arms Limitation Treaty (SALT) in its originally negotiated form: "The SALT treaty is seriously defective and should be corrected before it leaves Capitol Hill."

As former intelligence director, Bush advocated a strengthened CIA, but with stringent protections for the rights of U.S. citizens. He criticized Carter for stopping in 1977 the SR-71 flights over Cuba, saying that it weakened U.S. intelligence. He also criticized Carter for establishing diplomatic relations with the People's Republic of China. "For the first time in our history," he wrote in the *Washington Post*, "a peacetime American government has renounced a treaty with an ally [Taiwan] without cause or benefit."

All in all, however, the Bush campaign was unable to sustain deep popular support. After a startling upset of Reagan in the Iowa caucus, Bush was outflanked in New Hampshire. Reagan swept to the nomination. Still, Bush had succeeded in establishing himself as the orthodox alternative, which garnered him the number-two spot on the ticket.

One More Try

After two terms subordinating his moderate leanings to an immensely popular conservative president, Bush entered the 1988 race with the same strengths and liabilities that came with being a Republican establishmentarian. But he now faced a new difficulty in the lingering questions about his part in the administration's greatest failure: the Iran-contra affair. While he tried to campaign on his loyalty and performance as vice president, he said that he could not fully explain his place in the Iran controversy, claiming that his advice to the president had been confidential.

"I made the decision early on to stand with the president," he told the *Des Moines Register* in October 1987. "And frankly it's cost me, cost me in some rather hurtful ways. Because I'm unwilling to go out and criticize the president or say in public that which I tell him in private, that's cost me some identity."

In November, the congressional Iran-contra report found no evidence that Bush had been aware that profits from arms sales to Iran were being diverted to Nicaraguan insurgents. But the report hardly portrayed a vigorous leading light within administration policy circles either: "The vice president attended several meetings on the Iran initiative," it said, "but none of the participants could recall his views." Unable or unwilling to clarify the matter, Bush remained vulnerable; some questioned his complicity, others his competence.

To counter any appearance of being ineffectual, Bush pointed to other aspects of his performance within the administration. He concentrated on his leadership of presidential study groups, one on deregulation, another to investigate the slayings of young blacks in Atlanta.

On the foreign policy side, Bush pointed to his chairmanship of Reagan's "crisis management" team. There, according to anonymous administration officials who discussed Bush's record with the *New York Times*, Bush had indeed been more than a symbolic player. His role in the October 1983 invasion of Grenada, for example, had been far greater than publicly disclosed at the time. With the president out of town, it had been Bush who held a top-level meeting, recommended the military option and sent the proposal on for Reagan's approval.

Still, his leadership of task forces and study groups left him open to attacks from his chief rival for the nomination, Robert Dole. As Senate minority leader, Dole argued that he had been a "producer not an observer." He said he had been on the political front line, "not just standing there with the president."

Bush sought to counter Dole's attacks by sharpening his image and softening his erstwhile Reaganesque rhetoric with proposals that smacked of the old moderate. He continued to claim traditional conservative roots, opposing governmental growth and new taxes. But he increasingly emphasized arms control and a host of domestic initiatives that had held small place in the Reagan agenda.

"I'd like to be the follow-on president to complete a very broad and very aggressive arms-control agenda," he told Iowans. Beyond the administration's Intermediate Nuclear Forces treaty with the Soviets, Bush championed 50 percent reductions in strategic, long-range nuclear weapons, adding that he would then pursue negotiated reductions in conventional forces.

On the domestic side, Bush said he would make improved education programs the "cornerstone" of his administration. In formally announcing his candidacy Bush surprised some observers with the emphasis he placed on the issue: "If we have to spend a little more money on our schools, well, what could be a better investment?"

Among other things, Bush proposed additional money for Head

Start and other programs for needy preschoolers. He also supported Pell college-student grants, which the Reagan administration had tried to cut. And he called for tax-free college savings bonds, to be patterned after U.S. savings bonds.

The candidate also began stressing environmental protection, more federal support for child care and equal pay for women workers as goals of a Bush presidency. It seemed a clear break from the Republican far right, with the *Wall Street Journal* quoting the vice president as saying that he had "solidified the animosity of a handful of the extra-chromosome set."

Yet for all that moderation, Bush was not so willing to diverge from conservative thought on the issue of the deficit. "The best answer is to keep the recovery going," he told the *Des Moines Register*. "It is not to raise taxes." In fact, Bush even proposed a slice in capital-gains taxes, arguing that such a cut would spur investment.

Whether his delicate balance between conservatives and moderates would prove successful remained a big question as Bush pursued the 1988 nomination. Even with a substantial war chest and the vastly heightened name recognition that had come with the vice presidency, Bush was fighting an uphill battle at the first caucus in Iowa. And if he could not make a strong showing there, many observers thought he might quickly lose the expectations game.

Unable to marshal the fervent conservative support that had brought Reagan to the White House, Bush would appeal to the GOP center as he had eight years before. "I avoid being labeled," Bush said in January 1979 on ABC News' "Issues and Answers" when he was asked whether he was a liberal, moderate or conservative. "We Republicans—this is our death wish—we try to categorize some person, label them. I don't want to be labeled."

So the personable and casual man who had been able to get along with the diverse elements of the Republican Party found himself in many ways back where he had been in 1980: neither fervently supported nor opposed. "One would sooner look for the needle in the haystack than for someone who, having been exposed to Bush, dislikes him," wrote conservative columnist William F. Buckley Jr. Yet whether that lack of animosity could be translated into a base of support remained Bush's challenge.

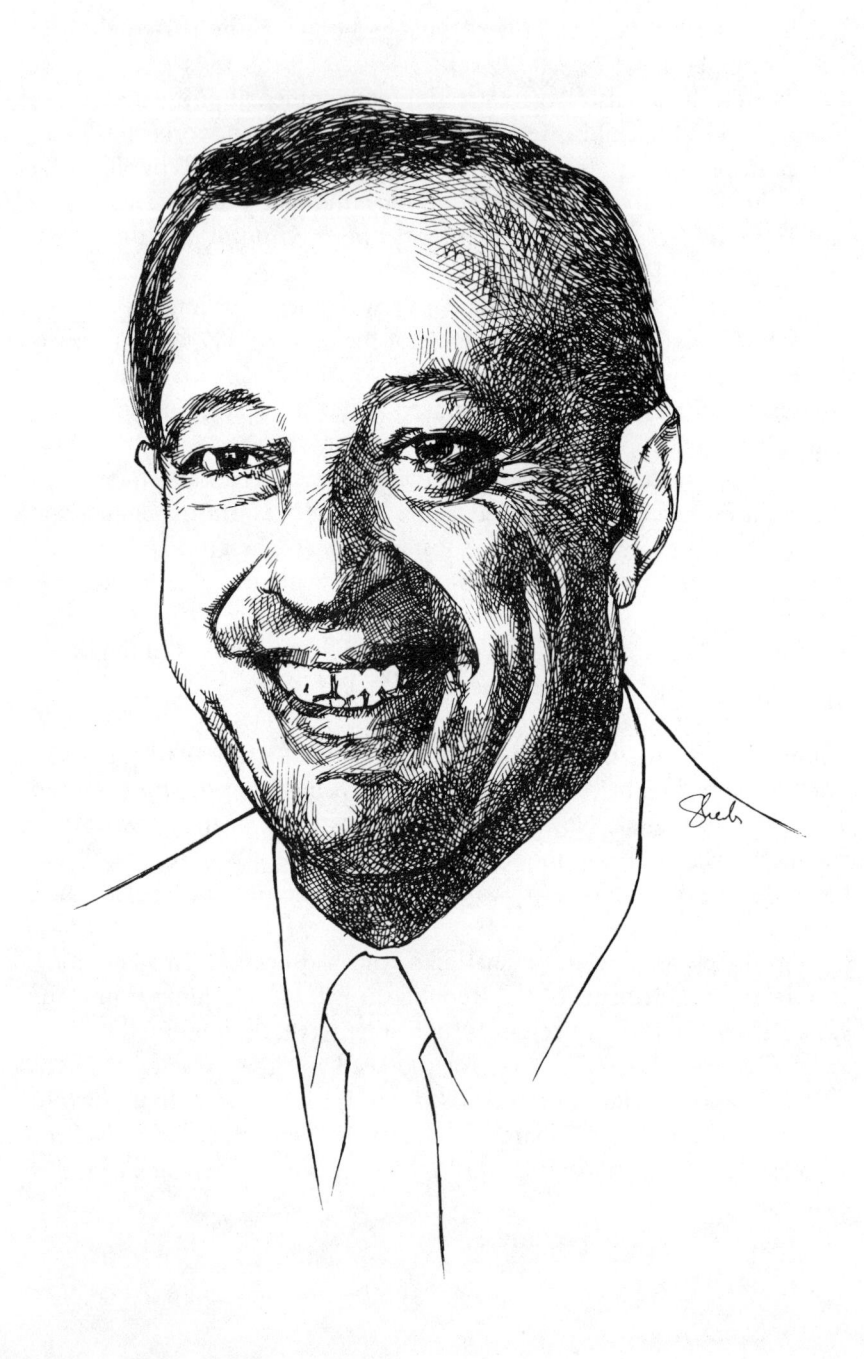

MARIO CUOMO

Despite His Protests, Draft Talk Persists

It was shortly before 8 p.m. and New York Gov. Mario M. Cuomo was winding up his weekly, hour-long radio call-in show at WCBS-AM in New York City. Sitting alone in the studio, Cuomo reached into his jacket pocket, pulled out a piece of paper and read, "I will not be a candidate" for president in 1988. He then turned and left the studio, ignoring the pack of stunned reporters waiting for him.

The reporters weren't the only ones who were surprised. Ever since Cuomo made his impromptu announcement on a February night in 1987, Democrats—and not a few Republicans—across the country have been struggling to suspend their disbelief. Cuomo, the 56-year-old son of Italian immigrants who was virtually unknown outside his home state a scant six years ago, has become one of the national Democratic Party's hottest properties, and a lot of people think he is his party's best hope of recapturing the presidency. They are having a hard time accepting Cuomo's decision not to run.

Such a hard time, in fact, that some of his supporters refuse to accept his announcement at face value. Under the proper political circumstances, and with the right amount of sweet-talking, they argue, Cuomo might still be coaxed into the 1988 campaign.

Even Cuomo's critics—and he has his share of detractors—seem to enjoy joining in the game of "will he stay or will he go?" As a result, every Cuomo action is interpreted for signs of his true presidential intentions; every speech is combed for clues.

For his part, Cuomo has stuck to his story, continually disavowing any ambitions to run this time around. "I think the candidate will come—and should come—from the pool of announced candidates," he said early in 1988.

But the governor has refused to make a Shermanesque statement,

Mario Matthew Cuomo

Profession: Lawyer.
Born: June 15, 1932, Queens, N.Y.
Home: Holliswood, N.Y.
Religion: Roman Catholic.
Education: St. John's University, B.A., 1953; LL.B., 1956.
Political Career: Sought Democratic nomination for lieutenant governor, 1974; New York secretary of state, 1975-79; sought Democratic nomination for New York City mayor, 1977; Liberal Party nominee for mayor, 1977; New York lieutenant governor, 1979-83; New York governor, 1983-present.
Family: Wife, Matilda Raffa; five children.

and he sometimes makes coy responses to questions about his political future that fan the very flames he claims to want extinguished. Asked about the possibility of a brokered convention—one in which no Democrat wins enough support in the primaries and caucuses to secure the nomination, putting the decision in the hands of the delegates at the convention—Cuomo leaves the door open to a draft candidacy. "I'll do the right thing," he said, setting off a whole new round of speculating.

The speculation has been fueled further by Cuomo's itinerary. He may be sincere when he says his political interests are limited to New York affairs, but his frequent speeches on national issues and trips around the country—and to places like the Soviet Union—do not exactly enhance his case.

Cuomo may yet become a presidential candidate; then again, reporters may wind up having wasted a lot of time and ink. But whatever happens, he almost certainly will continue to occupy a position of unusual influence in the 1988 campaign. Whether he is hosting forums for the other candidates, hinting at his favorites or merely being batted about in the rumor mill, Cuomo will still cast a long shadow over the current Democratic field.

Into the Spotlight

Actually, Cuomo has had some time to grow accustomed to all the attention. He first began hearing his name mentioned for national office back in 1983.

One reason for that is the interest traditionally showered upon New York's governor. By winning election to the office in 1982, Cuomo joined an elite club whose members have included some of the biggest names in American political history: Al Smith, Franklin Delano Roosevelt, Thomas Dewey and Nelson A. Rockefeller. Cuomo attained a certain amount of stature simply by virtue of where he sits.

Cuomo also attracted some attention by actively involving himself in the process of picking a Democratic presidential nominee for 1984. He held forums in New York to view his party's leading contenders, then grabbed headlines by endorsing Minnesota Democrat Walter F. Mondale shortly after the forums were completed. That move sparked a special interest in Cuomo in the Mondale camp.

Cuomo was placed on a list of politicians being considered by Mondale aides as a prospective running mate. That experience gave Cuomo some early practice at deftly demurring—a maneuver that has since become his specialty.

"I don't want to be vice president," Cuomo said in response to the running-mate rumors. "I want to be governor." He went on to explain that as vice president, "you would have to know about the IMF [International Monetary Fund] instead of the Buffalo Savings Bank. You would have to know about the Persian Gulf instead of Saturday night specials."

A Rousing Speech

But if Cuomo declined interest in the vice presidency, he was anxious to play some role in the 1984 campaign. He found his niche as keynote speaker at the Democratic National Convention in San Francisco, a role that vaulted him into prominence across the country and cemented his status as a party superstar.

His stirring speech gave Democrats who had been searching for ways to express the frustrations they felt in the Reagan era the words they had been looking for.

"A shining city is perhaps all the president sees from the portico of the White House and the veranda of his ranch, where everyone seems to be doing well," Cuomo thundered, alluding to Reagan's fondness for casting America as "a shining city on a hill." "But there's another part of the city, the part where some people can't pay their mortgages and most young people can't afford one, where students can't afford the education they need and middle-class parents watch the dreams they hold for their children evaporate."

Much of Cuomo's address was given over to an indictment of Reagan administration policies. He criticized the president for causing a recession and for racking up a federal budget deficit that "is the largest in the history of this universe," which he branded "a mortgage on our children's future that can only be paid in pain and that could eventually bring this nation to its knees." He said Reagan's foreign policy "drifts with no real direction, other than a hysterical commitment to an arms race that leads nowhere—if we're lucky. And if we're not it could lead us into bankruptcy or war."

But the address also revealed a good deal about Cuomo's own political philosophy. A scholarly man who cites Sir Thomas More and French poet Teilhard de Chardin as intellectual influences, Cuomo hammered home his belief in the traditional welfare-state obligations of the Democratic Party.

"We believe, as Democrats, that a society as blessed as ours, the most affluent democracy in the world's history, that can spend trillions on instruments of destruction, ought to be able to help the middle class in its struggle, ought to be able to find work for all who can do it, room at the table, shelter for the homeless, care for the elderly and infirm, hope for the destitute," he said.

Wary of his party's liberal image, Cuomo tempered his testimony on the legitimacy of federal spending with a dose of fiscal austerity. "We believe in only the government we need," he said, echoing a phrase aired during his inaugural speech in Albany, "but we insist on all the government we need."

He also explained his interpretation of the basic divide between Democrats and Republicans. "The difference ... has always been measured in courage and confidence," Cuomo said. "Republicans believe the wagon train will not make it to the frontier unless some of our old, some of our young and some of our weak are left behind by the side of the trail. . . . We Democrats believe that we can make it all the way with the whole family intact."

The Early Years

Cuomo's own family comes from the Provincia di Salerno, a stretch of south central Italy. His father emigrated to Jersey City, N.J., where he worked digging sewers and operating a push cart. Years later, the younger Cuomo would joke that his father had been greatly affected by the Great Depression of 1929. "A stockbroker jumped out the window and landed on his pushcart."

The elder Cuomo soon moved his family to Jamaica, Queens, an ethnic polyglot on the Long Island section of New York City. There he opened an all-night grocery. His family lived in an apartment behind the store.

Mario attended both public and Roman Catholic parochial schools as a boy and received a strict Vincentian education in his adolescence at St. John's prep school. He excelled in athletics, and his prowess on the baseball diamond soon attracted outside attention. Following his gradua-

Mario Cuomo keynoting the 1984 Democratic National Convention.

tion from high school, Cuomo signed a contract to join the Pittsburgh Pirates' baseball organization, as a player for their New Brunswick, Ga., farm team.

He distinguished himself as an able center fielder, and team scouts saw him as a man with a promising future. "Potentially the best prospect on the club, in my opinion, and could go all the way if he improves his hitting to the point of a respectable batting average," Pirate scout Ed McCarrick wrote of Cuomo.

McCarrick also provided some insights into the young Cuomo's character. "He is aggressive and plays hard. He is intelligent.... He is not an easy chap to get close to but is very well-liked by those who succeed in penetrating the exterior's shell.... He is another who will run over you if you get in his way."

Despite his promise, Cuomo soon abandoned his plans to play professional baseball. A fastball to the head—which left him laid up in the hospital for a month—helped him make his decision. He returned home to Queens and took a scholarship to attend St. John's University. But he did not give up sports entirely. He helped pay the balance of his education bills by playing semiprofessional basketball.

Early on, Cuomo had planned a career as a teacher. But after graduation he decided instead to pursue a legal path, convincing himself that he would better be able to provide for his family on a lawyer's salary. While enrolled at St. John's law school he started that family, marrying college friend Matilda N. Raffa. Her teaching position helped tide the two over until Cuomo graduated—tied for top honors in his class—in 1956.

Cuomo took a job as a law secretary for Judge Adrian Burke, who served on the New York State Court of Appeals. As Cuomo recalls it, those were halcyon days. "Maybe the happiest two years I ever had—writing law for the judges," he once told the *New York Times*.

After his stint with Judge Burke, Cuomo decided to strike out on his own as a lawyer. Unsuccessful in his attempts to land a position with a prestigious Wall Street firm, he settled for a spot in a Brooklyn outfit, where he soon began working with community groups that had disputes with the state and local government. Those disputes gave Cuomo the skills and the exposure that would launch his political career.

Cuomo's first major community dispute involved plans by New York City fathers to remove scrap dealers and junkyard owners from Willets Point, Queens, to make room for the 1964 World's Fair. Cuomo helped the dealers and owners win a settlement that saved many of their jobs.

The publicity from that effort helped attract the attention of a group of families from the predominantly Italian-American community of Corona, Queens. The families were up in arms over a New York City government plan to bulldoze houses in the area to make room for athletic facilities and a new high school. Following a protracted legal battle, Cuomo helped negotiate a compromise with New York City Mayor John V. Lindsay to build a smaller school, move the athletic facilities and spare most of the houses in the neighborhood.

Impressed with Cuomo's performance, Lindsay asked him to intervene in another community-government dispute in 1972. This one involved middle-class residents of Forest Hills, Queens, who feared that a public housing project—slated to be built in their midst—would bring poverty and crime to their neighborhood.

Cuomo, holding hearings with key participants that often stretched late into the night, crafted a compromise. He proposed that the housing complex be reduced in size by half, to preserve the project but reduce its impact on Forest Hills. His plan was adopted by the Lindsay administration, and the project was built as he proposed. Cuomo later published an account of the episode, entitled *Forest Hills Diary: The Crisis of Low Income Housing*.

In it he professed a distaste for politicians and complained that "the system" was insensitive to the needs and concerns of those caught in the Forest Hills controversy.

Overcoming His Objections

But Cuomo's disdain for politics evidently did not run too deeply. Basking in the publicity he received from his Forest Hills victory, he began plotting his own path to elective office.

He first set his sights on the Democratic nomination for the New York City mayoralty in 1973. But Cuomo scuttled those plans after Queens Democratic leader Matthew Troy endorsed another mayoral candidate, Rep. Mario Biaggi. Cuomo then examined his options statewide and decided to enter the 1974 race for lieutenant governor.

He won his party's endorsement for the post at the state Democratic convention, but that did not prevent a primary. Cuomo wound up losing that contest to state Sen. Mary Anne Krupsak, who went on to victory in November.

Cuomo did receive a consolation prize, however. Hugh Carey, an old friend from Brooklyn who tried to coax Cuomo into running for office in New York City in the late 1960s, had won election as governor, and he wanted Cuomo as part of his cabinet. Cuomo signed on as secretary of state, a post he used to investigate the nursing home industry, help overhaul the state's lobbying laws and wrangle a settlement on an Indian lands dispute.

Carey still desired a strong ally in New York City, and it wasn't long before he began thinking about Cuomo as mayor. According to the *New York Times*, Cuomo found out the hard way. "Without really checking with Mr. Cuomo," the *Times* reported, "he [Carey] called newspaper reporters and announced that Mr. Cuomo would be his candidate for mayor."

It was a difficult campaign. Cuomo had to contend with a field already crowded with able contenders, led by Edward I. Koch, who represented a patch of Manhattan's affluent East Side in the U.S. House at the time. Despite the endorsement of the *Times*, Cuomo finished second to Koch in the Democratic primary and failed to reverse that outcome in the subsequent runoff. Cuomo remained on the general election ballot as the Liberal Party nominee, however, and received a surprisingly strong 42 percent of the citywide vote in November.

Later, Cuomo critiqued his own candidacy. "I didn't belong in the race," he said. "I looked tentative because I was tentative. I looked around and said these guys [the other candidates] are as good or better."

It was not long before Cuomo's hat was back in the ring, this time as a candidate for attorney general in 1978. But Carey again intervened. Krupsak had announced plans to challenge Carey's re-election for governor. Carey asked Cuomo to drop his ambitions to become attorney general and run once again for lieutenant governor. Cuomo complied, and helped Carey pull off a come-from-behind re-election victory.

Although Cuomo's new job was largely ceremonial, he found ways to put it to political use. He studied the intricacies of the state budget process and made himself a statewide ombudsman, winning praise for helping citizens navigate the New York bureaucracy.

Running for Governor

By 1982 Cuomo's relationship with Carey had soured, and, like

Krupsak before him, he considered challenging the governor for re-election. But Carey's fading popularity convinced him to scrap plans to seek a third term, and Cuomo eagerly entered the race to succeed him.

He began the campaign as an underdog even for the Democratic nomination, largely because of the candidacy of his old nemesis: Koch. The feisty mayor of New York City laid claim to a powerful urban base; he had won re-election to a second term the year before with both the Democratic and the GOP nominations, pulling 74 percent of the vote citywide. That base would be crucial in the gubernatorial primary, for New York City usually casts roughly 60 percent of the Democratic primary vote.

Koch also appeared well positioned to build on his city base. Although he was known as an orthodox liberal during his five terms in the U.S. House, Koch had cultivated a somewhat more conservative reputation as mayor, embracing the death penalty and presiding over cutbacks in social spending. That image had given him entrée to suburbanites and upstate residents not normally enjoyed by politicians from the city.

But Koch squandered that entrée relatively early in the campaign, when he told *Playboy* magazine he considered life in suburbia "sterile" and branded rural life "a joke." Cuomo pounced upon the much-needed opening. "... New York City faces the worst deficit in its history, perhaps as much as $1.2 billion," Cuomo said in announcing his candidacy. "There will be no relief from New York City's fiscal despair if the two-thirds of the population that vote in November and live outside the city's limits are given reason to feel alienated." He hinted again at Koch's blunder by saying of himself that "no one knows the whole state better, no one loves the whole state more."

Cuomo also chipped away at Koch by questioning his Democratic credentials. He cited President Reagan's praise for Koch's fiscal management of the city as evidence that the mayor had strayed too far to the right to suit most New Yorkers.

Koch's hard line on crime kept him popular in the suburbs, despite his impolitic urban chauvinism, and he probably would have won had his city base remained firm. But some of his supporters there were unhappy with his decision to run for governor; they reminded him of a pledge he had made to remain 12 years in City Hall. Koch also suffered a hemorrhaging of support among blacks and Hispanics who resented his budget knife.

Capitalizing on his support among labor unions—whose members launched a massive canvassing drive on his behalf—white liberals and minorities, Cuomo posted an upset primary victory. He made a strong showing upstate, kept close to Koch in the outer boroughs of New York City and carried Manhattan, taking 52 percent of the vote statewide.

In the fall, Cuomo faced conservative Republican Lew Lehrman, a millionaire drugstore executive making his first bid for public office. Lehrman had clinched the GOP nomination easily, digging deep into his own fortune to finance television ads against a little-known moderate Republican, and his efforts gave him some valuable name recognition for the general election campaign. An ardent adherent of supply-side economics, Lehrman touted a drastic cut in state taxes to prime business' pump. He branded Cuomo a liberal in league with the unpopular Carey and argued that the Democrat was soft on crime.

It almost worked. Lehrman carried all but nine of the state's 62 counties. Only by making inroads into the normally Republican Italian-American vote, racking up strong margins in New York City and in upstate urban areas such as Albany and Buffalo—and by carrying the inner suburbs—was Cuomo able to salvage a victory. He edged Lehrman by just 180,386 votes out of nearly 5.3 million ballots cast.

A Pleasant Honeymoon

Cuomo's election as governor turned his career around. Going into the campaign, he was a four-time loser (counting primaries, runoffs and general elections) who had never won an election on his own. Coming out, he had overcome the odds and a financial disadvantage to pull out a victory.

His inaugural address in Albany on Jan. 1, 1983, provided some clues as to what sort of governor he wanted to be. "I believe government's basic purpose is to allow those blessed with talent to go as far as they can—on their own merits," Cuomo declared. "But I believe that government also has an obligation to assist those who, for whatever inscrutable reason, have been left out by fate—the homeless, the infirm, the destitute—to help provide those necessary things which, through no fault of their own, they cannot provide for themselves."

It was not long before Cuomo received his first taste of governing. On Jan. 8, 1983, inmates at New York's Ossining prison took a group of guards hostage, setting up a confrontation reminiscent of the 1971 Attica prison riots, which bedeviled then-Gov. Rockefeller and claimed 43 lives. Anxious to avoid an Attica rerun, Cuomo huddled with his advisers and, maintaining contact with those inside the prison, got the inmates to agree to a settlement. They let their hostages go in exchange for Cuomo's pledge to improve prison conditions.

Cuomo enjoyed a rather pleasant honeymoon—despite taking stands that would make most politicians unpopular. In his first year he presided over sizable tax increases and massive cutbacks in the state bureaucracy in an effort to curb the $1.8 billion deficit he inherited from Gov. Carey. But neither prevented him from winning the praise of legislative leaders in both parties in New York.

An important ingredient in Cuomo's success was the contrast he presented to Carey. The outgoing governor left a legacy of bitter executive-legislative relations that often threatened to bring New York government to a halt. In that acrimonious environment, leaders of the Republican-controlled Senate and the Democratic Assembly sometimes froze Carey out of decision-making altogether, teaming up to decide issues among themselves.

Although Cuomo inherited the split Legislature, he worked hard to improve ties to its principal players. He met frequently with Republican Senate President Warren M. Anderson and Democratic Assembly Speaker Stanley M. Fink, thrashing out issues over breakfast at the governor's mansion. The effort paid dividends when Cuomo signed the state budget into law on schedule in 1983—the first time that had happened in Albany in six years.

Cuomo offered few new government initiatives during his first term, focusing instead on increasing taxes, scaling back the state's short-term borrowing and cutting the state's work force to try to close the budget gap. Cuomo's campaign to cut state jobs was particularly galling to public employee unions who had helped him win election, but the two sides managed to come to terms.

Even after the financial crunch eased somewhat, Cuomo still showed signs of fiscal caution. He proposed increases in welfare assistance and low-rent housing in 1985 but mixed them with a tax cut to pacify those concerned about a sudden surge in state spending. Government should "serve the poor," he once said, "without crushing the middle class."

Cuomo had his share of setbacks during his first term. He had difficulty persuading the Legislature to pass several of his pet programs, including a plan to provide government subsidies to senior citizens for prescription medication. He also fell short in his attempts to win approval of a measure imposing mandatory sentences for certain crimes.

Critics accused him of being a better orator than a governor and said he was overly generous in assigning himself credit for certain accomplishments. The Legislature rebuffed his initial efforts to raise the legal drinking age to 21; it was only after the federal government threatened to cut off highway funds to states with lower age limits that the measure moved through.

He brought other problems on himself. When a group of sportsmen criticized the governor's support for a mandatory seat belt law, Cuomo lashed out. He said the sportsmen "drink beer, don't vote and lie to their wives about where they were over the weekend." Cuomo subsequently apologized, but the comment made him a few lasting enemies.

Despite those difficulties, however, it was widely regarded as a successful term. One Assembly aide branded Cuomo "Albany's great communicator.... An ethnic Ronald Reagan."

There was little doubting his ability at communicating. Cuomo made better use of television and radio than any other politician in New York history. At one point, according to the *New York Times,* Cuomo could be heard weekly on a public radio interview program, weekly on his own call-in radio show and several times a week on a program aired on Mutual Radio.

Playing Hardball, Winning Big

His efforts paid off. By the time 1986 rolled around, Cuomo was a shoo-in for re-election. With a second term ensured, the only real question was whether he really wanted to stay another four years in Albany.

For a time, Cuomo seemed content to let the suspense build. "It comes down to running for president or running for governor," Cuomo said at one point. "When you run for governor, that means you can't turn around in time and run a credible race for the presidency." Reporters in New York and across the country faithfully wrote down his remarks.

Cuomo eventually announced for re-election in May. After that, it was a relatively quiet campaign. The only real controversy involved Cuomo's old job of lieutenant governor, a position that took on added significance because Cuomo had refused to rule out a possible bid for the presidency; if he sought the White House, he would leave his second-in-command in charge.

His first-term lieutenant governor, Alfred B. Del Belo, left office after two years, complaining that he had been too isolated from the centers of power in the Cuomo administration. When it came time to select a running mate for 1986, Cuomo conducted an extensive search around the state. He settled on Democratic Rep. Stan Lundine, a five-term congressman from New York's GOP-minded southern tier.

Cuomo's selection of Lundine did not prevent a primary, however. Abraham Hirschfeld, a millionaire parking garage magnate who had run for many New York offices over the years, challenged Lundine and managed to make life a little difficult for both Cuomo and Lundine.

Without a primary of his own, Cuomo concentrated his energies on shepherding Lundine through. He challenged Hirschfeld's petitions for a place on the ballot, which had been approved by the state Board of Elections. Cuomo succeeded in forcing him off the ballot, but Hirschfeld did not go quietly. He accused the governor of an "un-American" attempt to deprive the voters of a choice, dipped liberally into his fortune to finance television advertisements that asked, "What happened to democracy?" and branded Lundine "a wimp."

Adding to the unpleasant publicity was a wave of criticism directed at Cuomo's political technique. Some New Yorkers felt the governor's decision to have his lawyers subpoena the Polish-born Hirschfeld's naturalization papers was overly aggressive; it triggered a backlash of sympathy.

Cuomo eventually acknowledged that his efforts to obtain Hirschfeld's papers were "a mistake" and the campaign proceeded without further incident. On Primary Day, Lundine went unopposed. Still, the whole episode left some critics feeling that Cuomo was a neighborhood bully who should pick on people his own size.

Republicans, meanwhile, were having a difficult time finding a formidable contender willing to take on Cuomo. Following a six-month talent search, state GOP leaders persuaded Westchester County Executive Andrew O'Rourke to wage a campaign.

O'Rourke, a lawyer and former county legislator with a reputation as an affable and articulate politician, came out swinging. He accused Cuomo of being stingy in funneling state funds to local governments and argued that the governor and others in his party had been insufficiently vigilant in cracking down on political corruption.

But O'Rourke never really got his campaign apparatus off the ground, and it wasn't long before the state GOP hierarchy began to wonder whether O'Rourke would drag the rest of their ticket down. National Republican strategists, dismayed by what they saw, declined to contribute much-needed funds.

As anticipated, it turned out to be a massive Democratic victory. Cuomo finished with 65 percent of the vote statewide, beating O'Rourke by some 1.34 million ballots—the largest plurality established by a governor in New York history.

The improved executive-legislative relations that marked Cuomo's first four years as governor began deteriorating early in his second term, the product of a power clash with Mel Miller, the new Assembly speaker.

Miller, who took over after Fink retired, challenged Cuomo's authority and sought to carve out a more powerful role for the Assembly. Miller even managed to negotiate passage of a tax cut while effectively keeping Cuomo on the sidelines. On many other issues, the result of the clash was a legislative logjam.

But Cuomo battled back, using efforts to create a new state ethics code as a vehicle. When Miller put together a coalition and passed a version of the code, Cuomo vetoed it, deriding the proposal as insufficiently stringent. He effectively forced the Legislature to pass a stronger version and rallied public opinion to his side.

Cuomo's supporters credited him with re-establishing political position by making an astute maneuver. His critics revived complaints that the governor sometimes seemed too eager to play political hardball.

The Critics Weigh In

That complaint, which has cropped up from time to time during Cuomo's tenure as governor, is one of several he would likely hear if he ever did decide to seek the presidency.

Just ask Republican members of the state Senate who opposed Cuomo on the so-called "toxic tort" bill in the summer of 1986. Cuomo supported the legislation—designed to make it easier for people exposed to toxic substances to take legal action seeking compensation from polluters—and encouraged the reluctant Republicans to do so, too. "How does it help to drive the governor into the position where he has to campaign against you?" Cuomo was quoted as saying in the

Washington Post. "He's going to come to your district with the toxic tort bill, with the victims who have been exposed to these substances, some of them in wheelchairs." The Legislature ended up approving the bill, with help from some of those GOP senators.

Candidate Cuomo also would have to contend with charges that he is overly sensitive to criticism. In 1986 Cuomo grew angry with reporters over some articles he felt were distortions intended to diminish him in the eyes of the public, and others he thought were unfavorable to his re-election campaign. He reacted by delivering a major address at the New York Press Club in which he called for better reporting, warning that a "reckless" press invited Supreme Court scrutiny.

Cuomo is particularly prickly on the subject of his ethnicity. He has occasionally lashed out at the press and political opponents for stereotyping Italians. "They always want to paint me as Latin, passionate, volcanic, unstable," Cuomo has said.

When some critics argued that there were natural limitations on the amount of national support an ethnic Catholic from the Northeast could command, Cuomo exploded. "If anything could make me change my mind about running for the presidency, it's people talking about, 'an Italian can't do it, a Catholic can't do it.'"

His concern about prejudice against Italians spills over into his analysis of organized crime. "You're telling me that the Mafia is the organization, and I'm telling you that's a lot of baloney," he told a group of reporters assembled in his gubernatorial offices one day. The remark took on a life of its own, fueling complaints that he suffered from hypersensitivity.

Critics also contend that Cuomo is too parochial to be president; until a fall 1987 trip to the Soviet Union, he had visited only one foreign country: Italy. Others argue that he is too insular, too arrogant and unwilling to delegate authority.

A Matter of Style

Those arguments do not faze supporters of a Cuomo bid for the presidency. His backers dispute the hardball charge, arguing that Cuomo's style of governing is marked much more by conciliation than conflict. They contend that he learned his basic approach to politics during his days as a mediator of community disputes.

"He often plays that role in Albany," Union College political scientist James Underwood told a reporter for *New York* magazine. "He puts himself in a position where he's trying to get two parties to agree. He'd be a conciliator as president. He has a knack for finding a common ground between disagreeing parties."

Those who feel Cuomo should run for the White House also argue that he has a trait rare among people in public life: a willingness to wade into controversial subjects regardless of the political consequences. Perhaps the best example they offer is a speech he gave on religion and morality in September of 1984.

The speech, which was part of a series of lectures at Notre Dame University, came in large part as a response to statements made by New York Archbishop John J. O'Connor. The archbishop had said that he did not see "how a Catholic in good conscience can vote for a candidate who explicitly supports abortion." He argued that Democratic vice presidential nominee Geraldine Ferraro had misrepresented the church's stance on abortion in her campaign.

Cuomo, who personally believes that abortion is wrong but is loath to overturn laws upholding a woman's right to choose, urged Catholics to be wary of imposing their religious and moral beliefs on others. "The Catholic public official lives the political truth most Catholics through most of American history have accepted and insisted on: the truth that to assure our freedom we must allow others the same freedom, even if occasionally it produces conduct by them which we would hold to be sinful," Cuomo said. "We know that the price of seeking to force our beliefs on others is that they might someday force theirs on us."

He went on to inveigh against people and political parties who sought to advance themselves by using religion as a vehicle, arguing that God should not be construed as "a celestial party chairman."

Perhaps more than anything else, however, Cuomo's supporters see him separated from the current field of Democratic candidates by an understanding of the symbolic side of politics. They feel he possesses the kind of image-conscious style that helped propel the candidacy and presidency of Ronald Reagan.

Even some leading Republicans share that view. "Cuomo's the only one they've got who is like Reagan," Republican National Committee Chairman Frank Fahrenkopf told a reporter.

"He hits people in their guts, and they use the same words to talk about him as they do when they speak of the president: 'He stands up. He's tough. He's strong.'"

The Talk Goes On

While Cuomo, as an influential non-candidate, may occupy an unusual position in the pantheon of presidential politics, his post is not unprecedented. Some observers see parallels to another New York governor.

"I think the closest analogy to Cuomo in 1988 is [Nelson A.] Rockefeller in 1968," said political scientist Norman Ornstein of the American Enterprise Institute. "Like Cuomo, he kept toying with running; he was in, he was out, he was thinking about it ... but Rockefeller didn't start with the assumption that there'd be a deadlocked convention. To win the nomination, he knew he'd have to be the popular choice," Ornstein said.

It is unclear, of course, whether that is also Cuomo's thinking. But it is clear that to count on a deadlocked convention is to ignore the historical odds.

The last time it happened was 36 years ago, when Democrats turned to Illinois Gov. Adlai E. Stevenson. Although Stevenson was the personal choice of outgoing Democratic President Harry S Truman, Stevenson repeatedly professed disinterest in the nomination both privately and publicly. In the end, he submitted to a draft movement in his behalf while the 1952 Democratic convention was under way. Stevenson managed to secure the nomination after three ballots—marking the last time either party has even had a multi-ballot convention.

Ornstein, and most others, warn that a 1952 rerun is extremely unlikely to happen. "The chances remain overwhelming that the convention in 1988 will be decided on the first ballot, and that the nominee will be somebody in the current field," he said.

But despite the weight of history, there remains an array of people around the country who continue to cling to the belief that Cuomo may yet find himself a 1988 presidential contender.

David A. Brock, chief justice of the New Hampshire Supreme Court, seemed to speak for that group when he introduced Cuomo as a commencement speaker at a New Hampshire law school in the spring of 1987. Brock, a good Republican, said he had not heard so much talk of a draft since the Vietnam War. "Should one emerge," he said, "I presume to speak for many here today, Governor, when I ask that you be neither a conscientious objector nor a draft-dodger."

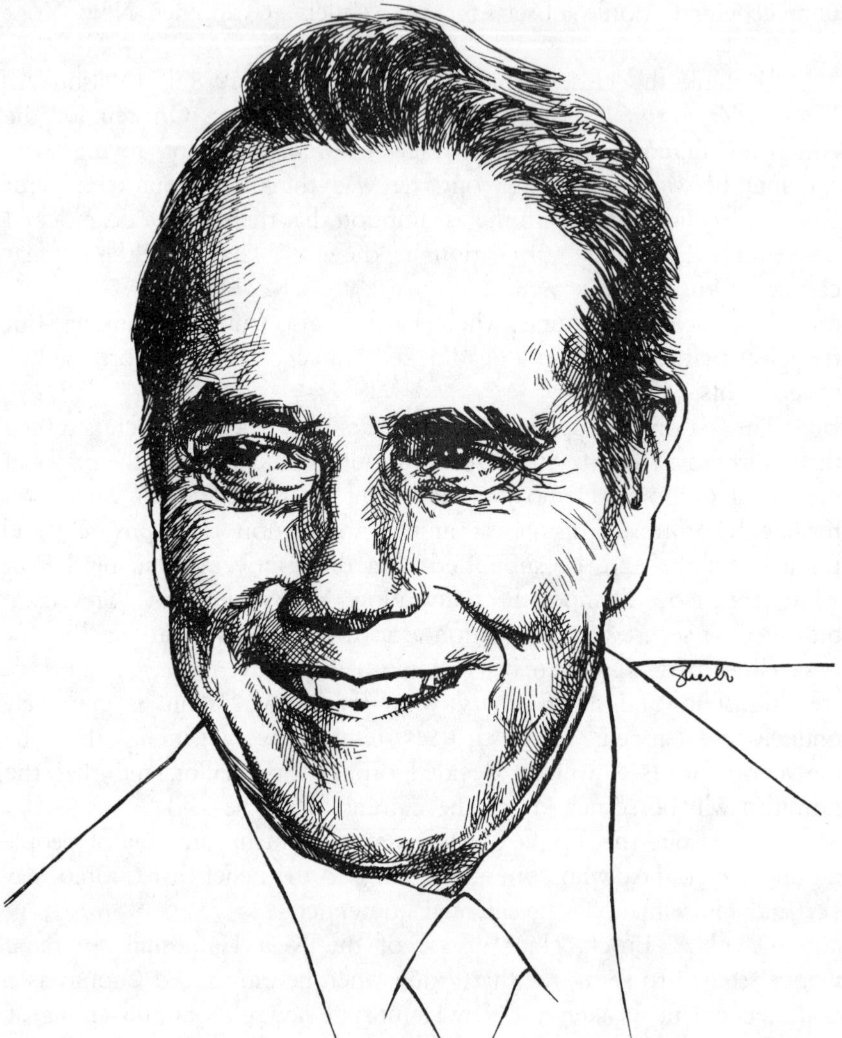

ROBERT DOLE

Great Peaks and Valleys Mark the Career
Of the Republican Democrats Most Fear

Ask any Democratic strategist which Republican presidential candidate would be toughest to beat in 1988, and the answer will probably be Robert Dole. This judgment conveys both the force and the flaw in the Kansan's candidacy.

Consider first the force. Although second to Vice President George Bush in opinion polling among Republicans, Dole does as well or better than Bush when matched against the Democratic candidates in polls of the general electorate. In a general election, tacticians say, Dole would have more maneuvering room than Bush. He could identify himself with Reagan when he wished and distance himself when necessary.

But will the Republican Party of 1988 be looking for a skilled broken-field runner, or a staunch standard bearer?

At his best, Dole evinces the steadiness and sophistication associated with the word presidential. He has earned this image the hard way, not by appointment to prestigious posts but through long years of trial in the military, political and legislative wars of his time. He has proven himself by winning more than a dozen local and state elections, over four decades.

But will the Republican Party of 1988 be looking for a veteran of electoral combat, or a successor to Ronald Reagan? The Republicans' nominee, if elected, must not only govern the country, but also determine the direction of his party. Only an outsider would say the first responsibility is more important to the party faithful than the second.

Dole has been both loyal and independent in turn, ceding to the White House at times and setting his own course at others. The prospect of entrusting Reagan's legacy to such an unpredictable loyalist remains anathema to the true believers of the party's right wing. For this core, winning with someone they do not trust is not winning at all.

Robert Joseph Dole

Profession: Lawyer.
Born: July 22, 1923, Russell, Kan.
Home: Russell, Kan.
Religion: United Methodist.
Education: Attended University of Kansas, 1941-43; Washburn Municipal University, A.B., 1952; LL.B., 1952.
Political Career: Kansas House of Representatives, 1951-53; Russell County attorney, 1953-61; U.S. House of Representatives, 1961-69; U.S. Senate, 1969-present; Republican nominee for vice president, 1976; candidate for Republican presidential nomination, 1980.
Military: Army, 1943-48.
Family: Wife, Mary Elizabeth Hanford; one child (by earlier marriage).
Senate Committees: Minority leader. Agriculture, Nutrition and Forestry, 1969-present; Finance, 1973-present; Judiciary, 1973-84; Public Works, 1969-72; Rules and Administration, 1984-present; Joint Tax, 1979-84.

There is real irony in this for Dole, who has always identified himself as a conservative. Throughout his lifetime, the party's poles have been its Eastern Establishment elite and its Western populist right. Having grown up poor in the rural Kansas of the Depression, Dole has never doubted which side he was on.

His voting record by any measure is consistently conservative. As the party's national chairman, he was an acolyte of President Richard Nixon. President Gerald R. Ford chose Dole as his running mate in 1976, in part to cover his right. And when Dole ended his own campaign for the presidency in 1980, he endorsed Ronald Reagan's. He has differed with Reagan at times in the 1980s, but he often has stood with him against the objections of Senate Republicans. Since 1984, he has been the point man for Reagan's legislative program as the GOP leader in the Senate.

But for the American conservative movement—sometimes called

the New Right—Reaganism has been more than just a legislative program. It has been a fundamental rethinking of the direction of American democracy. To be sure, Congress has had a role to play in retracting the overreach of government in the economy, restoring traditional social values and renewing American military and diplomatic might around the world. But to "movement conservatives," changing the law is more of a mopping up operation. The essence of the enterprise more closely resembles a crusade. And Dole will never be mistaken for a crusader.

Dole has diverged from movement doctrine most distinctly on taxes. He never subscribed to the supply-side economic theory, and often refers to it with undisguised contempt. In 1982 and 1983 he pushed packages of tax increases as an antidote to the federal deficit. Aside from his specific apostasies on taxes, Dole has offended the New Right by being too much a creature of the Congress—the second most senior Republican in the Senate, a power and a prisoner within the institution.

To overcome this, some say Dole must transcend his image. They say he must project the kind of individual stature and dedication to conservative principle that distinguished Barry Goldwater and Ronald Reagan—the Abraham and Moses of the contemporary Republican Party.

But it is difficult to imagine Dole doing this, or even attempting it. He has always been more attracted to the meat than the myth of politics, and he seems disinclined to change. So his challenge may be to change the party's perception of him. Daunting as that may be, Dole has been tested before. His very presence in the presidential field testifies to his resiliency and resourcefulness.

Prairie Roots

Dole was born and raised in Russell, a dusty town in west-central Kansas. Today, Russell has about 5,000 residents and serves the wheat growers and cattle and oil producers of the area. In 1923, when Robert Joseph Dole was born, prosperity had just arrived in Russell with a strike in a nearby oilfield. But it did little for the Doles, who lived in a two-room frame house on the lesser side of town.

Dole's father, Doran Ray Dole, had run in turn, a cafe, a grain elevator and a small creamery. His wife, Bina, took in sewing and sold Singer sewing machines door to door. It was a modest living, even before Bob's younger brother and two younger sisters were born. In their leanest times, the family met the mortgage by moving into the basement and renting the rest of the house to oilfield workers.

Although Dole's party has often been associated with privilege, he himself has never lost the particular sense of striving that characterizes those who have made their own way. He has eschewed the common demagoguery about welfare and was largely responsible for the current food-stamp program. Even when he had reached the heights of power in Washington, his words of concern for the underdog retained authenticity.

At age 12 Bob Dole was a soda jerk at Dawson's drugstore on Main Street. In high school, he went out for football, basketball and track. He was six-two, 180 pounds and unusually fast. Yet he is remembered most for his grit. One legendary tale has Russell defeating neighboring Ellis 6-to-0 on a last-second touchdown pass that Dole somehow managed to catch in a sea of mud.

Arlen Specter, a Republican senator representing Pennsylvania, also grew up in Russell.

"The reality of Russell is that it wasn't big, but it was highly competitive," Specter told the *Wichita Eagle-Beacon*. "There was a lot of pride in the town. You got a drive to be the best in whatever you did."

Sports took Dole to the University of Kansas, where he was soon threatening the collegiate indoor-track record for the quarter mile. He was also thinking about medical school. But the Japanese bombed Pearl Harbor during Dole's freshman year, and in 1943 he left school for active duty with the Army.

War Wounds

What followed has been widely interpreted as the turning point of Dole's life. Commissioned a second lieutenant, he found himself leading a platoon in northern Italy. A month before the German surrender in 1945, with the Russians already besieging Berlin, the Allies launched an offensive in the Po River Valley that involved Dole's unit.

In the midst of the advance, his platoon was caught in a hail of fire that left every man wounded.

Dole's right arm and shoulder were shattered. Five vertebrae were broken. He lay on the field eight hours before his paralyzed body was brought to a field hospital. "It was," Dole would say 20 years later, "kind of a long day."

When he reached a Veterans Administration hospital back in Kansas that summer, Dole had lost more than 60 pounds. He had also lost one kidney, all use of his right arm and most of the feeling in his left. Transferred to a Michigan hospital for rehabilitation, he got blood clots in his lungs. Doctors told his family he would die, but tried a then-experimental drug called streptomycin. Dole survived, but his limbs remained as lifeless as they had been on the battlefield.

"It got to me," Dole later told an interviewer. "Why me? And what did I do to deserve this?"

He would spend a total of three years, three months and two weeks in hospitals, much of the time in a body cast. Doctors told him he would

Bob Dole chats with onlookers during a visit to Woodbine, Md.

never walk again. Relatives recall his spending hours trying to get two fingers to close.

Dole was discharged a captain, decorated with the Bronze Star and the Purple Heart, both with oak leaf cluster. But there were more important contributions to his emotional convalescence. When he needed an expensive operation (to reconstruct part of his right shoulder and arm with muscle and bone from his legs), the townspeople of Russell raised $5,200.

In Michigan in 1948, Dole met Phyllis E. Holman, a physical therapist assigned to his case. They were married later that year. Phyllis enabled him to return to college, taking notes, transcribing tapes he made of lectures, substituting her hand for his until he had mastered writing with his left.

More than any other politician in our time, Dole carries the physical and emotional marks of the war that seared his generation. He still takes an hour or more to dress himself, tying his own necktie and shoes. Through nearly 40 years in politics, he has never reached out his right hand to shake hands with a voter. He carries a pen or a folder in that hand to divert the proffered hands of others.

When, in the 1976 vice-presidential candidates' debate, Dole referred bitterly to "Democrat wars" in this century, he was not speaking glibly. The bitterness in his voice was what made the ill-chosen words so difficult to recant.

Hardening as Dole's war experiences were, they have also had another effect—one far less well known. Throughout his career, Dole has championed the cause of the handicapped. Beyond his support for this cause in Congress, he established a foundation to assist the handicapped and has raised money for handicapped programs. And he has done these things without seeking the publicity he could obviously glean.

Taken together, the rough edges of Dole's boyhood and youth produced a man of unusual determination. "I do try harder," Dole once said. "If I didn't, I'd be sitting in a rest home, in a rocker, drawing disability."

A Determined Politician

Finally out of the hospital in 1948, Dole started back to school at the University of Arizona, then took his G.I. Bill benefits to Washburn University in Topeka, the Kansas capital. Already convinced he wanted to get into politics, and still a believer in students holding part-time jobs, he ran for a Russell-based seat in the state Legislature in 1950. He got elected and served while he finished his bachelor's and law degrees, both of which were conferred magna cum laude in 1952. Washburn added an honorary doctorate in 1969.

Dole's schooling and legislative term ended about the same time and he returned to Russell to settle down, start a family and build a political base. He got elected county prosecutor.

"I've lost 10 years out of my life," he told his brother, "and I'm going to make it up."

Years later, Dole would recall his early political decisions in terms one can read as cynical or naive.

"It was all sort of a game then," he told the *Wall Street Journal* in 1987. "You had to be Republican or Democrat, and you ran, and you didn't get into any philosophical discussions."

Dole's parents had been Democrats, and he himself admitted admiring Franklin D. Roosevelt. But when he returned from his long war, it was the GOP that recruited him. And it was the GOP that usually dominated politics in his part of the world.

If short on ideology, he was long on energy and personality. He loved to campaign. On a biographical questionnaire he listed his hobbies and other interests in one word: politics. Even Phyllis professed to enjoy the hours of stuffing envelopes and performing other volunteer tasks.

Dole was re-elected every two years until 1960. Then the district's Republican congressman retired and the 37-year-old prosecutor made a bid for the seat. In the *Journal* interview, Dole said this was when he first "started focusing on what the federal government did and what it could do."

The 26-county 6th District was thoroughly Republican, so the real fight was in the primary. Dole's main rival was Keith G. Sebelius from next-door Norton County, whom he defeated by just 982 votes. (Sebelius would win the seat when Dole got elected to the Senate eight years later and eventually serve six terms in the House.)

Dole got the committee assignment he needed, on Agriculture. This allowed him both to support farm subsidies and oppose the controls that often went with them. He was also well positioned to decry the Democratic ties to Texas wheeler-dealer Billy Sol Estes in the 1962 grain storage scandal.

Dole voted with his party 90 percent of the time and with the so-called conservative coalition (Republicans and Southern Democrats) virtually all of the time through his eight years in the House. The Americans for Constitutional Action gave him its distinguished service award. By contrast, he drew scores of zero from the liberal Americans for Democratic Action during most of his House service.

But Dole also backed the watershed civil rights bills of the mid-60s, supporting the Civil Rights Act of 1964 and the Voting Rights Act of 1965 (he would help put through its extension in the Senate 17 years later). He opposed other landmark liberal legislation, such as the Medicare Act of 1965 and the Civil Rights and Equal Employment Opportunity Act of 1966.

His mix of votes and rhetoric, heavy on conservative themes and farm needs, should have conferred electoral security in a GOP stronghold in a GOP state. But other circumstances were at work. The 1960 Census shrank Kansas' delegation from six House seats to five, combining the two western districts into one (now numbered the 1st District). So the two districts' representatives faced off in 1962 and Dole won, although by less than he had in 1960.

In 1964, with President Lyndon Johnson sweeping toward a landslide re-election, Dole found himself pressed by a Democratic challenger named Bill Bork. A farmers' co-op official, Bork insisted he was closer to farmers than Dole, whom he portrayed as a slick lawyer from the relatively big town of Russell. Dole got by, barely. A swing of 2,600 votes would have defeated him.

Times got easier after that. The off-year elections of 1966 marked the beginning of the GOP comeback, and Dole's winning percentage rose to 69 percent. That emboldened him to seek statewide office, and he got a chance when Republican Sen. Frank Carlson retired in 1968. The big competition was former governor William H. Avery, who had been defeated for re-election just two years earlier. Avery should have been a stiff test, but he ran as though seeking vindication and leveled his fire at the governor who had replaced him. Dole walked away with 68 percent of the primary vote.

The Democrat he faced that fall, Wichita attorney William I. Robinson, attacked Dole for opposing federal aid to schools. Dole saw the key issue as law and order in the face of the violence and social unrest of the time.

He worked hard to fix blame for that unrest on the Democrats in Washington. He won with 60 percent of the vote.

Making a Name

When Dole moved to the Senate, changes were under way. The Democrats' grip on Congress had been loosened, and there was a conservative Westerner named Richard Nixon ensconced in the White House. Without anyone knowing just who had delegated him the job, Dole became the Senate's self-designated hitter for the Nixon administration.

Nixon had come to Kansas to campaign during Dole's close-call election in 1964, and Dole remembered. But the freshman also seemed to relish the role. As he himself once observed: "The first six months it's 'How did I get here?' The next six months it's 'How did they get here?' "

So when Edward M. Kennedy of Massachusetts or Edmund S. Muskie of Maine rose to criticize the president, Dole would leap to the counterattack. His rebuttals were often funny, always biting. Some found them incompatible with the Senate's traditional decorum. Republican Sen. William Saxbe of Ohio said Dole was so disagreeable that he "could not sell beer on a troopship."

But the people around Nixon were a combative crew themselves, and they liked what they saw. One described Dole as "a hungry Doberman pinscher." The occasion of that remark was Dole's appointment, at Nixon's behest, as the party's national chairman in January of 1971. Just two years into his first term in the Senate, Dole was officially the party's national spokesman. He had reached the first true peak in what was to become a career of great peaks and valleys.

Dole's new station was not without disappointments. He was soon made aware he was to have no hand in Nixon's re-election strategy. That was to be handled by an entity separate from the party apparatus, called the Committee for the Re-election of the President. Dole, ever the wag, has been credited with coining the acronym by which the committee became known: CREEP.

Away from Home

The new job also entailed travel, national and almost non-stop, that strained Dole's already attenuated relationship with Phyllis. Their only child, Robin, had been born in 1954 and was now in high school. Dole has said he worried that the marriage was a worse influence on her than a divorce would be. But, as he himself admits, he feared the political

Dole's Interest...

Vote ratings by interest groups help to give a picture of Robert Dole's orientation during his career in the House and Senate.

This table shows how often Dole voted on key legislative issues in accordance with the positions of groups chosen to

	ADA	AFL-CIO	CCUS	ACA	ACU
House Service					
1961	0	—[1]	—[2]	—[3]	—
1962	0	0	—[2]	91	—
1963	—[4]	—[1]	—[2]	100	—
1964	4	9	—[2]	95	—
1965	0	—[1]	100	89	—
1966	0	0	—[2]	93	—
1967	7	9	100	96	—
1968	0	25	—[2]	90	—
Senate Service					
1969	0	18	—[2]	64	—
1970	13	17	89	76	—
1971	4	17	—[2]	71	—
1972	0	10	100	84	—

[1] *AFL-CIO did not compile vote records in some years.*
[2] *CCUS did not compile vote records in some years.*
[3] *ACA did not compile vote records in some years.*
[4] *ADA did not compile vote records in some years.*

consequences a divorce would have back home. Phyllis later told reporters her husband had been home for dinner exactly twice in 1972 before the night he came home and said: "I want out."

Phyllis moved back to Kansas, married a rancher named Lon Buzick and now lives about 40 miles from Russell. She supports her first husband's presidential aspirations, and has spent time making pins and buttons for the campaign.

...Group Ratings

represent liberal, labor, business and conservative viewpoints. They are the Americans for Democratic Action (ADA), AFL-CIO, Chamber of Commerce of the United States (CCUS) and Americans for Constitutional Action (ACA) or American Conservative Union (ACU).

	ADA	AFL-CIO	CCUS	ACA	ACU
1973	10	27	78	82	—
1974	19	18	80	84	—
1975	17	24	75	67	—
1976	10	16	75	87	—
1977	5	11	88	70	—
1978	20	22	83	58	—
1979	21	21	73/75 [5]	64	—
1980	22	28	90	77	—
1981	5	11	100	70	—
1982	15	20	62	71	—
1983	5	19	56	74	—
1984	10	0	83	88	—
1985	0	10	90	—	91 [6]
1986	0	0	89	—	91
1987	5	20	87	—	77

[5] *In 1979 there were two Chamber of Commerce scores for members of the Senate. The CCUS originally calculated scores based on 11 votes and excluded several procedural votes. Subsequently, the chamber revised its ratings, using 16 votes instead of 11. Revised score follows original score.*
[6] *Congressional Quarterly began publishing ACU ratings in 1985.*

Good Timing

Although never one of Nixon's intimates, Dole went on defending the Nixon program throughout the president's first term. He backed the president on Vietnam, including the invasion of Cambodia. He fought for the doomed nominations of Clement F. Haynsworth Jr. and G. Harrold Carswell to the Supreme Court. He supported Nixon's push for antiballistic missiles, a precursor of Reagan's Strategic Defense Initiative.

Dole was around to bask in Nixon's 49-state landslide re-election in 1972, but it was soon apparent that the White House staff had tired of him. In January of 1973, summoned to Camp David to be relieved of his chairmanship, Dole told Nixon he was quitting so as to concentrate on his own re-election.

Within a few months, Dole would realize the setback had actually been a stupendous stroke of luck. As the Watergate debacle exploded, Dole could step back and away from the wreckage. In May of 1973, Dole was telling Nixon to drop his fortress mentality and meet the problem squarely. He could even joke that "Watergate happened on my night off."

At this stage, Dole retreated somewhat from his aggressive partisanship and focused on Kansas' interests: wheat and cattle. He also joined forces with Sen. George McGovern of South Dakota, the Democratic presidential nominee he had roasted in 1972, in revamping the food stamp program.

Dole's return to his roots came none too soon. He had to run again in 1974, the year Watergate came home to roost. And, although never touched by the scandal, Dole was still associated with Nixon—who resigned in disgrace that August. Partly as a result, the Kansas Democrats fielded perhaps their strongest nominee for the Senate since the New Deal. He was Dr. William R. Roy, a physician and two-term House member who hung the sins of the Nixon administration on Dole like a wreath. When the newly installed President Gerald Ford granted Nixon a pardon, Dole labeled it "premature." But the polls still showed Roy with a double-digit lead.

Dole brought in Sen. Lowell Weicker of Connecticut, a GOP hero from the Watergate investigating committee, to campaign on his behalf. He also aired a TV ad in which his own picture was obscured by mud. As Dole's voice spoke of Dole's integrity, the mud was gradually wiped away. The ad became a genre classic.

But the race's decisive factor may have been a negative tactic of Dole's own. Stressing his own pro-life record, Dole noted that Roy, a Catholic, had admitted performing some legal abortions. Just before Election Day, Kansans were inundated with anti-abortion literature featuring pictures of dead fetuses. Dole disavowed the literature, but it was widely believed to have made a difference. When the votes were counted, a fraction more than 50 percent were for Dole.

Lofty Heights, Tough Fall

Back in the Senate in 1975, Dole seemed subdued by his close brushes with political death. Nonetheless, it was his reputation as a gunslinger—his choice of words—that brought him back to the national limelight just 18 months later.

President Ford began his quest for a term in his own right by beating challenger Ronald Reagan in the early Republican primaries and caucuses. But GOP primary voters of the South and West felt differently. And after the North Carolina primary turned things around in March, Reagan staged a rally that carried him to the brink of victory at the nominating convention.

In the restive atmosphere that followed Ford's nomination, the choice of a vice president appeared critical. Ford was then trailing the Democratic nominee, Jimmy Carter, by 20 points or more in the polls. The nominee wanted help in the farm states. And he wanted to pursue a "Rose Garden" strategy, manning the White House and being presidential while other party leaders did the dirty work. Who better than Dole?

But just as important, Ford needed someone to placate the passionate Reagan delegates—many of whom felt cheated by the convention. So, ironically in current hindsight, the characteristic that clinched the second spot for Dole was his conservatism. His credentials with the right were thought strong enough to appease the Reagan wing.

Dole was, by all reports, as surprised as anyone in America when Ford turned to him. Overnight, he became a household word. In a matter of 10 weeks, he might be the proverbial "heartbeat away." And, if the ticket won, he would have the opportunity that automatically attaches to the vice presidency: the opportunity to run for the presidency himself someday, to run and have instant credibility.

But if this peak was higher than any he had known before, it was also more slippery. Dole went after his task with relish, and before long he was in trouble. The focus became his debate in Houston with Carter's running mate, Sen. Walter F. Mondale of Minnesota. Besides his ill-received remark about "Democrat wars," for which he was slow to apologize, Dole joked about Carter's interview with *Playboy*. He was obliged to defend Ford's pardon of Nixon, and at times his sullenness seemed vaguely reminiscent of his former mentor.

Mondale, no barnburner as a televison performer, was generally conceded to have had the better of the debate. Later, when Ford had lost the election by a surprisingly slim margin, Dole got a lot of the blame. It had to hurt, but he kept it in.

Dave Owen, who has worked in all of Dole's campaigns, later told the *Wichita Eagle-Beacon* about the morning after that defeat. "No apologies. No self-pity. He just said: 'Well, what does the next [Senate] election look like?' "

A Fresh Start

If Dole was able to rebound quickly after the disappointment of the Ford campaign, one reason may have been Elizabeth Hanford ("Liddy") Dole. A bachelor for nearly four years after his divorce, Dole in 1975 married Elizabeth Hanford, a Nixon appointee to the Federal Trade Commission. Originally a Democrat, she had worked for the Johnson administration and then been retained as a consumer advocate in the Nixon White House. She had changed her party registration to independent. After marrying Dole, she became a Republican.

The new Mrs. Dole had for years been one of the most sought-after women in Washington. A Phi Beta Kappa graduate of Duke, she held both a law degree and a master's degree from Harvard. In the years ahead, as Dole achieved new stature, she would become a liaison official in the Reagan White House and then be elevated to Secretary of Transportation in 1983. Quitting that job four years later to campaign full time for her husband, she offered personal charm, an opening to women and new appeal in the critical region from which she hailed—the South.

But all that still lay ahead when the Doles surveyed the damage of the 1976 campaign. Before long, and especially after the Republican gains of 1978, it became apparent that new opportunities for the Republican Party were in the making. All that remained was to position oneself to take advantage of them.

Few did that as well as Bob Dole. Having concentrated throughout his Washington career on the House and Senate Agriculture committees, Dole found himself gaining seniority with surprising speed. In 1979, still in just his second Senate term, he was the ranking Republican member of the committee. That meant that a GOP takeover of the Senate would make him chairman of one of the upper chamber's foremost committees. And such a takeover was looming, much closer than anyone knew.

He may not have foreseen the dimensions of it, but Dole believed 1980 would be a Republican year. Carter had never consolidated his power within his own party, and the Iranian hostage crisis seemed to have crippled him. A big line of would-be challengers was forming for 1980, and Dole decided he might as well be part of it.

But he had relatively little money and even less organization. He seemed incapable of delegating real authority to what organization he had. He was frequently stuck in Washington, attending to Finance Committee business. Worse yet, the field was dominated by Reagan, back for another try and looming larger than ever. Also on hand were Bush, Howard Baker, then a senator from Tennessee, and John Connally, who had been in the Nixon Cabinet and before that a Democratic governor of Texas. Dole never found a clear lane in which to run.

Nevertheless, he seemed to need the feel of the track again, and he wanted to move beyond the memories he had left with the national electorate in 1976. As it turned out, his 1980 campaign scarcely penetrated the national consciousness. After getting an unbelievably dismal 600 votes out of 150,000 cast in New Hampshire, Dole pulled out, endorsed Reagan and filed for re-election.

It would be presumptuous, however, to say that Dole's weak outing in 1980 accomplished nothing. At the very minimum, he reiterated his own personal claim to national office. If the electorate was not yet ready to validate that claim, there might still be other opportunities.

A New Era

Once again, a valley led Dole to a new peak. Not only did the Kansan win a third term in 1980 with 82 percent of the vote, but Reagan's smashing victory that fall brought a Republican takeover in the Senate. It was the first GOP majority in either body of Congress since 1954, and it gave Dole the first real power he had ever had in Washington.

The first challenge was passing Reagan's 1981 tax cuts, a relatively simple matter in a Senate where the new majority had gained power largely by campaigning against taxes. Dole's greatest feat that year may have been persuading Reagan to scale back the cut from 30 percent over three years to 25 percent.

The next year, with the tax cut taking effect and federal spending still climbing, Dole crossed swords with the "supply side" theorists by urging a tax increase to lower the budget deficit. Supply siders, including Rep. Jack Kemp of New York, insisted the lower tax rates would so stimulate the economy that tax revenues would still go up. Dole argued that they were not going up fast enough and the deficit was headed for unprecedented levels.

After a prolonged struggle within the Senate and the White House, Dole got Reagan to sign a bill that closed tax loopholes, tightened various rules and brought in about $100 billion in revenue over three years. It may have seemed a modest move in retrospect, but many in the New Right called it "the biggest tax increase in history." Republican Rep. Newt Gingrich of Georgia ripped Dole as "a tax collector for the welfare state"—a dart that stuck. Dole will feel its sting again in 1988.

Senate Republican Leader

In 1984, Majority Leader Howard H. Baker Jr. announced he would retire from the Senate, presumably to prepare a presidential campaign for 1988. Dole was a natural choice to succeed him, but such power is rarely transferred by acclamation. Dole had to contend with several of his senior colleagues before emerging as Baker's successor just after the elections of 1984.

Along the way, he picked up the support of Sen. Jesse Helms of North Carolina, a debt that Dole would dutifully repay by protecting the rights of the irascible archconservative on the floor. Dole may have won because other senators also believed he would defend their prerogatives in conflicts with the White House. But Dole's record as leader was decidedly mixed in this regard. As the 1986 elections approached, he proved unexpectedly loyal to the White House on issues such as aid to farmers and economic sanctions against South Africa—much to the distress of colleagues who would have preferred to skirt hard votes on such issues.

In his two years as the Senate's boss, Dole strove to make the institution work. He was criticized by some for trampling individuals' rights in the process. Ironically, others said he tried too hard to curry favor with senators whose support he would need in the coming presidential season. Still, he produced. He accomplished a cherished goal of Baker's, television coverage of the Senate, by attaching it to other changes in Senate procedure that won over anti-TV votes. And the big bills of the 99th Congress were passed with his help, including the tax reform and immigration reform measures of 1986, the 1985 farm bill and aid to the Nicaraguan "contras."

Tax and farm legislation were natural concerns for Dole, who never retreated from his committee assignments even as party leader. He even functioned as de facto leader of the Agriculture Committee, because its chairman, Helms, had few friends on the panel and remained preoccupied with narrow issues within farm legislation and broader issues beyond.

Dole's greatest frustrations were in dealing with the deficit. Reagan's no-tax pledge in the 1984 election left him with little room to maneuver, but he wrenched concessions on defense spending from the White House nonetheless. He helped pass the Gramm-Rudman-Hollings deficit reduction bill in 1985, although he also supplied one of the more telling remarks for the opposition. Late in a nocturnal floor debate, Dole told the Senate: "We can't let this bill sit around too long, people may start to read it."

At times, Dole's drive to dominate the proceedings seemed to strain the Senate's vaunted traditions of "comity." During debate over the South Africa sanctions, Dole had the official copy of the bill locked in a safe. That blocked further action temporarily and infuriated the bill's backers. Dressed down for his ham-fisted tactics on another occasion by Democratic leader Robert C. Byrd of West Virginia, Dole announced that he "did not become majority leader in order to lose." And: "I think it's time we asked ourselves, in all honesty, what kind of game we are playing."

The Democrats' recapture of the Senate in 1986 has been viewed as both a help and a hindrance to Dole's presidential hopes. No longer the focus of Senate activity, Dole has been somewhat less of a figure in the Capitol. But that has freed him to spend more time out where the voters are. It has also allowed him to pick his shots with respect to the White House's current occupant.

When the Iran-contra scandal erupted early in 1985, Dole was swift to call for complete cooperation with the investigation. Sounding very much like a veteran of the Watergate era, Dole strove to avoid any semblance of cover-up and received the back of many Republicans' hands as a result. But he did stand by the president's veto of a popular highway bill (which the Senate overrode anyway) and fought to the futile finish for Supreme Court nomination of Robert Bork.

As the demands of his 1988 presidential campaign increased, Dole faced the question of whether to remain in his leadership post or give it up to concentrate on winning the White House. Many had thought he would have chosen the latter far earlier. But Dole's political career has been a long lesson in caution. And with Bush still well ahead in the early betting, Dole seemed loath to gamble everything he had worked so long to build in 19 years in the Senate.

Back to the Track

Dole quickly made some major changes from his campaign of eight years ago. First, he raised serious money, $4 million in the third quarter of 1987 alone. He got started at it when he was Senate Finance Committee chairman, one of the best seats from which to hold fund raisers in Washington. He kept it up as majority leader and stayed in thereafter. Second, he brought in a peer, former senator Bill Brock of Tennessee, to be his campaign chairman and bolster his Southern front.

For those to whom politics remains the rough-and-tumble of getting elected, Dole deserves a hard look. Those who measure first the man will be struck with how Dole has survived, how he has come back. The years have begun to elevate him above regionalism, above his days as a hit-man and beyond the usual labels of conservative and liberal.

Still, Dole cannot win the nomination with crossover votes. And the very qualities that political professionals respect in him—his ability to reach out in all directions, for example—make Republican partisans suspicious.

Dole remains rough-hewn as a personality. He does not write books and makes little pretense of reading them. He is an old-fashioned tough guy in an era of fuzzy, feel-good politics—Humphrey Bogart miscast in a part written for Jimmy Stewart. Still, there are those who find this contrariness as welcome as others find it woeful. And by the time the Republican delegates gather in New Orleans in August, Dole may have forced many to reconsider their assessment of him.

After all, as 1988 began, the GOP field had no clear philosophic heir to Reagan. Kemp struck some Reaganauts that way, and Pat Robertson filled the bill for others. Some Reagan adherents have even been willing to embrace Bush, who, after all, is Number Two in a party that traditionally honors hierarchy.

But no one had displayed Reagan's knack for uniting all points of the party's compass within himself. With the force of the movement thus diffused, Dole hopes to have a chance to win. If his early advantage holds up in Midwestern neighbor-states Iowa and South Dakota, it could lend leverage to move the bigger stones in New England and the South.

And if his zest for a campaign comes through as a heartfelt defense of the Reagan philosophy, movement conservatives may find him more appealing—not just as a potential occupant of the White House who happens to be a Republican, but as a species of heir to Reagan.

Busy as they will be on their own, it is a safe bet the Democrats will be watching what happens to Bob Dole.

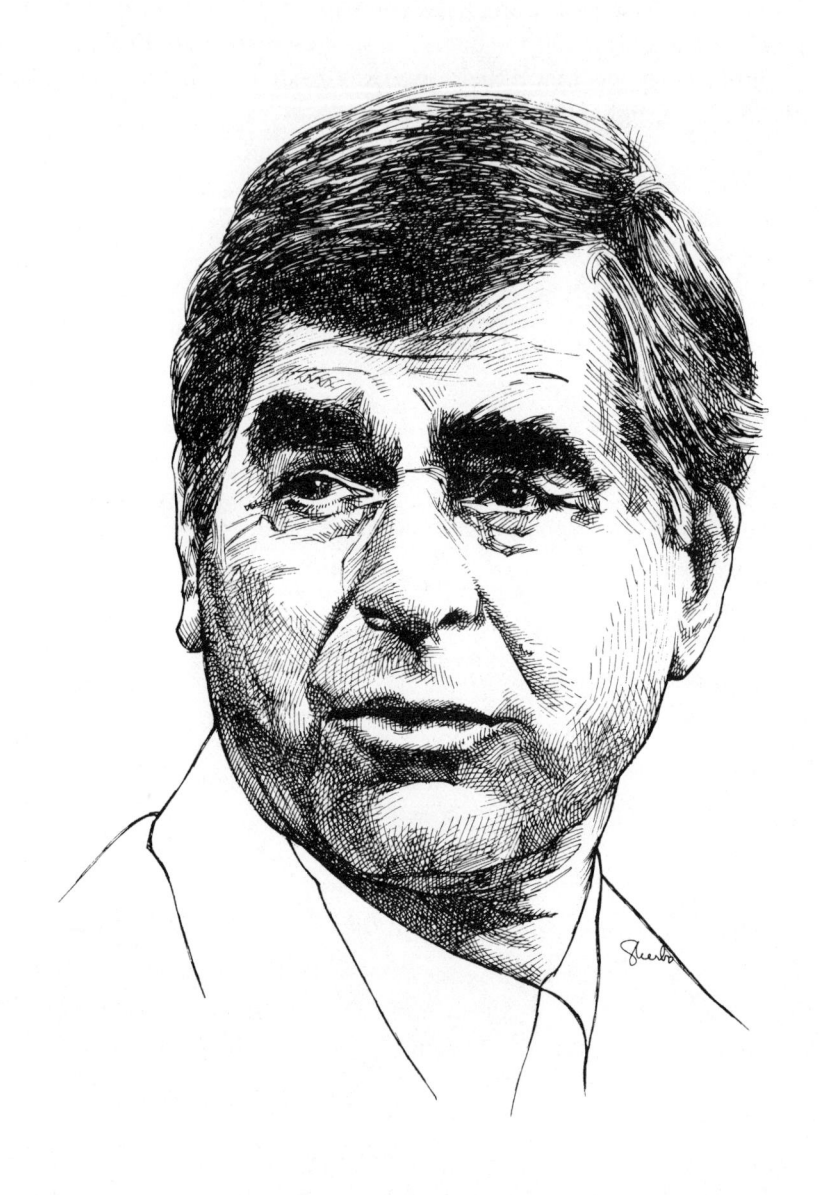

MICHAEL S. DUKAKIS

Marketing Massachusetts To a National Audience

Michael S. Dukakis, a son of Greek immigrants, is seen by many New Englanders as the embodiment of their region's most cherished values—thriftiness, diligence and integrity.

But for others, Dukakis, who was re-elected in 1986 to serve a third term as governor of Massachusetts, remains an enigmatic figure whose political positions fluctuate—a man who can be shrewd and arrogant, and who is riding an economic revival the making of which was not his and the components of which he opposed.

When you ask people in Massachusetts what they think of Michael Dukakis as governor, they are liable to ask, "Which one?" It is an acknowledged aspect of Massachusetts politics that there have been, in fact, two Michael Dukakises—Dukakis I, the young reformer who swept into office in the Watergate year of 1974 on a platform of clean government and fiscal restraint, and Dukakis II, the chastened pragmatist who reclaimed his old job in 1982 after learning the politics of compromise in his four-year exile.

Clearly, it is that second incarnation who is seeking the Democratic nomination for president. His message of business-government cooperation as the pathway to economic recovery and prosperity is hardly unique—but it is one that Dukakis-watchers in the 1970s would have been somewhat startled to hear.

His first term featured anything but cooperation. During his four years in office, 1975 to 1979, Dukakis won favorable national attention for his urban redevelopment policy and open style. People found refreshing this low-key, workaholic anti-politician who rode the subway to work. His frugality became legendary: the governor who shopped for suits in Bostonians' haven of bargains, Filene's Basement, and argued with his wife over credit card bills.

Michael Stanley Dukakis

Profession: Lawyer.
Born: Nov. 3, 1933, Brookline, Mass.
Home: Brookline, Mass.
Religion: Greek Orthodox.
Education: Swarthmore College, B.A., 1955; Harvard University, J.D., 1960.
Political Career: Massachusetts House of Representatives, 1963-71; Democratic nominee for Massachusetts lieutenant governor, 1970; Massachusetts governor, 1975-79; defeated for renomination, 1978; Massachusetts governor, 1983-present.
Military Career: Army, 1955-57.
Family: Wife, Katharine 'Kitty' Dickson; three children.

But many people in state government were finding Dukakis difficult to deal with. Critics said he was a stubborn, sometimes overbearing, perfectionist, flashing an aura of intellectual superiority that repelled potential allies among the traditional labor-oriented "lunch bucket" Democrats in the Legislature. His outsider's posture against the Democratic establishment—particularly his refusal to reward supporters with patronage positions—annoyed party loyalists. He alienated his liberal constituency by slashing welfare programs and outraged conservative Democrats by reneging on a campaign pledge not to raise taxes. When his re-election was at hand, Dukakis was ripe for a fall.

In his challenge to Dukakis in the 1978 primary, conservative Democrat Edward J. King sought to unite the assorted pockets of resentment. King employed his strategy of inflaming Dukakis-haters with considerable effectiveness in blue-collar neighborhoods. His pitch went beyond the call for tax limitations, embracing social issues that have long stirred the emotions of the state's heavily Catholic middle class. King stressed his adamant opposition to abortion and attacked Dukakis for opposing capital punishment.

Dukakis, in contrast, ran a poorly organized and ineffective campaign. According to some Democrats, the governor believed that his image as an honest and intelligent public servant would earn him renomination, without need for any unseemly boasting about his accomplishments.

Massachusetts Democrats, however, were dissatisfied with Dukakis' approach to governing. King won the Democratic primary with 51 percent to Dukakis' 42 percent—an outcome that was at least as much a rebuff of Dukakis as it was an endorsement of King. In November, King defeated liberal Yankee Republican Francis W. Hatch Jr. to become governor.

To be sure, Dukakis' troubles were not entirely of his own creation. After pledging not to raise taxes, he had come into office and met a $400 million deficit left behind by the previous administration. Nevertheless, the voters were clearly sending him a message. As it turned out, he was listening.

Back to the Drawing Board

The loss to King in the 1978 primary was a watershed in Dukakis' political career. His wife, Kitty, described it as "a public death," a telling assessment in two senses. For one, the unexpected defeat humiliated Dukakis as no event had ever done. In another sense, it forced Dukakis to re-evaluate every aspect of his political style and his method of governing: It was the death of Dukakis I.

That a politician can overhaul his views to suit the voters he seeks to attract is not remarkable. What is noteworthy in Dukakis' case, however, is that his principal liability was his personality—his unyielding approach to issues that scuttled coalitions and antagonized neutral parties. Dukakis summoned the pragmatism necessary to overcome those traits, a not inconsiderable political feat.

Dukakis retired to Harvard University's John F. Kennedy School of Government, where he became a lecturer and director of intergovernmental studies. He worked on his personal and political regeneration, with his gaze riveted on a rematch four years later.

In the ensuing months, friends and family noticed a marked change in Dukakis. The most common observation was that he had found humility, a quality decidedly lacking in the former governor. But he had also matured in his perspective toward management, discovering the virtues in consultation and conciliation.

In 1981 Massachusetts was in turmoil. Proposition 2-1/2, a ballot

Candidates '88

measure approved in 1980 that limited property taxes to 2.5 percent of a community's full property values, had had a drastic effect on state government. The measure sapped cities and towns of up to 75 percent of their operating budgets.

The Legislature and the governor, divided on how to offset some of Proposition 2-1/2's impact on municipalities, failed to reach an agreement on the state budget before the fiscal year ran out on June 30. State employees, welfare recipients and pensioners stopped receiving their checks, leading to huge demonstrations at the Capitol and eventually a four-day work stoppage by 22,000 state employees. National Guard troops were summoned to fill in for striking state workers in prisons and state hospitals. In the meantime, Gov. King's administration was being buffeted by charges of corruption.

Over the preceding year, Dukakis had been working nearly full time trying to reassemble his organization and raise money. By the beginning of 1982, he had put together a formidable operation that spread into each of the state's villages and towns. His primary campaign ads hammered away at King and the "hidden costs" of corruption. "The corruption tax ...," the ads intoned, "the tax you'll never hear Ed King mention."

As had happened in 1974, Dukakis' campaign was boosted by events on the national front. The national recession was in full swing and, although Massachusetts weathered it better than most states, many Democrats were more than willing to exact their retribution on the abrasive King, whom President Reagan had called his "favorite Democratic governor."

Dukakis' strength in the primary was aided greatly by his use of corruption as a central campaign theme. That enabled Dukakis, whose integrity as governor was granted even by his detractors, to prevent King from going on the offensive as he had in 1978. On primary day, Dukakis won by more than 82,000 votes out of nearly 1.2 million cast, 53.5 percent to 46.5 percent. He showed surprising strength in older industrial cities that had been presumed to be King strongholds. The general election was little more than a formality, as Dukakis overwhelmed Republican John W. Sears with nearly 60 percent of the vote.

A New Day, A New Way

Early in Dukakis' second administration, it became apparent that in his four years away from politics he had gotten the message that voters in

1978 were transmitting. The *Washington Post* has related Dukakis' own account of the fruits of his sabbatical:

"I learned how to listen, how to think a little bit longer before I do things. I learned to do better at building coalitions. I understand a lot better than I did that you've got to involve people from the beginning in what you're doing—legislators, constituency leaders—and if you involve them, you get not only greater commitment but a better product."

One of Dukakis' first tasks in his new administration was to propitiate the business community, which he had enraged in his first term with his efforts to regulate the banking and insurance industries. Since 1975, when Massachusetts had the third highest unemployment rate in the nation at 11.2 percent, the state's economy had rebounded, fueled not only by measures of fiscal austerity implemented in Dukakis' first term, but also by two elements Dukakis adamantly opposed: Proposition 2-1/2, which helped stem the tide of businesses migrating to New Hampshire and the South to escape the high property levies of "Taxachusetts"; and the Reagan administration's defense buildup, which poured millions of dollars' worth of military projects into Bay State high-tech companies

Michael Dukakis and wife, Kitty, having breakfast on the campaign trail.

and defense contractors. By 1983 it was the business community—notably the high-tech companies around metropolitan Boston's Route 128 that had rejuvenated Massachusetts' economy—that wielded the most potent economic and political leverage; Dukakis saw he could not afford to allow a return to the antagonistic business-state relationship of the mid-1970s.

One clear sign of Dukakis' new approach to governing came when one of his favorite old constituencies, environmentalists, was pitted against the constituency he was trying to court, business.

In 1977 a high-tech corporation had signed an agreement to buy part of a historic farm outside of Boston to build its headquarters, enraging environmentalists. Gov. Dukakis moved to prevent construction by having the state take the property by right of eminent domain. But the company won a court order blocking Dukakis' move and by 1983 it was building a $20 million office on the farm. In 1984, however, the state's highest court overturned previous court rulings that had allowed the company to build, freeing the state to take the farm by eminent domain.

Confronted with the dilemma of supporting business or environmentalists, Gov. Dukakis this time sided with the company; he negotiated an agreement that permitted construction to continue in exchange for strict environmental and employment concessions.

While some environmental groups bitterly denounced Dukakis' decision, the business community applauded it as responsible and pragmatic. Dukakis said the decision represented his "personal effort to forge a result that links the goals of a strong economy and environmental quality." It is this emphasis on forging coalitions that is the hallmark of Dukakis II.

Dukakis would attract the ire of environmentalists for other actions as well, such as approving the construction of a mall in a wetlands section in southeastern Massachusetts, supporting trash-to-energy incinerators as the primary way to dispose of the state's rubbish, and not expediting cleanup of Boston Harbor. Gay activists routinely picket his appearances around the state for his administration's policy that effectively prevents gay couples from becoming foster parents.

This is not to say that Dukakis has abandoned his liberal underpinnings. But even during his first term it was difficult to pin him down ideologically because he would address problems more from a technical standpoint than from a political one. In that term, for example, he implemented a limited and controversial mandatory workfare program that was attacked by liberals as harsh and unfair. While there is little question that for the most part his politics fall to the left side of the spectrum, it is equally true that his independent approach to problem solving defies ideological pigeonholing. "People are confused as to whether he's liberal, moderate or conservative," political consultant Edward Reilly told the *Boston Globe*.

Spreading the 'Miracle'

The story of his state's resurgence from economic stagnancy to vitality—at around 3 percent, Massachusetts has the lowest unemployment rate of any industrial state—has become known as the "Massachusetts Miracle," and Dukakis is touting the virtues of business-government cooperation as well as his innovative approaches toward welfare reform and tax enforcement as he campaigns around the country. His pitch to voters in his first campaign for national office is direct: It works in Massachusetts; let's try it nationwide. His campaign ads echo that theme: "What he did for Massachusetts, he can do for America."

One of Dukakis' most ambitious initiatives is his welfare-to-work program, Employment and Training Choices, known as "ET." Dukakis calls ET his proudest achievement. His administration boasts that the program has placed 30,000 in jobs, saved the state $125 million in one year, helped reduce the welfare caseload by 4 percent and shown that welfare recipients want to work. It provides vocational training, transportation vouchers and child care to welfare recipients on a voluntary basis. While some have questioned the estimated savings and criticized the program for failing to produce better results for its cost—about $3,400 per job placement—most have praised ET as being a good, innovative program.

Dukakis defends ET against critics who argue that the results do not justify the investment made by the state. "We don't club people off the welfare rolls into dead-end, make-work jobs," he wrote in February 1987 in the *Wall Street Journal*, "because the only future in those jobs is dependency and a return to the welfare rolls. ET has placed more than 30,000 welfare recipients and applicants into good jobs, at decent pay, with a future. The average starting wage is $12,000, more than twice the average welfare grant. And 86 percent of our ET graduates who leave the welfare rolls are still off one year later."

Another Massachusetts program that Dukakis is promoting on the campaign trail is his tax compliance program, Revenue and Enforcement and Protection, or "REAP." The program, which combined tougher tax-collection methods with a 90-day tax amnesty, is credited with broadening the state's tax base by 5.2 percent and increasing revenues by 15 percent.

Dukakis argues that federal tax compliance can be improved and that, through the same methods of stricter enforcement and a one-time amnesty, the government could collect $105 billion over five years and $35 billion annually thereafter.

"Hokum," snorts Democratic rival Richard A. Gephardt of Missouri, a coauthor of tax-overhaul legislation in the House, who has joined others in disputing Dukakis' numbers and deriding his deficit-cutting proposal as a gimmick. Dukakis argues that REAP worked in Massachusetts, so it should be given a chance to work nationally.

Dukakis has found mixed support for his positions on energy policy. He adamantly opposes an oil import fee, which he argues would boost oil-producing states in the South and Southwest while hurting New England states, which rely on imported oil for winter fuel.

There is little divergence among the Democratic candidates, however, on Dukakis' position on the Seabrook nuclear power plant in southern New Hampshire. Convinced that an accident at the $4.8 billion facility would wreak untold devastation in the area, Dukakis has refused to submit emergency plans for six Massachusetts communities within the 10-mile evacuation zone around the plant, effectively blocking the plant from beginning to produce power. Many nearby New Hampshirites applaud Dukakis' efforts at preventing Seabrook from operating. In recent months, senior Dukakis aides have discussed with Texas energy executives the possibility of converting Seabrook into a plant that would burn Southwestern natural gas.

Learning While He Goes

Although he lacks any specific grounding in foreign policy or on domestic issues outside New England, Dukakis has a reputation as a quick study, something he has manifested on the campaign trail as he grapples with issues brand new to a governor of a small industrial state.

When he toured Iowa farm land in the months before he entered the presidential race, he demonstrated his unfamiliarity with agricultural issues by suggesting to hard-hit corn and soybean farmers that they try growing apples, blueberries, flowers or Belgian endive to diversify their crops. Arkansas Gov. Bill Clinton, who was accompanying Dukakis, scoffed that it was "yuppie agriculture."

A month later, Dukakis met with farm-state legislators in Washington, D.C., and won plaudits from South Dakota Democratic Sen. Thomas A. Daschle for his grasp on the subject of feed grains. "In fact," Daschle marveled, "he made reference to a 30-year-old [farm] plan that only the hard-core agricultural advocate would refer to."

A few weeks later, Dukakis unveiled a five-point plan aimed at aiding farmers, although he has continued to receive some flak in farm states for his reluctance to support a controversial program placing federal controls on production and marketing of farm products.

Moving Up

As he never did in any of his statewide races, Dukakis in his White House bid is selling himself as the product of the classic immigrants' American dream, donning the mantle of the campaign's ethnic candidate. "With your help and with your prayers," he said in announcing his intention to run for the nomination, "a son of Greek immigrants named Mike Dukakis can be the next president of the United States."

Dukakis was born in 1933 in Brookline, a suburb west of Boston. His father, Panos Dukakis, was born in Turkey and came to the United States at age 15 with no money and unable to speak English. Eight years later, he was attending Harvard Medical School. He died in 1979 at age 83 after a long career as a family doctor. Dukakis' mother, Euterpe, emigrated from Greece at age 9 and grew up in Haverhill, near the New Hampshire border. She went on to Bates College in Maine; according to Dukakis, she was the first Greek girl from that town ever to go to college. She became a teacher and now lives in Brookline.

An honor student at Brookline High School, Dukakis went on to Swarthmore College, outside Philadelphia, where he became a campus leader, serving as sports editor of the college newspaper and president of the student government. Originally a pre-medical student, Dukakis soon shifted his attention to political science.

To earn money while at college, he set up a barber stand in a dormitory hall, where he would cut the hair of his classmates as well as that of black students whom local barbers refused to serve. He supplemented his Greek by learning French and Spanish, and spent time studying in

Peru. He graduated from Swarthmore Phi Beta Kappa and with highest honors in 1955.

From 1955 to 1957 Dukakis served in the Army, stationed at Munsan, South Korea. On his return, he enrolled in Harvard Law School and graduated with honors in 1960. After law school, he joined the Boston law firm of Hill and Barlow and became involved in Brookline town government. Two years later he ran for state representative, finishing second among six candidates in a three-member district.

Dukakis was a maverick from his earliest days in politics. In the state House, he acquired a reputation as a bright, principled outsider who was a skilled debater but did not play by the Democratic hierarchy's rules. His most significant achievement in the Legislature was his sponsorship of a bill creating the nation's first no-fault insurance program.

In 1966 he ran for the Democratic nomination for attorney general, losing at the state convention. In 1970 he left his seat in the Legislature to run for the nomination for lieutenant governor. He defeated a more senior state legislator for the nomination, but he and Boston Mayor Kevin H. White, the Democratic nominee for governor, were soundly defeated in the general election by GOP Gov. Francis W. Sargent, 57 percent to 43 percent.

Following the election, Dukakis worked to maintain the political organization he had built up in hopes of mounting a future campaign. He remained visible to voters by moderating a public-television debate program, "The Advocates."

In 1973, he began his first campaign for governor. His primary opponent was Robert Quinn, the state's attorney general and a former Speaker of the state House. Quinn was identified with the regular organization wing of the Democratic Party, while Dukakis, a relatively new face to voters—candidates for lieutenant governor generally do not leave lasting impressions—was the insurgent. It was a year when voters across the nation were expressing their dissatisfaction with the political establishment. And in Massachusetts, the one state to vote for George McGovern for president in 1972, that mood was reflected in Democrats' voting 58 percent to 42 percent for the anti-establishment candidacy of Dukakis.

Dukakis' primary victory over the regular Democrats' favorite did not leave lasting scars and the factions joined in support of the winner with relatively little friction. Dukakis found an important ally in then-House Majority Leader Thomas P. O'Neill Jr., who called on party regulars to support the gubernatorial ticket. O'Neill had a personal stake in backing Dukakis: His son, Thomas P. O'Neill III, was Dukakis' running mate. With a unified party supporting him, Dukakis overcame his 1970 statewide loss by trouncing Sargent with 54 percent of the vote to the Republican's 42 percent.

1986: A Launching-Pad Election

It was well into the 1986 campaign season before Dukakis even had an opponent in his re-election bid. King, who had switched parties, was widely expected to be the Republican nominee, but he decided early in the year not to seek a rematch.

The GOP quest for a candidate became a tragicomedy, as the party conducted its fall primary between two men who were no longer candidates. The first-place finisher was anti-tax activist Gregory S. Hyatt, whose candidacy had been sunk by negative publicity. Before the spring GOP convention, a former employer said he had fired Hyatt for alleged bizarre behavior, including sitting nude in his office and talking to himself on the telephone. Later, it was reported that Hyatt had sought campaign funds from an alleged organized crime figure.

Shunning Hyatt, the party endorsed state Rep. Royall H. Switzler. But in June, Switzler ended his campaign, admitting he had lied about his military record. GOP leaders had struggled for so long to find a viable candidate that their eventual choice, businessman and former King aide George S. Kariotis, was regarded as merely a sacrificial lamb.

The combination of GOP ineptitude and Dukakis' bounding popularity pushed Dukakis to a 69 percent to 31 percent victory, the largest in Massachusetts history. It was a resounding endorsement both for the booming economy over which Dukakis was presiding and for the changes Dukakis himself had undergone.

Local Hero

A six-state region that appears to have been plastered onto the body of the country by an impatient potter, New England can seem somewhat isolated from the rest of the nation. Home to some of the most liberal congressional delegations and voters—two of the three lowest statewide percentages for Reagan in 1984 came from Massachusetts and Rhode Island—New Englanders have garnered a reputation for quirky independence in the face of national trends. (Many recall the time in 1984 when White House Chief of Staff James A. Baker III was asked if his trip to China was his first visit to a communist country. "No," he replied, "I've been to Massachusetts.")

A byproduct of this independence is a strong regional parochialism that attaches itself to everything from sports teams to driving habits. When a New England college football team takes on a national powerhouse from the South or Midwest, many will perceive it as a triumph of regional values if the local school prevails. By the same token, many New Englanders have added Dukakis to their pantheon of parochial products to be flourished proudly at the rest of the nation.

This treatment of Dukakis as a kind of regional commodity has been particularly noticeable in the print and electronic media in Boston, which buttressed the Massachusetts governor's home-field advantage in the New Hampshire primary. Many voters in populous southern New Hampshire tune in to Boston TV stations for their evening news, and the *Globe* and *Boston Herald* sell close to 100,000 copies in that part of the state.

In the months before Dukakis announced his candidacy, the *Globe* would recite a wide-eyed litany of major national news organizations and columnists courting Dukakis for appearances and interviews. The *Atlanta Journal and Constitution* charted the *Globe*'s coverage between Feb. 1 and May 22, 1987, and counted articles about Dukakis' presidential campaign on 78 of the 111 days, or 70 percent. Sensitive to charges of boosterism, the *Globe* has moved toward taking a more expansive view of the presidential campaign, treating Dukakis more as one candidate in a field rather than as a provincial favorite. During the six-week period leading up to May 22, according to the *Journal and Constitution*, only six of the 34 stories about Dukakis made the *Globe*'s front page, compared with 17 of 43 in February and March.

The *Washington Post* counted 41 pictures and 44 stories in Boston's Murdoch-owned tabloid, the *Herald*, for the four days around Dukakis' entry into the race. Still, much of the *Herald*'s coverage is not positive; analysts note that the tabloid has run some of the toughest stories about Dukakis, and *Herald* columnists such as Howie Carr and Peter Lucas are renowned for pulling no punches when Dukakis is the subject. (When two biographies published late in 1987 revealed that Dukakis, while he was out of office in 1979, had approved the leaking of damaging information about Gov. King's questionable use of state expense accounts, Carr slammed Dukakis for claiming to shun negative campaigning and postulated that the governor's middle initial stood for "Sanctimonious" or "Sleazy." It stands for Stanley.)

A guiltier party in the media boosterism of Dukakis is Boston's local television news programs, which have been criticized for having contracted "Duke fever" and trying to transmit it across the state line into New Hampshire. The *Washington Post* quoted Richard M. Gaines, editor of the weekly newspaper the *Boston Phoenix*, as describing the TV reporting as "breathless, mindless and worthless." "When Dukakis is anywhere," he added, "there are live reports from corn fields, beaches, fund-raisers, and it's all very immediate—the context is about 20 seconds long." In a promotional ad, the CBS-TV affiliate in Boston, WNEV-TV, described its political team as Dukakis' "running mates."

Even the real hometown team has joined the campaign. Minnesota native Kevin McHale, an all-star forward on the Boston Celtics, has stumped his home state for Dukakis.

The impact of the Boston media's coverage of Dukakis is difficult to gauge, but it has stirred plenty of grumbling in rivals' camps. A Gephardt adviser complained to the *Post*, "Everyone has their hometown press, but what's the responsibility when they move over into New Hampshire?"

'Cool' Is What Counts

To some New Englanders who have watched him in action, Dukakis' viability as a national candidate comes as a surprise. With his rapid-fire delivery and expressionless visage, he strikes many as the antithesis of the 1980s "blow-dried, fair-haired" media model, regardless of *Playgirl* magazine's description of Dukakis as one of the country's "10 sexiest men."

But Dukakis is not quite so mismatched as some believe. The medium of presidential campaigns is television, and Dukakis' cool technocratic equanimity is tailor-made for TV news "sound bites" and half-minute commercials. His work on "The Advocates" served as a training ground for his modern-day media campaign. A few years ago, he had a walk-on role on the TV program "St. Elsewhere."

Democratic leaders picked Dukakis to moderate the Democratic response to Reagan's 1984 State of the Union address, primarily due to the governor's mastery of the medium on which the president excelled.

Dukakis was roundly lauded for his work on the broadcast. One party official effused, "He is probably the best TV Democrat we've ever had."

Many Massachusetts residents warmly recall Dukakis' reassuring, sweater-clad presence during the blizzard of 1978 that crippled the state for several days. For a week in February, Dukakis dominated local television, giving reports of storm damage, issuing orders to arrest anyone who violated the driving ban and assuring viewers that the state would pull through.

While a capable television performance is helpful, it is not an electoral panacea; Dukakis, after all, went on to lose renomination in 1978. But no one would dispute that in a campaign to be waged largely across the airwaves it is an advantage to appear comfortable on a TV screen.

Hand on the Throttle

One thing Dukakis need not worry about in running for president is losing his job. Re-elected in 1986, he is not up for re-election until 1990. When he is out of the state, Massachusetts' constitution designates the lieutenant governor, Evelyn Murphy, as the chief executive in the governor's absence. Dukakis, however, has said he would retain control while out of state. The reasons go a bit beyond a desire to maintain contact over day-to-day state operations.

Tensions between Murphy's and Dukakis' forces have been no secret. The roots of any bad feelings toward Murphy are said to go back to the days following Dukakis' renomination loss to King. Murphy, unlike other Dukakis loyalists, tried to keep her job as secretary of environmental affairs (a bid King rejected). Murphy apparently was not forgiven by the Dukakis camp. She merited additional opprobrium from the Dukakis camp in her unsuccessful 1982 primary run for lieutenant governor by saying that she could work with either Dukakis or King. In winning the 1986 election, Murphy became the first woman in Massachusetts history to win statewide office. If Dukakis were to be elected president, she would fill out his term as governor.

Dukakis has taken pains to avoid being labeled an absentee governor. His first major appointment after announcing his candidacy was C. Hale Champion, executive director of the Kennedy School, as chief of staff. Champion replaced John Sasso, a respected political strategist who left to become Dukakis' campaign manager.

Sasso, dubbed by many Dukakis' alter ego, resigned from the campaign on Sept. 30, 1987, after admitting he had given reporters a videotape juxtaposing nearly identical speech passages by Delaware Sen. Joseph R. Biden Jr. and British Labor Party leader Neil Kinnock. Biden later withdrew from the field of Democratic presidential aspirants amidst revelations of earlier allegations of plagiarism. Paul Tully, Dukakis' (and, formerly, Sen. Gary Hart's) political director, also resigned over the tape furor.

The incident rocked the Dukakis campaign. Earlier instances of Sasso's use of controversial campaign tactics were cited, and Dukakis' assertion that he strongly opposed negative campaigning was called into question. Sasso's and Tully's abrupt resignations forestalled a protracted scandal, however, and the flap died down after a few weeks.

With Dukakis not devoting full time to gubernatorial duties, and especially with Sasso gone, some glitches arose. In April 1987, Democratic leaders in the state House rejected Dukakis' fiscal 1988 budget. His ambitious universal health plan, which would make Massachusetts the first state to guarantee health insurance coverage to all its residents, was nearly killed in the Legislature.

On the other hand, Dukakis took the lead in the summer of 1987 in writing complex legislation to replace the state's $5 billion-a-year mechanism for reimbursing hospitals and controlling health costs. And Dukakis' presidential bid has not generated much feeling of neglect among the Massachusetts public. An August 1987 *Globe* poll showed that 57 percent of state residents felt that Dukakis had paid enough attention to his job despite his frequent trips outside the state, and that 77 percent said they felt favorably or somewhat favorably toward him.

For his part, Dukakis showed few signs of wear from the long grind of greeting torrents of faceless people and spending night after night in featureless motels far from home. Dukakis has compared his presidential bid to a favorite avocation, running marathons. As he told an Iowa crowd in May, "They're long, they're grueling, but they're a lot of fun. And when you cross that finish line, there's a sweetness to them."

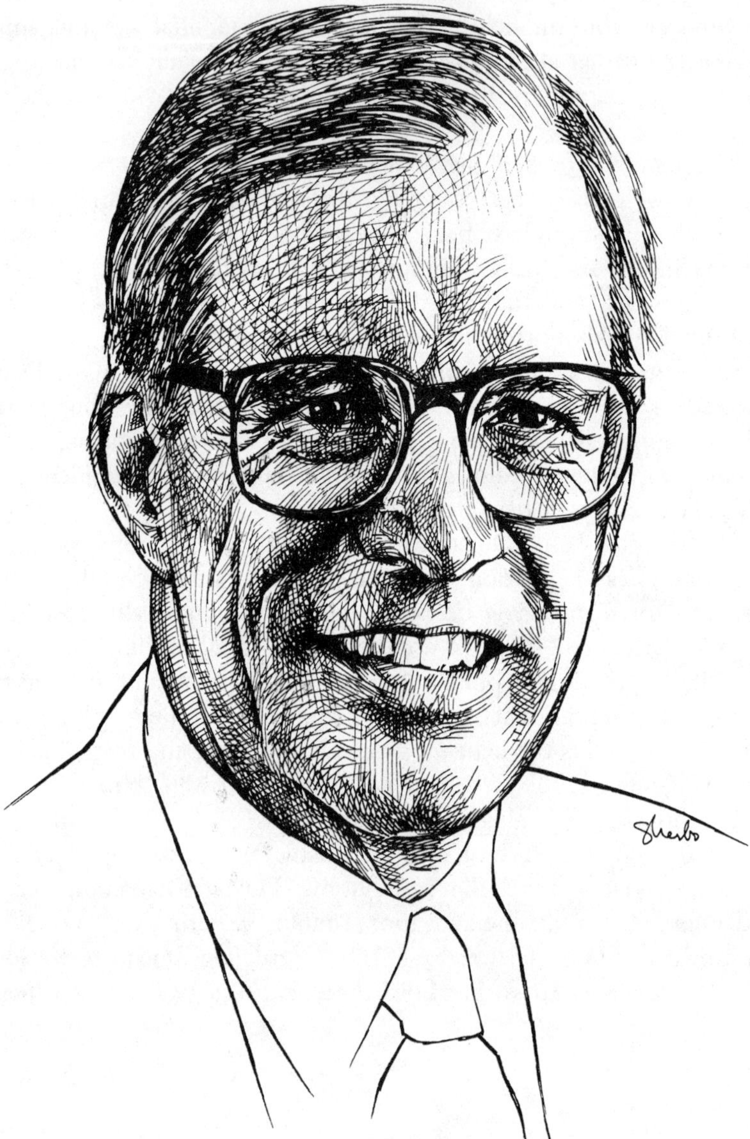

PIERRE S. 'PETE' DU PONT IV

Eastern Establishment Republican Offers Unconventional Proposals

The tall, aristocratic, bespectacled man stood before 1,000 supporters in Wilmington's Grand Opera House. "I'm unknown," he said. "I'm underrated, and there's nowhere to go but up." Thus did Pierre S. "Pete" du Pont IV make public his wish to run for the presidency. It was June 3, 1986, and du Pont was the first Republican to announce his intentions.

"Assuming we can assemble the necessary resources this summer, in the fall I will become a candidate for the presidency of the United States," he said. The decision to go ahead did come, and du Pont made his formal announcement on Sept. 16. Fully one year later, however, the former Delaware governor was still known by a mere 2 to 5 percent of the electorate, and he drew only some 5 percent in most preference polls.

His obscurity, of course, ended at state's edge. In tiny Delaware—which has three counties, one at-large representative in Congress and a population about the size of Pittsburgh (roughly 600,000)—the name du Pont emblazons the state's major industries, as well as schools, hospitals, parks, hotels, roads and museums. Sales by E. I. du Pont de Nemours & Co. Inc. totaled $27 billion in 1986, roughly 27 times the state's annual budget.

Bucking a Famous Heritage

Given his family's commercial prowess, Pete du Pont's decision to embark on a political career came as a surprise to many. Most friends and observers had expected him to go into the family business, as had most of his relatives. But after a short stint as a quality control engineer, du Pont found the lure of politics simply overwhelming.

Apprenticing for a term in Delaware's Legislature, du Pont served six years in the U.S. House of Representatives (1971-77) and in 1977 was

Pierre Samuel 'Pete' du Pont IV

Profession: Lawyer.
Born: Jan. 22, 1935, Wilmington, Del.
Home: Rockland, Del.
Religion: Episcopalian.
Education: Princeton University, B.S.E., 1956; Harvard University, J.D., 1963.
Political Career: Delaware House of Representatives, 1969-70; U.S. House of Representatives, 1971-76; Delaware governor, 1977-85.
Military: U.S. Navy (lieutenant), 1957-60.
Family: Wife, Elise Ravenel Wood; four children.
House Committees: Foreign Affairs, Merchant Marine and Fisheries, 1971-77.

inaugurated to the first of two four-year terms as governor. Barred by the state constitution from running for a third term, he toyed briefly with challenging incumbent Democrat Joseph R. Biden Jr. for the Senate in 1984. But, according to aides and observers, the presidency was the plum du Pont had long sought.

In deciding against a Senate race in July 1983, du Pont said: "Being a senator is a high honor and an important responsibility. But it is a full-time job by itself. Its very nature forces attention to the issues of the day rather than the agenda of tomorrow."

Somewhat of a political chameleon, du Pont was considered a moderate Republican during his days in the House. But after becoming governor he was won over to the supply-side economic philosophy (tax cuts along with reductions in government spending) that also was embraced by Ronald Reagan.

While du Pont has been called the most conservative Republican presidential contender, he describes himself as a populist. His major themes are attention-grabbing ones that include: overhauling Social Security; phasing out farm subsidies; eliminating welfare programs and putting all able-bodied persons to work; mandatory random drug-testing for high school students; and providing parents vouchers to pay for their children's education at public, private or church-supported schools of their choice. The last major presidential candidate to talk seriously about voluntary Social Security and an end to farm subsidies was Republican nominee Barry Goldwater in 1964.

The former Delaware governor provided some indication of how difficult it would be to pin philosophical labels on him when, in an interview with the conservative weekly *Human Events*, he commented: "I think there have been two great leaders as Presidents in this century. One was Franklin Roosevelt, who led us out of the Depression, and one is Ronald Reagan, who led us back to a more sensible government philosophy."

With other displays, du Pont has tried to downplay his privileged background. For example, he drove an old Buick during his tenure in the House. Yet it would be nearly impossible for him to escape the reality that his name is associated with immense wealth. Indeed, the issue still tends to hound him politically. He is the richest of the candidates; a detailed financial statement du Pont released in 1987 put his net worth at $5.78 million.

Du Pont's ancestors arrived from France nearly 200 years ago and almost immediately established themselves as shrewd entrepreneurs. His great-great-great grandfather, Éleuthère Irénée, founded the E. I. du Pont de Nemours gunpowder company; and the first Pierre S. du Pont was instrumental in suggesting the Louisiana Purchase.

In the early 1900s the family branched out into explosives and automobile manufacturing; a half-century later, its holdings included chemical, plastics, paint, textile and oil companies. By the late 1940s the family had put together what the U.S. government said, disapprovingly, was "the largest single concentration of industrial power in the United States." The Supreme Court broke up the family holdings in 1961. Although the du Ponts (now numbering around 2,000) no longer control their namesake company, *Forbes* magazine has called them America's "first family of wealth."

Company executives of du Pont spent $1 million trying to defeat Franklin D. Roosevelt in 1936—though a du Pont daughter married Franklin Jr. In other political activity the family contributed heavily to the arch-conservative Liberty Lobby.

For his own part, Pete du Pont is a skilled yachtsman (he was at the helm of an American entry at two Olympic trials in the 1950s) who attended all the "right" schools: Phillips Exeter Academy, Princeton University and Harvard Law School. In 1957 he married Elise Ravenel Wood, herself a wealthy heiress and descendant of Benjamin Franklin. She graduated from law school during Pete's first term as governor and was appointed by President Reagan as an assistant administrator in the U.S. Agency for International Development. Her own political connections and conservative credentials have made her a principal ally and asset in the campaign, according to observers.

Though trained in engineering, du Pont's tenure with the family company was not satisfying to him. "I think that the scientific gene kind of missed my generation in the family," he says. "I got a little bored.... [A]t age 34 I was right on track to becoming a senior vice president at age 63. And somehow, I thought to myself, there must be more to life than 30 years of carefully moving up the [corporate] ladder."

Mr. du Pont Goes to Washington

After serving in various local and state GOP committees, the national Republican Finance Committee and the state Legislature, du Pont ignored the advice of party leaders in 1970. He wrested the GOP congressional nomination from the party favorite with a "down home" and folksy campaign style that he was to adopt in succeeding campaigns.

During his run for the nomination, du Pont visited every one of the more than 400 delegates to the state convention. His appearances in the delegates' own living rooms helped him win the 20 percent he needed to get on the primary ballot. Having won the nomination he was elected with 53.7 percent of the vote, a count that was to increase in later re-election bids.

"I learned a valuable lesson then, that if you work people one at a time you can accomplish a lot," du Pont has said, in comparing his first major race with his presidential bid. "That's what I'm doing now. That's the fun part, building. I like campaigning. I like people. They refresh you."

A strong opponent of receiving PAC (political action committee) money, du Pont organized "Pete's 3,000" to finance his 1974 House re-election bid. He sought and received 3,000 individual contributions of $100 or less. Again, the campaign was a success.

As for his record in Congress, du Pont generally took a middle-of-the-road position on major issues. He earned ratings that hovered near 50 percent from both the liberal Americans for Democratic Action and the conservative Americans for Constitutional Action.

He joined liberals and moderates to support a number of significant bills: higher gasoline taxes, campaign reform, federal funding of abortions, tax reform, public works employment, an increase in the minimum wage and establishment of the Consumer Product Safety Commission. He voted with them against the oil depletion allowance, against government loans to bail out the ailing Lockheed Corp. and against assisting anti-communist rebels fighting in Angola (a position he has since reversed).

Du Pont also stood with liberals to override President Richard Nixon's veto of the War Powers Act, which had been designed to give Congress a greater voice in overseas military commitments.

At the same time, du Pont voted against school busing and in favor of voluntary school prayer—positions he still takes. Generally pro-environment, du Pont as a freshman led a successful floor fight against the Tocks Island Dam on the Delaware River, a major East Coast environmental issue. "In Congress I'm about in the center," he said at the time. Yet that was to change during his tenure as governor.

Pete du Pont and his wife, Elise, enjoying the snow in Manchester, N.H.

Governorship: A Rocky Road

Campaigning in 1976 for the Delaware governorship under the slogan "Leadership for a Change," du Pont limited campaign contributions to $100 (the amount was increased to $1,000 for his re-election). He was swept into office with nearly 58 percent of the vote on a wave of dissatisfaction with Democratic Gov. Sherman W. Trippett.

The state's economy was in shambles; bad management was rampant in the statehouse. High level officials "were not party hacks. But they were only one step above," noted Robert L. Byrd, a Democratic legislator at the time, and now lobbyist for the Delaware Chamber of Commerce. The top marginal income tax rate was 19.8 percent, the nation's highest, as was the state's debt service. Although 22 tax increases had been enacted during the previous six years, Delaware's $424 million budget was $19 million in debt, amounting to $1,000 per capita. Unemployment stood at 9 percent.

Du Pont's tenure began inauspiciously. First, he announced to the state Legislature that Delaware was bankrupt, "face to face with economic disaster." However true, it was a disastrous admission.

"When Wall Street heard that, they pulled the plug on our bond market. It took eight years for it to recover," said Richard Cordrey, the Democratic president pro tem of the state Senate at the time.

During du Pont's first year in office, Democrats stalled much of the governor's legislative agenda (Democrats controlled both houses for six of du Pont's eight years in office) and held up confirmation of 15 major appointments. And, in a devastating blow, the Legislature overrode a governor's veto of the budget for the first time in the state's history.

"Democrats in the Legislature thought him elitist," explained Byrd. "He was being taught a lesson and learning that he had to work with people." Detractors nicknamed the governor "Champagne Pete." And when he referred to the average voter as "Joe Six Pack," the response was another epithet: "Pierre S. Six Pacque the 4th."

Du Pont himself admits that his first months in office "were tough.... I had been elected governor by a state that was clearly tired and disgusted by where we have been.... But in the people's wisdom, they gave me the same Legislature that had created the problem."

The trials of the initial six months apparently hit home. Thereafter, du Pont worked to hone a functional relationship with his opponents, succeeding in persuading them to abandon an expensive cost-of-living increase for public employees. He scored other victories as well, including passage of a prison reform bill. He also installed management controls and made appointments on the basis of merit, rather than patronage. He brought in outsiders for top jobs and appointed the state's first female and black cabinet officers. Probably the most important coup of his first term was passage of two amendments to the state's constitution. One limited expenditures to 98 percent of projected revenues, with a 2 percent contingency fund to be tapped only in emergency; the second required a 60 percent vote for new or increased taxes.

Sweeping to Re-election

Like his previous campaigns, du Pont's bid for a second gubernatorial term was characterized by handshaking at street corners and circulating at county fairs. It cost only $245,000, and du Pont won with 71 percent of the vote, the largest plurality in the state's history.

"Du Pont meets people well, and he's not afraid to roll up his sleeves at a bowling alley or a fire hall," observed one high-ranking state official. "People, while they respect him, don't think he's looking down his nose at them."

Even du Pont's Democratic opponent, William J. Gordy, admitted, "He was a good governor, and one of the best politicians I've ever seen. He's got a great personality and can sit with chicken catchers or lawyers and talk their language."

On du Pont's legislative agenda during his last year in office, pay freezes and a no-growth policy for state agencies topped the list. At the same time he proposed an 8 percent increase in the Aid to Families with Dependent Children Program, a reduction in the size of elementary school classes and initiation of a statewide computer education program. He also started a pilot project that would give vouchers to unemployed workers who were unlikely to get their old jobs back: the first of its kind in the nation. The vouchers could be cashed at vocational or community colleges for training in a new field.

One of the most important pieces of legislation signed during du Pont's second term was the Financial Center Development Act, passed in February 1981. The measure removed usury limits on banks' interest rates and credit card operations, while providing tax incentives for banks to locate in the state if they employed at least 100 people within their first year.

Twenty major national banks subsequently opened offices in Delaware, creating 18,000 new jobs. A Delaware Development Office also was created to lure other new businesses to the state, which became the nation's credit card headquarters.

When du Pont left office in 1985 to join the law firm of Richards, Layton & Finger, and ponder his future political prospects, the state was booming with a 20 percent increase in employment. His own approval ratings approached 90 percent. Three reductions had resulted in a 30 percent cut in personal income taxes. Unemployment was among the nation's lowest.

Du Pont could point to eight budget surpluses, the one in his last year amounting to $180 million in a budget of $800 million. Many Republicans and Democrats alike sang his praises. "He was a strong leader who believed in balanced budgets and stuck to his guns as far as spending was concerned," commented Delaware state Rep. Robert Gilligan, leader of the House Democratic majority during du Pont's last two years in office. "If du Pont is the Republican candidate for president ... 80 percent of the Democrats in Delaware would vote for him."

Campaign Strategy: Getting the Message Out

Du Pont's national aspirations probably date back at least to the late 1970s, when he founded COPAC to help Republican candidates for local and state offices. The theory was that it was essential for the GOP to gain control of more state legislatures if the party was to have greater influence on congressional redistricting after the 1990 Census. Du Pont called the effort political "venture capital." And he reaped its profits too. The effort helped him build a range of contacts for the presidential race.

Nonetheless, du Pont's 1988 presidential campaign was to be somewhat of a shoestring affair. It would be run out of a one-story building by young enthusiasts inexperienced in presidential politics, who fondly refer to du Pont as "the Duper."

An air of unconventionality seemed to hover about du Pont's campaign and, although wealthy, he was to have difficulty raising money. Part of the reason was his personal opposition to accepting PAC money, despite his earlier support for COPAC. "I don't like being funded by interest groups. That kind of bothers me," he said in a March 1987 interview.

Personally, du Pont is energetic, an impeccable dresser, a good listener and an intense speaker. He displays the easy, self-deprecating sense of humor coveted by many politicians. He also makes a point of noting his executive experience as governor, which other Republican presidential hopefuls lack. "My experience as governor was a tremendous education," he noted in an Oct. 1, 1987, article in the *Boston Globe*, entitled, "Why I'm Running."

A hard-working campaigner, du Pont is eager to get his message out although some may find irony in such a wealthy man telling bankrupt farmers in Iowa that subsidies are bad for them. "How can someone named du Pont, who went to all those fancy schools, understand the problems of ordinary people?" he said while campaigning in Iowa. "That's a good question. Some people from wealthy families who go into politics feel guilty about their money. They become liberals and believe in spending their money and yours. I'm not that kind of person. I believe in creating opportunity."

Calling himself the next leader of the "American conservative majority," du Pont appeared to relish the controversy his ideas tended to cause. And he recognized from the outset that he was a long shot: "We have no machine. We have no grand public office. We have no front-runner status. And we don't think we need them. We can get along listening and learning and offering suggestions, offering our campaign as a means of accomplishing what America wants to do."

Gaining national exposure was to become du Pont's major obstacle. "We had a wonderful break this morning," he commented wryly in October 1987. "The *Boston Globe* wrote an editorial attacking me." (The editorial said his ideas were "a recipe for unwise government and disastrous politics.") "If you're attacked," he concluded, "you know you're doing better."

The campaign did get a minor boost in May 1987, when du Pont debated former Arizona governor Bruce E. Babbitt, a Democratic presidential aspirant, in Iowa. "National television exposure cannot do anything but help," observed Glenn C. Kenton, du Pont's campaign manager and closest political adviser. Kenton, who began working for du Pont in 1968, served as his administrative assistant in the U.S. House and was appointed secretary of state during his governorship.

Du Pont's strategy was to concentrate on Iowa, where he spent more days than any other Republican candidate, supported by the second-largest paid staff of any in the field. But his campaign seemed to lack momentum and he failed to develop an obvious constituency.

Candidates '88

Du Pont's Interest Group Ratings

Vote ratings by interest groups help to give a picture of Pierre S. "Pete" du Pont's orientation during his House career. This table shows how often du Pont voted on key legislative issues in accordance with the positions of groups chosen to represent liberal, labor, business and conservative viewpoints. They are the Americans for Democratic Action (ADA), AFL-CIO, Chamber of Commerce of the United States (CCUS) and Americans for Constitutional Action (ACA).

	ADA	AFL-CIO	CCUS	ACA
1971	41	0	—[1]	82
1972	50	36	70	39
1973	52	36	73	48
1974	61	55	50	36
1975	53	24	56	59
1976	35	32	54	33

[1] CCUS combined vote records for 1971 and 1972.

Nonetheless, a number of people gave his performance high marks.

"People who've actually listened to what he's saying and thought about it are very much impressed," said Iowa's Franklin County Republican chairman Tom Latham. Du Pont "is the only one among the Republicans saying anything different. With the rest of them, there's little more than personality differences between them. Sure, he's got ideas that some would consider radical. But at least he's come out and taken some stands on things."

"He came off more statesmanlike than I've ever seen him," said Roger Huetig, active in Iowa's Republican Party, after viewing a televised debate among the GOP contenders Jan. 9, 1988. "Everything Pete du Pont had to say tonight, I liked," said another viewer. "He's right about the education system being messed up, and he's right that the Soviets haven't changed. They still lie and cheat, and they still can't be trusted."

Du Pont's campaign was to revolve around a few carefully crafted positions, which some political commentators criticized as peripheral. Based on his conversion to supply-side economics, du Pont's policy prescriptions became a mixture of right-leaning and liberal philosophies. Du Pont sought advice from specialists at the conservative Heritage Foundation and libertarian Cato Institute. So, not surprisingly, he subsequently won high marks from spokesmen of those groups.

"One of the most exciting candidates of the last decade of either party is Pete du Pont," said Burton Yale Pines, a vice president of the Heritage Foundation.

"He's more creative and substantially more courageous than the others, talking about Social Security reform in Florida and agricultural reform in Iowa," commented William A. Niskanen, chairman of the Cato Institute.

Although du Pont displayed passionate devotion to what he referred to as his "damn right" ideas, some critics questioned his conservative credentials. They pointed to his moderate-to-liberal record in Congress. "All of us were different in the 1970s," du Pont responded. "There really are very few issues where I've changed my position. In fact, on most issues from gun control to right-to-work laws to drug enforcement to fiscal constraint I've always had conservative views."

Some of du Pont's change was due to "conviction, some has been blowing with the wind," observed former Du Pont company chief executive officer Irving S. Shapiro (a Democrat). "You can sort of trace some of Pete's movements to turns in the country."

Added Jim Leach, R-Iowa, of du Pont's House performance: "Pete was a classic, liberal, Rockefeller Republican. Now it appears he's decided to wrap himself in New Right political cloth."

An Agenda of 'Damn Right' Ideas

Whatever the mix of belief and opportunism, du Pont did take his case to some of its least receptive audiences.

"I believe the government should be out of the agricultural marketplace in five years," du Pont said in announcing his candidacy. "In the meantime, we should stop playing politics with price-fixing schemes and start making payments directly to farmers during this transition period. Our farmers are the most productive in the world. They can out-plant, out-harvest and out-sell any competitor. It's high time we gave the American farmer the chance to be his own master once again."

Writing in the Feb. 1, 1987, edition of the *Sioux Falls Argus Leader*, du Pont argued: "The biggest folly is the very foundation of federal farm policy: the target price system that has farmers addicted to government aid."

Instead, du Pont offered a "Farm Opportunity Plan" to phase out price supports over five years. According to his estimates, such a system would save the government $25 billion. Commodity price support programs would be replaced with "market transition payments" made directly to farmers, with gradually reduced amounts. Deficiency payments, paid diversions, set-aside requirements and marketing quotas would be ended immediately.

Although du Pont's attack on farm subsidies frequently encountered a lukewarm and sometimes cold reception in Iowa, Dean Kleckner, president of the American Farm Bureau Federation, voiced qualified approval. "The Farm Bureau also wants to move toward dependence on the market and not on government," he said, "but we can't get from here to there overnight, and five years is probably too fast."

On Social Security, as with farm subsidies, du Pont stepped in where most politicians fear to tread. His solution to what he foresees as a coming crisis, due to the retirement of the "baby boom" generation, was to make Social Security voluntary. To stave off bankruptcy of the system he would offer people the alternative of paying into a private, interest-bearing account, similar to individual retirement accounts (IRAs). A family paying $1,000 a year in Social Security taxes would put up that amount twice, once to the system and once to a private account. In return, it would receive a $1,000 tax credit. Those currently contributing to Social Security would continue to be guaranteed benefits.

Du Pont estimated that the reform, dubbed the Financial Security Program, would add $20 billion to the federal budget deficit in the first year—if, say, 20 percent of eligible workers took the option. In the long run, however, du Pont contended that the scheme would save money for the government.

On the issue of drugs, du Pont's hard-line approach has been welcomed by conservatives. He proposes mandatory drug testing in high schools; students who fail would be barred for a year from receiving their driver's license. To critics who argue that his plan would jeopardize individual rights, du Pont was to respond: "There is a constitutional right to be free from unreasonable searches and seizures. But the United States Supreme Court decisions make it clear that what is reasonable depends very much on the situation and on the objective served by the search.... There is no more compelling need than getting drugs out of America's classrooms."

Some skeptics questioned whether postponement of a driver's license would suffice to deter drug use. "What if they [teenagers] don't have a car?" queried GOP presidential contender Robert Dole somewhat sarcastically during a televised debate.

"I'm worried about a druggie stealing my car; he doesn't need a driver's license," commented another Republican presidential hopeful, Alexander M. Haig Jr.

Almost as controversial was du Pont's plan to establish a federal jobs program that would substitute mandatory work (at 90 percent of minimum wage) for Aid to Families with Dependent Children and other welfare programs. Ironically, some observers have likened it to the Works Progress Administration (WPA) of the New Deal era. Du Pont's philosophy is: "If you don't work, you don't get a check."

Elaborating during a speech in Philadelphia on June 19, 1987, du Pont said his basic intent was to change the underlying incentives for work: "As it stands now, government actually penalizes low-income families which stay together; discourages poor people from taking that initial entry-level job needed to build work experience, confidence, and self-respect; and breeds hostility toward the traditional American ethic of building and achieving through hard work.... Why take a job as a dishwasher at a restaurant if one can receive about the same amount of money from the government for not working at all? Our government is actually rewarding people for staying poor."

At the same time, du Pont would argue that anyone who needs help financing higher education or job training should be able to obtain government-guaranteed loans at market rates from local financial institutions. He would also increase the Earned Income Tax Credit from the existing $800 to as much as $3,300 a year for a family of four. In addition, he was to propose guaranteed medical coverage for any family whose income fell below the poverty line. And he would toughen child support enforcement laws. "Instead of a handout, we need to provide poor people with a job and everything that comes with it—a paycheck, a boss, responsibility for mistakes, rewards for initiative and a chance to move up to a better job," he said.

The candidate brushed aside such criticisms as the inadequacy of existing day care programs and the fact that low-paid make-work might seem undignified. And from a fiscal standpoint, du Pont estimated that his "Work and Family Responsibility Plan" would cost about $7 billion in the first year, with a break-even point in the third year and "substantial savings" thereafter.

On education, a similar faith in the private sector could be discerned in du Pont's approach. "I think one of the problems of education is, it's a monopoly still, run by the government," he would say. "There's no competition in it."

Du Pont was to suggest giving parents government vouchers worth the federal share of the cost of an education. Parents could use the vouchers to finance their children's education at public, private or religious schools of their choosing. The program would not be mandatory, however; states and local school boards would decide whether and how to implement it. Beyond that, du Pont was somewhat vague on the specifics of how the plan would work. Instead, he clung to the underlying principle: "Giving parents a greater say in where their kids go to school," he said, "will force schools to improve."

On other issues, du Pont was to present an amalgam of conservative and liberal ideas. Monogamy, he would contend, is the best way to prevent the spread of AIDS (acquired immune deficiency syndrome). "AIDS is not a civil rights issue. It's a deadly issue," he warned. "If we all decided today to limit our sexual partners to one person, there wouldn't be any more spread of AIDS." The candidate was to support screening for AIDS during routine blood testing, but he opposed mandatory universal testing. Education, he insisted, would be the key to eradicating the disease.

As for abortion, du Pont expressed his moral opposition. Nor did he favor federal funding of such surgery, arguing that the Supreme Court's decision to permit the procedure in *Roe v. Wade* should be overturned. States, he contended, should rule on the issue for themselves.

Du Pont was to speak out less frequently on foreign policy and defense issues than he has on domestic policy. However, he became an ardent advocate of Reagan's Strategic Defense Initiative (SDI), popularly known as "Star Wars." If elected, he said, he would deploy SDI by 1996.

He also opposed the U.S.-Soviet agreement to eliminate intermediate- and short-range nuclear missiles in Europe (the INF accord). Du Pont warned that "Fifteen years of arms control negotiations with

Moscow have left America vulnerable to attack as the Kremlin has cheated on every agreement."

In Central America, du Pont strongly supported U.S. aid to the "contra" guerrillas fighting the leftist Sandinista government in Nicaragua. And in the Persian Gulf, he backed the Reagan administration's policy of protecting Kuwaiti tankers. As for the policy of trading arms for hostages, du Pont deemed the Iranian arms affair ill-advised.

On the eve of Soviet leader Mikhail Gorbachev's visit to the United States in December 1987, du Pont wrote an article calling on Moscow to hold free elections in Poland, withdraw from Afghanistan, end Cuban aid to Nicaragua, destroy the Soviet SS-25 missiles, permit free emigration of Soviet Jews and tear down the Berlin Wall. Yet, he was to break with conservatives by supporting pressures on South Africa to end its apartheid policy.

On the domestic side, du Pont favored stricter laws on acid rain. He also has offered a rather novel proposal to put the Audubon Society in charge of national parks.

True to his enthusiastic support of supply-side economics, du Pont vigorously opposed tax increases. "I don't think the people of this country need more taxes.... What they need is for the government to tighten its belt and get its spending under control," he said.

Critical of the Gramm-Rudman-Hollings balanced budget act, du Pont argued: "The secret is to have a mechanism to restrict spending, not to balance the budget, which can force you to raise taxes."

He is a strong advocate of deregulation, noting that "one job in five in Delaware today was created in our eight years because of deregulation and tax-cutting efforts."

Commenting on his reform plans, du Pont once said, "I don't think my ideas are liberal or conservative." But were they radical? "There's nothing more dangerous than conventional wisdom in a time of crisis," he responded. Indeed, he would quote his mother, who told him: "In life, no matter what you do, half your friends will say you're right and half your friends will say you're wrong. So you might as well do the right thing."

Whether the electorate would agree with what du Pont thought right, or "damn right," seemed a dubious proposition as the first primaries and caucuses approached. On the other hand, some speculated that his vigorous prosecution of the campaign may have opened a Cabinet door for Pete du Pont in a future Republican administration.

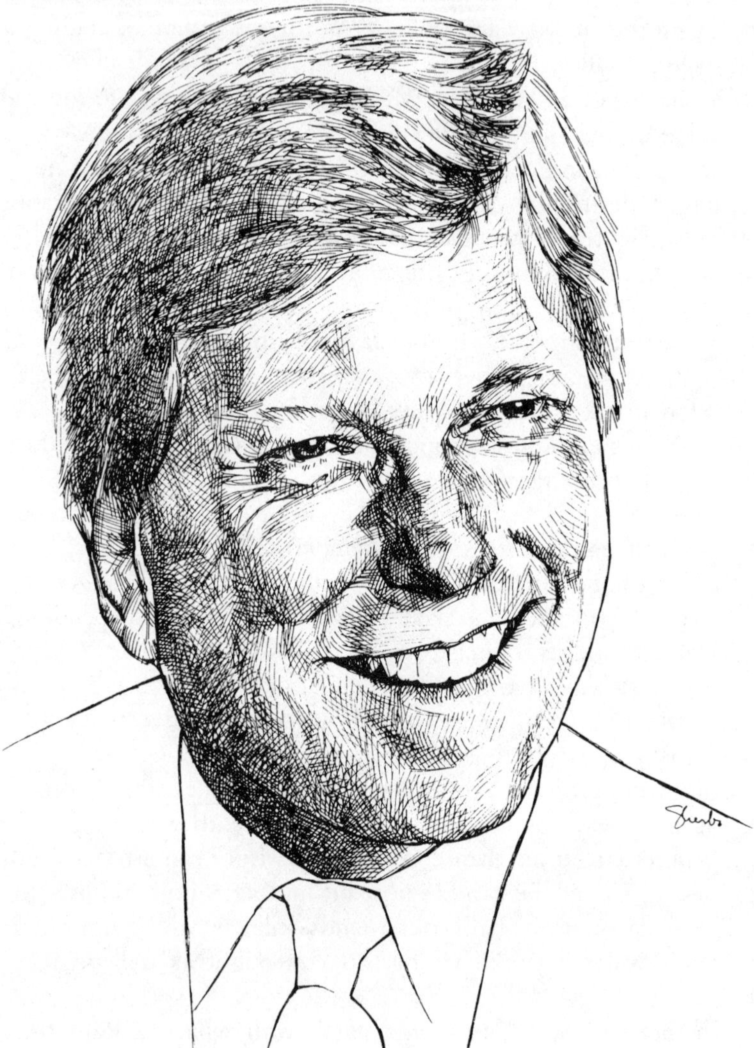

RICHARD A. GEPHARDT

A House Insider Aims for the Top, Adjusting His Message and Manner

To an American electorate still learning his name, Richard A. Gephardt seems to have walked out of a Norman Rockwell painting and onto the national political stage.

His boyhood pictures suggest a 20th-century Huck Finn, a modern child of the Mississippi River. Even now, his looks evoke his days as an Eagle Scout and his year as straight-arrow president of his college's student body. And when Dick Gephardt introduces his wife, Jane, he sometimes jokes that "Spot and Fluff are in the car."

The Gephardt résumé has a storybook quality. After law school he joined a prestigious hometown firm and served in the Air National Guard. A St. Louis alderman at 30, he became a Democratic member of the U.S. House at 35. A decade later, he set out to become the first member of the House to go directly to the presidency since 1880.

At times, the 47-year-old legislator with what House colleague Claude Pepper calls "a good, square face" seems confined by his image. Perhaps an aspirant to the ultimate power in the Free World should seem tougher, more weathered. But Gephardt still uses expressions such as "work harder than heck." And when the candidates were all asked whether they had tried marijuana, Gephardt grinned boyishly and said his college crowd "had trouble getting beer."

Yet Gephardt has enlisted in his cause more than 60 of his Democratic House colleagues, an unusually exacting jury. Charm alone did not make him chairman of the House's Democratic Caucus and a major player on the Ways and Means Committee. He got there with years of homework and legendary patience in the councils of policy and party politics.

Hard work has been the genius of his presidential campaign, as well. Formally announcing his candidacy in February 1987, Gephardt

Richard Andrew Gephardt

Profession: Lawyer.
Born: Jan. 31, 1941, St. Louis, Mo.
Home: St. Louis, Mo.
Religion: Baptist.
Education: Northwestern University, B.S., 1962; University of Michigan, J.D., 1965.
Political Career: St. Louis Board of Aldermen, 1971-76; U.S. House of Representatives, 1977-present.
Military: Air National Guard, 1965-71.
Family: Wife, Jane Ann Byrnes; three children.
House Committees: Ways and Means, 1977-present; Budget, 1979-84.

vowed to be "the first to work each day and the last to quit each night." He has been praised for what one reporter called his "highly disciplined energy," and he has spent it without stint—sometimes giving six or more speeches in a day. Focusing on the early caucuses in next-door Iowa, he canvassed that state more than any rival from either party—achieving the unprecedented feat of visiting all 99 counties.

Gephardt's decision to seek the presidency at this stage of his career surprised many political observers. He had twice rejected chances to run for the Senate, and he had turned away from a fight for the next rung on the House leadership ladder. But in shunning those contests, it now seems clear, the young congressman was heeding an inner voice that told him 1988 could be his year for something bigger.

Through much of 1987 Gephardt's sense of timing seemed prescient. The potential field narrowed, as bigger-name candidates dropped out or declined to enter. Moreover, his early attention to Iowa seemed to be paying off. Although a distant second among Democrats in fund raising, he was able to expand his campaign into critical states that were to hold their primaries on March 8—"Super Tuesday."

The withdrawal of Gary Hart in May moved Gephardt toward the front of the pack. Taken more seriously by national commentators, he also found himself taken to task for some of his issue positions. His controversial proposals on trade were portrayed as hurting the world economy. And he was accused of changing his stands on issues, particularly on abortion. Gephardt's position in Iowa was shaken by the emergence of Sen. Paul Simon of Illinois, and then by the return of former front-runner Hart.

True to his strategy, however, Gephardt simply renewed his concentration on Iowa and predicted that his natural strengths of competence and appeal would pull him through. With that redoubled effort, Gephardt got himself back into contention as the Iowa voting drew near.

The Early Years

Gephardt grew up in the 1940s and 1950s on the south side of St. Louis, a working-class section of a city just past its peak of population and importance. The Germans here were called "Scrubby Dutch" for their reputed practice of scrubbing the concrete sidewalks in front of their homes.

Gephardt's father, Louis, had come to town when the family farm in rural Washington, Mo., was foreclosed during the Great Depression. Louis Gephardt worked as a milk delivery driver and later sold real estate and owned some modest income property. He died just after Christmas of 1984, even as rumors of his son's presidential ambitions were gaining currency.

Perhaps the more influential of Gephardt's parents was his mother, Loreen, who worked as a legal secretary and raised two sons. Dick was the younger, and her confessed favorite. A devout Christian, Loreen Gephardt says she sensed early that God had great things in store for this boy. She took a hand in proving herself right, too. When Dick ran for the Board of Aldermen, and then for Congress, she was out knocking on doors for him. And when he decided to run for president in 1987, Loreen, now 79, took an apartment in Des Moines to campaign in Iowa full time.

Gephardt's boyhood was baseball, Boy Scouts and the Baptist Church. He went to Mason Grade School and Southwest High School, where he lettered in tennis and played the lead in "Arsenic and Old Lace." His parents, neither of whom had graduated from high school, saved and sacrificed to send their sons to college. Dick won a scholarship to Northwestern University, a prestigious private school in Evanston, Ill., where he majored in speech (he played Henry Higgins in "Pygmalion") and earned a B average. He washed dishes, waited tables and worked as a night motel clerk to pay bills.

He met Jane Ann Byrnes when he was a senior helping freshmen women move into their dorm (her suitcase fell open when he picked it up). He became president of his high-status fraternity, Beta Theta Pi. And late in his junior year "Rich" Gephardt was elected president of the student body. In a fashion later to be called characteristic, he finessed a tough election confrontation by striking an agreement by which his main rival ran for vice president instead.

He graduated in 1962, at the height of the heady Kennedy era now referred to as America's Camelot. But if the young Gephardt shared the restlessness of his generation, he found conventional channels for it. He enrolled in law school at the University of Michigan and got his law degree on schedule three years later. He joined the Air National Guard (receiving an American Spirit Honor Medal at Lackland Air Force Base) and the law firm of Thompson & Mitchell (one of St. Louis' largest). In 1966, he married Jane.

Climbing the Ladder

In the America of 1968 young people of political passion seemed everywhere on the march. Some supported the anti-war presidential candidates, Sens. Eugene McCarthy and Robert Kennedy—or, at the other end of the spectrum, Republican Richard Nixon. But Gephardt, the young lawyer, supported Hubert Humphrey, Lyndon Johnson's vice president and the choice of the party establishment.

He became a Democratic committeeman in St. Louis' 14th ward upon the death of a man who had held the post for 40 years. "Jane and I would walk into a ward meeting in those days, two young kids, and people would think we were lost," Gephardt recalls. They were not lost; they were learning. Within two years, Gephardt was St. Louis coordinator for the re-election campaign of Democratic Sen. Stuart Symington.

The next year, 1971, he sought and won the 14th ward seat on the Board of Aldermen. Once there, he became point man for the "Young Turks" of the board, a new generation with a neighborhood-oriented agenda. But he also learned the ways of power in City Hall. In 1973 the *St. Louis Globe-Democrat* would report: "First-termer Gephardt has been the spark plug of the board. The hard-working alderman is a consummate politician, but a conciliatory force able to deal with the crusty, impervious veterans."

During these years, Gephardt's son Matthew (1970) and first daughter, Christine (1973), were born. At the age of two, Matthew was diagnosed as having terminal cancer. He struggled through months of hospital treatment, much of it experimental chemotherapy. And, although Matthew beat the odds, his illness left a deep mark on his father.

"It made me think that, number one, family is the most important thing in your life," Gephardt later told the *St. Louis Post-Dispatch*. "And number two, life is fragile and if there are things you think are important, you ought to do them. And three, that if you think there is all the time in the world, well, you don't know that. Life could be taken away in a day."

As these years went by, the Gephardt résumé grew. He was honored by the Kiwanis, the Jaycees, Downtown St. Louis and the Metropolitan

Richard Gephardt visiting senior citizens in Portsmouth, N.H.

St. Louis Senior Citizens. He was chairman of the young lawyers of the St. Louis Bar and then the Missouri Bar. And he became vice president of the St. Louis Council of the Boy Scouts of America.

Though barely into his mid-30s, Gephardt chafed. He began to consider running for mayor. Then, in the spring of 1976, his break arrived unexpectedly. Leonor K. Sullivan, the legendary congresswoman who had represented St. Louis' south side for 24 years, suddenly announced her retirement. A former associate remembers calling to urge Gephardt to drive down to the state capital and file for Sullivan's seat. Replied Gephardt: "I just got back from there."

The prospect of a safe Democratic seat in Congress drew a big field, but the heavyweights were Gephardt and a state senator, Donald J. Gralike, who was also president of an electrical workers local in the district. Gralike had the backing of the AFL-CIO, but Gephardt had a network of community activists on one hand and a host of downtown law connections on the other. The former provided footsoldiers, the latter came up with cash to put Gephardt ads on television.

Gephardt also had secret weapons named Loreen and Jane. Together, the three canvassed more than 60,000 homes that year. The young-Turk alderman won an absolute majority of the 85,000 votes cast in the primary. In the fall, he won 64 percent of the vote against the Republican nominee, Joseph L. Badaracco, two-time president of the Board of Aldermen. Gephardt ran 15 percentage points ahead of the Democratic national ticket in his district.

The 1980 census caused the district to be redrawn, adding suburban territory that was more Republican. But Gephardt attracted only token opposition in his re-election bids, when there was any opposition at all.

Congress: Quick Starter, Inside Player

When the freshman from St. Louis arrived in Washington, he was swiftly adopted by Richard Bolling, dean of the Missouri delegation and one of the most powerful men in the House. Bolling had come close to being majority leader (and, eventually, Speaker), and in 1977 he was one term away from becoming chairman of the pivotal Rules Committee. As chairman of the Democratic Caucus in the House, he got Gephardt a rare freshman appointment to Ways and Means. Two years later, he put Gephardt on the House Budget Committee, as well.

Gephardt's closeness to Bolling, and to Bolling's successor as caucus chairman, Gillis Long of Louisiana, recreated his successful relationships with older aldermen in St. Louis—but on an even more productive scale. Although inevitably identified with younger members, Gephardt was unfailingly appreciative of his seniors. It was a trait frequently noted by observers, some of whom attributed it in part to the contribution such men could make to Gephardt's success. But even the more cynical of these consistently remarked that Gephardt's deference seemed also to spring from genuine respect. Unfailing courtesy to all—senior and junior, ally and adversary—was a defining Gephardt trait.

As was also typical, Gephardt lost no time in making use of his opportunities. Marked early as a rising star of Ways and Means, a committee with wide-ranging power even beyond taxation, he startled many with a major coup in just his second term. Having watched House leaders and the Carter White House negotiate a deal on hospital cost containment, he quietly constructed a coalition to kill the deal in the crucial committee session.

In its place, he offered a plan to heighten competition among health care providers rather than increasing governmental control over them. His co-sponsor was GOP Rep. David Stockman of Michigan, later to gain fame and notoriety as Ronald Reagan's first budget director.

The collaboration with Stockman symbolized Gephardt's willingness to cross party lines and defy political convention. Once, he even voted against increasing the minimum wage, an almost unthinkable act for a labor-oriented Democrat. Similarly, on economic issues, he joined forces with younger Democrats and Republicans to offer plans calling for a leaner federal government. One of these was an alternative to the Reagan tax cuts of 1981. It lost, and Gephardt subsequently went along with the House-amended version of those cuts.

In 1982 Gephardt teamed with Democratic Sen. Bill Bradley of New Jersey to introduce a modified "flat tax" as an alternative to the 14-bracket income tax. The plan attracted little attention in the popular media at the time, but it became the model on which the Senate built its breakthrough version of the 1986 tax reform. The plan was primarily Bradley's, but Gephardt was the ideal House sponsor. He was well positioned, he knew the issue and he was willing to speak out for the plan and endure the howls from interest groups that saw their oxen about to be gored.

As his stature rose, Gephardt would find himself involved in formulating Democratic policy beyond his committee assignments. He had a hand in the compromise on the MX missile and in developing the Democratic position on aid to the "contra" rebels in Nicaragua.

He earned a reputation for helping reach compromises when everyone else seemed ready to give up. He seemed ready to keep talking—and listening—long after everyone else's patience was exhausted. One admirer said Gephardt could dominate a meeting with the intensity of his listening.

Mike Synar, a friend and House colleague from Oklahoma, has joked that Gephardt gave himself a well-placed shot of novocaine before sitting down for a meeting. But Gephardt's attentiveness was more than courteous, it had an element of interest. One former Gephardt aide liked to say that "everybody goes away from Dick Gephardt feeling like he's just talked to his best friend."

All this made Gephardt a logical candidate for the caucus chairmanship when Long announced that, at the end of 1984, he would retire. Gephardt declared early for the post and his main rival, David Obey of Wisconsin, dropped out a full year before the vote. That gave Gephardt time to consolidate his position and enjoy some heightened prestige—even before taking the job.

This good fortune almost led to trouble. As the 1984 election neared and another Reagan landslide looked inevitable, a group of Democrats dissatisfied with the leadership of Speaker Thomas P. O'Neill Jr. began holding secret meetings. They believed the party would need a new leader if Reagan's expected victory also cost Democrats too many seats in the House. Gephardt's name was said to have been mentioned, although he himself quickly denied any interest. In the end, the Democrats' majority in the House held up well that year, O'Neill set his retirement date two years in the future and the rebellion dissipated. Gephardt's elevation to caucus chairman took place smoothly on schedule.

Going for Broke

While Gephardt was slowly emerging as a man to be dealt with in Washington, his political stock was appreciating in Missouri as well. In 1980, there was talk that he might challenge incumbent Republican John C. Danforth in the 1982 Senate race. Gephardt ruled that out early, perhaps too early. Recession made 1982 a Democratic year, and another Democrat from St. Louis County, state Sen. Harriett Woods, came close

Gephardt's Interest Group Ratings

Vote ratings by interest groups help to give a picture of Richard Gephardt's orientation during his House career. This table shows how often Gephardt voted on key legislative issues in accordance with the positions of groups chosen to represent liberal, labor, business and conservative viewpoints. They are the Americans for Democratic Action (ADA), AFL-CIO, Chamber of Commerce of the United States (CCUS) and Americans for Constitutional Action (ACA) or American Conservative Union (ACU).

	ADA	AFL-CIO	CCUS	ACA	ACU
1977	50	70	29	30	—
1978	35	75	22	48	—
1979	74	85	24	16	—
1980	56	61	64	33	—
1981	45	73	11	39	—
1982	55	80	35	36	—
1983	85	94	25	23	—
1984	75	92	38	5	—
1985	60	88	19	—	19 [1]
1986	70	100	18	—	0
1987	20	100	0	—	0

[1] *Congressional Quarterly began publishing ACU ratings in 1985.*

to upsetting the incumbent.

Late in 1984, Gephardt's political future became a favorite topic for speculation among political insiders. Some in the House still wanted him to challenge the order of succession after O'Neill's departure. Missouri's Democratic Sen. Tom Eagleton, who was about to retire, wanted Gephardt to succeed him. And O'Neill himself was letting it be known that the young Missourian might be majority whip, the next step up on the career ladder to Speaker.

But another ambitious young Democrat, Tony Coelho of California, also had his eye on the whip's job. Coelho had distinguished himself as chairman of the House Democrats' joint campaign committee, and especially as a fund raiser for his colleagues. Gephardt seemed reluctant to test his popularity, based on issue work and relationships, against Coelho's fat ledger of IOUs. Besides, both Coelho and Gephardt were disinclined to duel. By nature, each prefers symbiosis.

These calculations aside, however, the Missourian seemed to hear another call. Early in 1985, before making his plans public, Gephardt told his staff he would seek neither the Senate seat nor a higher position of leadership in the House. He was thinking seriously about the presidency, he said, because he thought the time would be right for him. He said the country would want a relatively young president after Ronald Reagan, the oldest man ever to hold the office. He also said he thought the country would not want a conventional liberal—a Mondale or a Ted Kennedy— unless the election coincided with generally adverse economic times.

A lane seemed to be open on the presidential racetrack, one Gephardt might fill. So, in his first months as caucus chairman, he traveled as much as his Washington responsibilities would allow (he still answered 81 percent of the roll-call votes that year).

Soon the press took notice. It was not the extent of Gephardt's travel (30 states in 1985) so much as his frequent stops in Iowa and in New Hampshire, where the first caucuses (Feb. 8) and primary (Feb. 16) would be held in 1988. Gephardt was also hitting the fund-raising centers in Texas, New York and California. He met with political professionals associated with presidential campaigning, including Hamilton Jordan, who had engineered Jimmy Carter's nomination in 1976.

For a time, Gephardt explained his national travel and exposure strictly in terms of the caucus. Appearing on national news programs, he downplayed any talk of a presidential race. When, in February, the *St. Louis Post-Dispatch* printed a page-one banner headline proclaiming Gephardt's presidential ambitions, Gephardt acted aghast.

But as the year wore on, the fig leaf fell away. Gephardt's intentions soon became manifest in more than just his itinerary.

Changing Priorities

Gephardt continued to devote considerable time to tax reform into 1985, but during that year his priorities underwent a noticeable shift.

Apparently convinced he could play a greater and more visible role on other issues —including trade and the Gramm-Rudman-Hollings deficit reduction law—Gephardt was often absent when Ways and Means got down to cases on Reagan's tax-reform proposals.

To some degree, that decision represented a realistic assessment of House mechanics. The chairman of Ways and Means, Dan Rostenkowski of Illinois, was making an immense personal investment in the fate of tax reform. He would be disinclined to share the spotlight with Gephardt. And, on at least one occasion, when Rostenkowski personally asked Gephardt to help out in a tough committee bargaining session, Gephardt was there.

Still, those who followed the issue most closely were saying that Gephardt had lost faith in the bill's chances for passage in the Senate. When the bill, by a near miracle, was enacted late in 1986, Gephardt's name was nearly lost on the list of legislators deserving credit. That may have been disappointing enough, but insult was swiftly added to injury. It was suggested that Gephardt had dropped tax reform because it contributed less to his political calculus than other issues might. Suddenly, the clean-cut overachiever from Middle America was being portrayed as not so much savvy as shrewd, not so much flexible as fickle.

Gephardt had come to Washington a self-described conservative. He knew his district well and represented it carefully. As recently as 1985 he had co-founded the Democratic Leadership Council, a group of elected leaders who wanted to pull the party to the right—especially on questions of national defense and economic growth. To some degree, they also wanted to restore the party's appeal for white males, whom studies had found disaffected with the party.

In the House, Gephardt had earned his spurs with an ability to reach in several directions that was pluralistic and relatively non-partisan. In the Bradley-Gephardt phase of tax reform, he had stood up to a host of interest groups trying to protect their precincts within the tax code. Organized labor, a power in his home district and certainly a key constituency for any presidential hopeful, objected strenuously to the taxation of fringe benefits. But for a long time, Gephardt stood firm.

As 1986 wore on, however, longtime observers began to see a change. Gephardt seemed to steer clear of those controversies in the tax debate that might damage him with groups he would need in the nomination process. And, although this deviation was a subtle one, it reinforced an impression that was coming to be seen as an Achilles' heel.

Candidates '88

In March 1987, *National Journal* observed that Gephardt, "who began with a conservative tilt on foreign policy and social issues and a centrist position on economic issues ... by 1986 ... was in the Democratic mainstream on foreign policy and had a perfect liberal score on the others." The American Conservative Union, a lobbying group that compiles ratings based on congressional voting, had rated Gephardt as high as 33 (out of a possible 100) in 1982. In 1986 it had dropped him to a flat zero. For the same year the Chamber of Commerce had downgraded him to an 18 (from a high of 64 in 1980). Meanwhile, his rating from the liberal Americans for Democratic Action, which had rated him as low as 35 early in his career, had risen to 70.

Gephardt argues that his position as Democratic Caucus Chairman required him to vote with the leadership more often than he would have previously. He has also contended that the party as a whole has moved more towards his philosophy, and that the issues themselves have changed as the Reagan years wore on.

Perhaps the country has moved, as in a sense it always does. But by 1987 the young Gephardt, who in 1976 told the *St. Louis Globe-Democrat* "my particular philosophy is conservative when stacked against the Democratic platform or Sen. [Walter F.] Mondale," had clearly moved a long way on his own.

The 'New' Gephardt

That movement was apparent within his staff. One by one, most of the longtime Gephardt aides with roots in St. Louis or Missouri politics had moved on. The presidential aspirant once viewed as an alternative to the liberalism of a Mondale or a Ted Kennedy is now staffed by political professionals such as William Carrick, the campaign manager, Joe Trippi, Robert Schrum, David Doak and Richard Moe—all of whom worked for either Kennedy or Mondale.

In his presidential campaign, he has become increasingly identified with the causes of organized labor, farm activists and disarmament groups. These groups tend to dominate the nominating process, especially in Iowa. So Gephardt was seen by some to have rewritten his political ticket so as to be admitted through the campaign's first gate. He stood accused, not so much of doctrinaire liberalism, but of tailoring himself to fit critical states or support groups. Thus his 1987 endorsement of a tax on imported oil was portrayed as a gesture toward Texas, the biggest producer of domestic oil and the biggest electoral prize on Super Tuesday.

Such shifts may make a candidate more palatable in certain precincts, but they rarely win steadfast friends. Purists, after all, are partial to those of their own pedigree. And whatever gains are made must be measured against corresponding losses. Exhibit A for Gephardt in this regard was the fallout from his modified position on abortion.

Elected to represent a blue-collar, 50 percent Catholic district, Gephardt had opposed both abortion and the busing of children to achieve racial balance in schools. More to the point, he had supported passage of constitutional amendments to ban both. The busing issue has since faded, but the abortion issue still burns bright.

In 1985 anti-abortion activists wanted Gephardt to run for the Senate. Woods, the Democrats' Senate nominee in 1982, was running again (she would be nominated but defeated in November). She was pro-choice. The activists were disturbed to learn that Gephardt would not oppose Woods and, worse, would not reintroduce the constitutional amendment banning abortion. But they still thought he was their man. A year later, some still hoped he would run for president on a pro-life platform. But in a series of painful meetings, Gephardt made it clear he would no longer commit himself even to supporting such an amendment.

That stirred a rage of protest from the activists. Not only had they considered him one of their surest votes, but they had hoped his ascent would carry their fortunes higher—in the House and beyond. One of his first acts as a freshman congressman had been to co-sponsor the Human Life Amendment. He had renewed that support in each succeeding Congress. But now he was backing off, saying the amendment had no realistic chance of passage and saying, "I do not feel there is a consensus in the country or in Congress to initiate an amendment."

Although Gephardt continued to oppose abortion personally and to vote against federal funding for abortions, he was pilloried in national anti-abortion newsletters as a traitor nonetheless. Although he attended endless meetings to explain his position, the anger did not subside. Anti-abortion picketing dogged his campaign appearances intermittently through 1987.

Whatever weight such activists carry, no politician relishes losing part of his or her support base. Yet this is always a hazard for candidates trying to expand their constituencies without alienating old friends.

Sometimes, even the Gephardt forte of sincere diplomacy can seem to rankle.

During the 1987 World Series, Gephardt asked a crowd in northern Iowa if they liked his hometown team, the St. Louis Cardinals. A few cheered for the Cardinals, but more cheered for the Minnesota Twins. Someone shouted a question about Gephardt's allegiances and he said he hoped the best team would win. When a wire news service carried that small item back to St. Louis, it left a lot of mouths agape.

More Controversy

By 1987 Gephardt's name was principally known not for tax reform but for two other legislative initiatives that bore his name. One was a proposal for decreasing the U.S. trade deficit with certain competitor nations, notably Japan. The proposal required trading partners with big surpluses to negotiate reductions in the surpluses and lower barriers to U.S. goods. If they failed, the proposal said, they would face trade sanctions to be imposed by the president that would include higher tariffs and quotas.

The proposal had evolved from legislation drafted by the United Auto Workers and supported by other unions that had suffered from the loss of manufacturing jobs. Opponents said such measures would bring on retaliation from trading partners and depress world trade in general, causing a global depression. They also likened it to an import-protection bill passed in 1930 called the Smoot-Hawley Act, which all but barred foreign products from American markets.

Although the comparison was strained at best, it was especially harmful after the stock market collapse in October. That heightened the historical, if not the substantial, parallel. And, because most historians believe Smoot-Hawley brought on and deepened the Great Depression, any association was negative.

The so-called Gephardt amendment was not made part of the trade bill that emerged from Ways and Means. But the Rules Committee allowed it to be considered as an amendment when the bill went to the floor of the House. It was adopted by a vote of 218-214, an achingly close vote given all that Gephardt had gambled in momentum and stature.

The other legislation was actually the handiwork of Democratic Sen. Tom Harkin of Iowa, who believed the only way to rescue the failing farm was to raise the price of farm products. The bill, which Gephardt co-sponsored, would create a farmers' referendum on production restraints. Although controversial in the agricultural community at large, the idea was popular among politically active farmers, especially in Iowa.

At the same time, commentators noted that restrained supply would raise prices to consumers. And, because the oil-import tax and trade legislation might have the same effect, Gephardt became vulnerable to an "anti-consumer" label as well as to accusations of political opportunism.

The Campaign

The House member who came closest to a major party's presidential nomination in this century was James B. "Champ" Clark, another Democrat from Missouri. Clark, who was the Speaker at the time, got 40 percent of the delegate vote at the 1912 nominating convention, losing out to Woodrow Wilson.

The process has entirely changed since then. The great majority of delegates now are chosen by primaries and caucuses in which millions of rank-and-file voters participate. Gephardt has been, as always, a student of the process. At one time, he even considered introducing a bill to reform the system around a one-day nationwide primary.

As he approached his own run, Gephardt looked carefully at the system's internal structure and decided his strategy was obvious. The key would be the Iowa caucuses. In 1976 Carter had risen from almost total obscurity by scoring well in the caucuses held in that state before the first primary in New Hampshire. That positioned him to win New Hampshire (political light-years from his base in Georgia) and become the focus of media coverage. A version of that one-two punch enabled Carter to hold off Kennedy's challenge in 1980. And yet another variation worked for Gary Hart in 1984. Hart had run a distant second in Iowa, but he was not expected to do even that well. A sudden spurt of interest in his lightly regarded prospects propelled him to an upset victory in New Hampshire.

That same dynamic—the exceeding of expectations—was the Gephardt goal. In 1988, he and his advisers reasoned, there would be an even greater payoff for doing well in Iowa. Because so many states had moved their primaries to March 8, the early front-runner (as determined by Iowa and by the New Hampshire primary a week later) could score an early knockout before his rivals had recovered.

A corollary to this theory was that an early leader could command more support from the so-called "superdelegates," the 643 members of Congress, governors and party officials who would be automatic delegates to the national nominating convention in Atlanta in July. Gephardt was already doing well within this group, which would include nearly all his nucleus of House supporters.

Gephardt also saw himself as a natural beneficiary of Super Tuesday's Southern accent. Of the 16 Super Tuesday states, 13 are Southern or Border states. Gephardt considered his own Border State roots an asset, along with his DLC ties and his ability to project himself as a mainstream politician. And he could count on more than 30 House Democrats from below the Mason-Dixon line who were ready to work for him.

In one sense, the Gephardt strategy has had to contend with an overabundance of success. The decisions of Kennedy and New York Gov. Mario Cuomo not to run allowed Gephardt and other dark horses greater access to money, political talent and potential supporters.

Moreover, Gary Hart and Sen. Joe Biden of Delaware were driven from the field by adverse personal publicity. And several potentially formidable Southerners—Sens. Sam Nunn of Georgia and Dale Bumpers of Arkansas and Gov. Bill Clinton of Arkansas—also took seats on the sideline.

Hopeful as these developments seemed, they also undercut Gephardt's strategy, which had assumed the presence of a clear front-runner. The benefit of winning early has largely been in eclipsing another, better-known candidate. Instead, the vacuum left by the party's biggest names in 1987 has been filled with candidates who, like Gephardt, are still struggling for recognition.

Moreover, the Gephardt campaign, once thought remarkably well organized and funded for all its long odds, seemed to stumble toward the end of 1987. Fund raising fell off and Gephardt had to borrow against the federal matching funds he expected to receive in 1988. And his matching funds were already somewhat smaller than his fund raising would suggest, because the government matches only the first $250 contributed by any individual. Gephardt's finances had depended heavily on larger checks, and on gifts from political action committees (PACs).

And Gephardt suffered from two unexpected, almost perverse developments: a burst of interest in Simon and the stunning return of

Hart, whose re-entry heightened the competition for votes, media coverage and campaign resources. (Gephardt's political coordinator for the Northeastern states deserted to rejoin Hart.)

Simon, who also represents a state bordering Iowa, rose quickly in several polls of Iowans, including that of the *Des Moines Register*. After Hart dropped out, Dukakis had moved ahead in New Hampshire while Gephardt took the lead in Iowa. That split made sense in Gephardt's scheme of things. But by autumn of 1987 Simon had taken over the lead in Iowa—with Gephardt reduced to a virtual tie for second with Dukakis.

It was this development that some observers saw motivating a change in tactics for Gephardt, whose campaign persona developed a harder edge. Gephardt started taking swipes at both Simon and Sen. Al Gore of Tennessee. "Simonomics is really just Reaganomics with a bow tie," he said. Some thought they saw Gephardt getting nastier on the hustings, as well. But Bill Lambrecht of the *Post-Dispatch*, who has watched Gephardt as long as any reporter, thought it more likely the candidate was using lines urged upon him by advisers. "If left to himself," Lambrecht said, "Dick would go the rest of his life without being anything but nice to people."

In addition to sharpening his message, Gephardt dramatically concentrated his resources: He shuttered his offices in the South and poured nearly everything into Iowa and, to a lesser extent, New Hampshire. While this effort was consistent with his long-held strategy to run well early, it meant that the quick-strike victory had become more than just the best way for Gephardt to win; it had apparently become the only way.

If Gephardt should falter in the early stages of the nominating process, he would not be without consolation. He had until March 31 to file for re-election to his House seat.

Moreover, his years of travel and fearsome schedules will not go unrewarded. His national name recognition has added to his standing in Missouri, where he still might choose to run for governor or senator—or even for mayor of St. Louis.

Most importantly, his emergence as a national figure makes it possible for him to think of being president in the not-too-distant future. Among presidential nominees since 1960 who were not incumbents, only Jimmy Carter was nominated on his first try. It has become almost a given that a contender who shows well at all will be back.

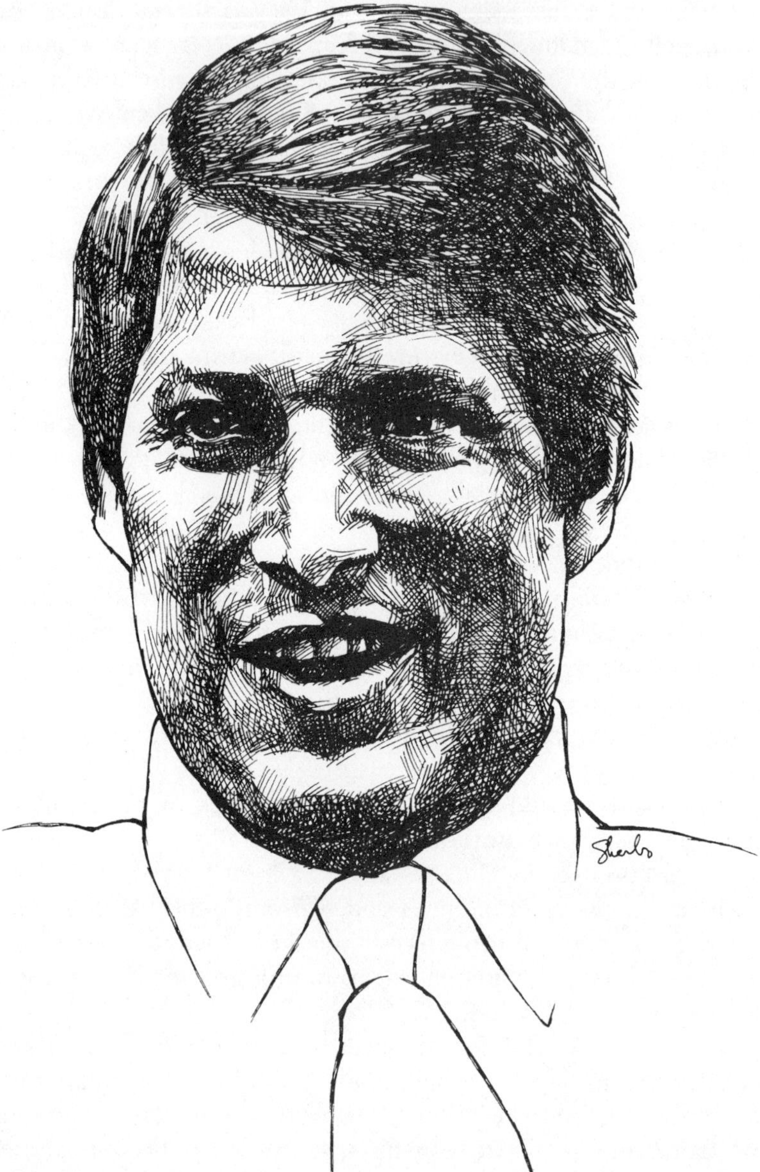

ALBERT GORE JR.

Tennessee's New Good Ol' Boy, Washington's Raging Moderate

Sen. Albert Gore Jr. is a presidential candidate of contradictions. Raised a congressman's son in the rarefied atmosphere of Washington, he still claims rural Tennessee roots. Projecting the air of an urbane political professional, he has staked his White House bid on the support of Southerners traditionally skeptical of such sophistication. And though he has campaigned to the right of his Democratic colleagues on military and foreign policy issues, his congressional voting record is well in line with the national Democratic Party's liberal bent.

Undaunted by accusations of inconsistency, Tennessee's junior senator has proclaimed himself the "raging moderate" among his party's presidential contenders. Gore has pursued a centrist candidacy that he has said will revivify Democrats while yielding something quite rare in the past two decades: an electable Democratic nominee.

During a 1987 campaign stop in Kentucky, his home state's northern neighbor, Gore told the *Chicago Tribune* how he planned to walk to the White House along the fine line separating South and North. Fittingly, the senator stood in Frankfort's capitol rotunda between statues of two Kentucky-born presidents, the Union's Abraham Lincoln and the Confederacy's Jefferson Davis. He admitted that he was exploiting creation of a "Super Tuesday," the March 8 concentration of 20 primaries, including 12 in Southern states. "I am testing the theory behind Super Tuesday," said the senator. But, he added, "I am running as a national candidate who happens to be from the South."

Touching on that subject in a later interview with North Carolina writer Garrett Epps, Gore responded to those who mused that his Tennessee heritage might be more contrived than real. "I always felt rooted there," he said. "Maybe that was because it was an easy choice for a kid to make between a 250-acre farm with a pony and a horse and a

Albert Arnold Gore Jr.

Profession: Journalist; home builder.
Born: March 31, 1948, Washington, D.C.
Home: Carthage, Tenn.
Religion: Baptist.
Education: Harvard University, B.A., 1969; attended Vanderbilt University School of Religion, 1971-72; attended Vanderbilt University Law School, 1974-76.
Political Career: U.S. House of Representatives, 1977-85; Senate, 1985-present.
Military: Army, 1969-71.
Family: Wife, Mary Elizabeth "Tipper" Aitcheson; four children.
Committees: (House) Interstate and Foreign Commerce, 1977-84; Science and Technology, 1977-84; Select Intelligence, 1981-84; (Senate) Commerce, Science and Technology, 1985-present; Government Affairs, 1985-86; Armed Services, 1986-present.

river and a canoe on the one hand, and the eighth floor of the Fairfax Hotel on the other, where I played on the roof and threw water balloons on cars at 21st and Massachusetts Avenue. It would have been an easy choice for you too."

An Unprecedented Strategy

A junior senator of divided upbringing was hardly what the Southern Democrats who first coordinated Super Tuesday had in mind. Those strategists had hoped their power play would attract the likes of Georgia Sen. Sam Nunn. A congressional heavyweight with solid conservative credentials, Nunn probably would have had the best chance of any Dixie politician to thumb his nose at early-voting Iowa without jeopardizing his chances across the South.

But Nunn declined to run. So, at the behest of a moderate and moneyed consortium, in stepped the more liberal, lesser-known Gore. The question became whether Super Tuesday could be captured by this graduate of elite Northeastern schools—where, it was joked, he had taken Southern as a foreign language.

Gore also came in as the youngest of the bunch. A veteran of the Vietnam War, the senator in some ways represented the "new generation" so often touted by presidential contender Gary Hart and Democratic pollster Pat Caddell.

Ironically, though, Gore's strategic dependence on a bloc of Southern states meant that he would have to win the votes of Democrats both older and more conservative than himself. The senator tailored a centrist candidacy in hopes of swelling his region's traditionally low primary turnout. Such a strategy, he hoped, would shift the nomination's source of momentum from Iowa or New Hampshire to the South.

In Gore's mind, the 1988 Democratic nominating process was a tale of two parties. The Iowa caucuses, he argued, were dominated by liberal activists and interest groups that had produced Democratic nominees who were usually unelectable. On the other side rested the senator's home region, laden with moderate-to-conservative Democrats.

As in the past, Iowa inevitably would garner early attention because of its lead-off spot on the delegate-selection calendar. But this time Dixie's one-day regional vote would elect more than five times as many Democratic delegates as Iowa and the other early-voting states combined. Stressing that new calculus, Gore sought to convince Southerners that he would be a viable candidate for the nomination even if he ran poorly in Iowa and other early contests up North.

Skeptics of this "Iowa bypass" strategy contended that a poor showing in the Hawkeye State would quickly saddle Gore with a loser's image, leaving him dead in the water. Defenders countered that the effect of small Northern primaries would be mitigated in 1988, precisely as the creators of Super Tuesday had planned.

"After New Hampshire," explained Chris Verenes, executive director of the South Carolina Democratic Party, "the story will be Super Tuesday, not who won New Hampshire. It will be like two ball games.... If a moderate doesn't do well in Iowa or New Hampshire, he's not dead. And if a liberal does well, he still has to work hard Super Tuesday. You can throw out past experience."

Notwithstanding that assessment, Gore backers knew his strategy would be a gamble. True, the Super Tuesday turnout was potentially huge, with 40 million registered voters in the South (including Maryland and Missouri). Yet in 1984 fewer than 5 million voters participated in the

Democratic primaries and caucuses in those states, producing an electorate that often was disproportionately influenced by liberal elements, especially blacks and union members.

The result in 1984 had been that Walter Mondale and Jesse Jackson divided much of the South, with Mondale winning most of the delegates. Then, in the November general election, when the turnout was much larger, Mondale did not come close to carrying any Southern states.

Equally foreboding for Gore's prospects were the performances of the two Southern contenders for the 1984 Democratic nomination. South Carolina Sen. Ernest F. Hollings and former Florida Gov. Reubin Askew faltered in early voting outside the South and folded their campaigns before Super Tuesday. Moreover, Ohio Sen. John Glenn, the "raging moderate" of that year's Democratic race, did not find the votes he needed in Dixie to keep his candidacy alive.

On the other hand, there was precedent for a Southerner receiving regional support in presidential primary voting. Alabama Gov. George C. Wallace easily carried all the Southern primaries in 1972; Georgian Jimmy Carter swept them all in 1980 and nearly all of them in 1976. Still, both were political heavyweights when they won the support of Dixie Democrats: Carter had proved national voting appeal in early 1976 contests in Iowa and New Hampshire, while Wallace was riding the wake of a major third-party presidential bid.

Gore represented a yet longer long shot. The cultured, well-coiffed senator might have a much tougher time drawing support from blue-collar Wallace voters. "Gore has the persona of a guy with every hair in place," said Merle Black, a University of North Carolina political scientist. "Wallace voters might respond to a Southern candidate, but it is questionable whether Gore is that candidate."

The Fortunate One

Gore hardly could deny his golden boy image. His political aspirations clearly were aided by the stature of his father—whose career, conversely, had been built up from the ashes of family disaster.

The elder Gore had struggled steadily after the day in 1929 when his own father's savings were wiped out by bank failures. Albert Sr. worked his way through teachers' college, taught his way through the Nashville YMCA Law School and then was elected to Congress at age 29.

Following seven terms in the House, he was elected to the Senate in 1952.

During more than three decades on Capitol Hill, Albert Sr. epitomized a liberal progressivism that ran counter to much of his region's prevailing philosophy. He refused to sign the segregationist Southern Manifesto of Strom Thurmond. Later, he became a leading antagonist of the Nixon administration.

A legacy of liberalism and professional politics was passed to the younger Gore, just as surely as the wealth that let him buy 250 acres of cow pasture near the Middle Tennessee town of Carthage.

Born in 1948, the younger Gore was groomed for national leadership from the outset. While his father was extremely successful, he likewise was insecure. He wanted his son to bear none of the rough edges that had etched his own political profile.

Albert Sr. had climbed from the House to the Senate and even been

Al Gore sought to win the nomination through a Southern strategy.

nominated for vice president in 1956. He also served as President Kennedy's delegate to the United Nations. But, as the elder Gore explained to Epps: "I keenly felt my lack of linguistic ability. I was often embarrassed because I would be in conference with people who could switch to my language or another, while Tennessee hillbilly was all I could accommodate. So I undertook to provide for my children a better education than I had had."

The result: Albert Jr. was taught at St. Albans, an exclusive boy's prep school of the Washington elite. There, the senator's son fulfilled his father's expectations as an honors student and captain of the football team.

Yet the boy was not all sheen or grind. While some classmates dubbed him "Ozymandias," after the vain tyrant of Shelley's poem, others tagged him "Gorf"; they knew the senator's son less as the fortunate one than as the fellow famous for balancing a broom on his nose while lying on the floor.

Gore's summers, meanwhile, were spent in Carthage. There he lived with a tenant farmer, working the fields and hunting. In an interview with the *Wall Street Journal,* Gordon Thompson, the farmer's son, summed up Gore's youth as well as anyone: "He lived two different type lives." Of course, the more time-consuming aspect of that divided existence was training and tutelage—particularly after the boy entered Harvard.

Intending to become a writer, Gore in college turned his pen toward politics. In 1968 he became chairman of "Tennessee Youth for Eugene McCarthy." His opposition to U.S. involvement in Southeast Asia naturally confronted no yawning generation gap at home. His father was a clear, if moderate, critic of the Vietnam War.

That said, when Gore graduated from Harvard in 1969, his father's upcoming re-election bid was clouded precisely by the family's anti-war posture. It was a record the GOP would do everything to exploit. Despite a low draft number and his participation in anti-war protests, the younger Gore felt compelled to enlist. Not only would the lottery simply put someone else in his place, thought Gore; his father's campaign could be strongly threatened by the appearance that his son was a draft-dodger.

Gore married his college sweetheart, Mary Elizabeth "Tipper" Aitcheson, and reported for Army training. Albert Sr. still lost his re-election bid, in part due to his anti-war record. Today, the younger Gore is quick to identify himself as a Vietnam veteran, even though his tour entailed just six months as a reporter in an engineering unit. "We were constructing roads in runways in hostile environments," he told Epps, "but I didn't see the kind of combat that made heroes out of people."

Gore never witnessed a casualty. Nor did he ever fire the rifle that he holds in a campaign brochure photo. Instead, he wrote about subjects such as Army paving techniques in the Mekong Delta or reconstructed stories about guerrilla attacks. Nevertheless, Gore told the *Journal*, "I had no feeling these guys had gone through it and I didn't."

Whatever his peril, Gore's experience stood him in good stead upon coming home. He was hired as a reporter by a family friend who was then editor of the *Nashville Tennessean*. He spent the next five years working his way up from the police beat to covering City Hall. Intent upon that career, Gore still found time to study some religion and law at Vanderbilt University.

Then, one day in 1976, Gore's editor called with word that Joe Evins, a Democrat who had represented Carthage's congressional district since the elder Gore's graduation to the Senate, would retire.

The senator's son never hesitated, though he did throw up before announcing his candidacy. At the same county courthouse where his father had begun his public career nearly 40 years before, Albert Jr. started up the political ladder.

The Reporter Goes to Congress

Gore's family name did not exactly scare away competition. Eight other Democrats entered the contest. They soon found out, however, that they were opposing not only a family tradition, but also a born campaigner.

Gore's themes had a populist flavor. He called for higher taxation of the rich and tighter strip-mining laws. He criticized "private power trusts" who wanted to dismantle the Tennessee Valley Authority. He also favored cuts in defense spending and said the government should create more public jobs.

Gore's chief rival in the crowded field was state House Majority Leader Stanley Rogers, who tried to make an issue of Gore's wealth (net worth $273,000 at the time) and claimed Gore's father was tied to energy monopolies. On top of that, Rogers stressed his legislative experience in hopes of casting Gore as a political amateur.

But Rogers' political base was in the southern part of the district and several other candidates from that area drew votes away from him.

Gore, who was not seriously challenged in his more northerly Smith County base, came in first, just 3,559 votes ahead of Rogers.

Although he had barely captured his party's prize, the nomination was tantamount to victory. No GOP nominee was forthcoming. And Gore quickly tightened his grip on the seat with three successive re-election landslides. Among other traits, he was legendary in the House for the frequency of his trips to his home district; in 1982, he held his 1,000th open meeting there.

As for his performace on Capitol Hill, Gore quickly became known in the House as a sensational—and sometimes sensationalistic—investigator. Drawing on the skills and techniques that he had honed while reporting, he almost annually came up with a dramatic inquiry of one sort or another.

One set of hearings resulted in a bill cracking down on the sale of worthless insurance to uninformed senior citizens. Another led to the requirement that infant formula sold in the United States meet certain nutrition and safety standards. Gore's investigation of influence peddling in the contact lens industry led to a grand jury probe, and his work on the long-term effects of radiation brought a measure to compensate veterans exposed during wartime atomic testing.

The common thread to all this investigative work was a populist belief that an unwary public needs federal help in dealing with the business community, and that corporate offenders ought to pay substantially when something goes wrong. It was largely the legacy passed down from his father, who had railed so long against corporate abuses and supported the New Deal and its legislative descendants.

Beyond his innate panache and sense of the newsworthy, the younger Gore demonstrated a technical competence unusual in Congress. After a couple of terms crowded with one-man investigations, Gore became a leader in the realm of nuclear weapons policy.

He first became interested in that issue in 1980, when he was disturbed to find that an audience of Tennessee teenagers nearly all expected a nuclear war in their lifetime. After taking a seat on the Intelligence Committee in the 97th Congress, he began mastering the subject of arms control and gained a reputation for expertise in the field.

Exploiting his connections in the Northeast Corridor's intellectual and political circles, Gore evolved into a significant contributor to the arms control debate. He soon became known as the political champion of a proposal for "Midgetman" missiles. If either or both sides used such

Gore's Interest Group Ratings

Vote ratings by interest groups help to give a picture of Albert Gore's orientation during his career in the House and Senate. This table shows how often Gore voted on key legislative issues in accordance with the positions of groups chosen to represent liberal, labor, business and conservative viewpoints. They are the Americans for Democratic Action (ADA), AFL-CIO, Chamber of Commerce of the United States (CCUS) and Americans for Constitutional Action (ACA) or American Conservative Union (ACU).

	ADA	AFL-CIO	CCUS	ACA	ACU
House Service					
1977	45	78	41	30	—
1978	65	70	22	15	—
1979	74	80	22	12	—
1980	50	79	67	29	—
1981	70	93	11	14	—
1982	70	90	18	26	—
1983	70	88	28	44	—
1984	65	62	31	25	—
Senate Service					
1985	65	86	41	—	17 [1]
1986	70	87	32	—	9
1987	60	50	10	—	6

[1] *Congressional Quarterly began publishing ACU ratings in 1985.*

single-warhead mobile rockets, reasoned Gore, nuclear tensions would be stabilized. Mobility would protect Midgetmen from attack, preserving their deterrent value. But their offensive capability would be much less threatening than that of multiple-warhead devices, which theoretically threaten 10 sitting rockets.

Early in 1983 Gore joined a small group of Democrats who had sought a middle ground in the MX missile debate. President Reagan was then pushing hard for deployment of 100 of the missiles in existing silos; MX critics in the House seemed within striking distance of doing in the president's plan entirely, a move that Gore feared would enable Reagan to brand Democrats as soft on defense and then withdraw from arms negotiations with the Soviets.

Working with other Democrats usually identified as liberals, including Norman D. Dicks of Washington and Wisconsin's Les Aspin, Gore decided to back some MX production in return for a White House promise of greater U.S. flexibility at the strategic arms reduction talks in Geneva. He also won promises from a reluctant administration that it would produce the Midgetman.

The stance of Gore and his allies proved crucial to the MX's survival, although at funding levels below what Reagan wanted. Their work frustrated arms control liberals, who said the administration was not living up to its end of the bargain. But Gore gained credibility with defense policy conservatives that he had never had before. And he was to carry that new-found stature into the U.S. Senate.

The Next Rung

Gore's 1984 Senate election bore the mark of inevitability from the moment Howard H. Baker Jr. announced his retirement, creating an opening nearly two years before the vote. In many past statewide campaigns, Tennessee Democrats had cut themselves to ribbons in primary competition, paving the way for GOP victory in November. But Gore, with his immense popularity in Middle Tennessee and a name that needed no introduction anywhere in the state, had the Democratic field to himself. It was the Republicans, struggling to hold the seat, who were divided over the nomination.

While they squabbled, Gore campaigned. Starting early in 1983, he worked the grass roots, lining up rural Democratic courthouse networks and urban party organizations. The eventual winner of the GOP nomination was state Sen. Victor H. Ashe, a wealthy, Yale-educated lawyer from Knoxville whose acerbic manner and habit of needling colleagues in the Legislature had offended even some Republicans. Ashe did tone down his manner in the primary and, with the support of the state party establishment and an early endorsement from the National Republican Senatorial Committee, he easily won the nomination. But serious Republican divisions remained. New Right activist Ed McAteer, angered by national GOP backing for Ashe, withdrew from the primary and mounted an independent November campaign.

Gore campaigned in the fall as if he were the incumbent. He pointed to his work on issues such as nutritional standards for baby formula, toxic-waste cleanup and the MX, all of which played well to most audiences. And despite his record of liberal populism, he demonstrated a remarkable ability to attract the contributions of corporate political action committees.

Ashe, meanwhile, seemed outmaneuvered at every turn. When he called a press conference to accuse Gore of speaking out against busing but voting for it, Gore ignored the charge and announced that Reagan had just signed three of his bills—creating a national organ donor program, requiring stronger warning labels on cigarette packages and strengthening penalties against repeat criminal offenders.

The election was a rout. Gore won 61 percent overall while Reagan was carrying the state with 58 percent. Ashe lost even his home base, the longtime GOP stronghold of Knox County.

As he entered the Senate, Gore began by furthering the arms control credibility he had brought with him. Early in 1985, he and fellow Democrats Sam Nunn, David L. Boren and Robert C. Byrd helped produce an agreement with the Reagan administration holding MX deployment to 50 missiles.

The White House was not thrilled with that compromise, but by then its attention was shifting to another item on the nuclear arms agenda—the strategic defense initiative (SDI), the space-based defensive missile system. Gore tried to find a middle ground on this issue as well in 1986, asking the Senate to "exercise caution" on SDI even while admitting that "the political climate . . . is such that a great deal of money is going to be authorized."

To Reagan's $3.7 billion SDI request, Gore offered $2.5 billion and sought assurances that work on SDI would not violate the 1972 ABM treaty. Gore's funding level, however, was too high for many liberals and too low for SDI boosters; it lost, 59-36.

In other Senate business, Gore's muckraking urge remained strong. After the space shuttle *Challenger* crash in January 1986, he was one of the harshest critics of the National Aeronautics and Space Administration (NASA). Despite his junior status on the Commerce Subcommittee on Science, Technology and Space, he grabbed headlines from more senior colleagues by cultivating his own anonymous contact in the space agency, who told him that NASA had sharply reduced personnel devoted to quality control in the years before the *Challenger* explosion.

In May 1986 Gore was one of nine senators to oppose Reagan's nomination of James C. Fletcher to return as administrator of NASA, which he headed in the 1970s. Gore said many of the management problems that contributed to the *Challenger* crash began under Fletcher's earlier tenure.

Gore also continued his call for a significantly more active federal role in the realms of science and medicine. Having steered through a complicated bill to ease the difficulties of critically ill patients and their families in seeking organ transplant surgery, Gore frequently criticized the Reagan administration for failing to implement the computerized transplant network. He repeatedly fought for federal money to finance it and to help poor patients buy the expensive drugs that prevent rejection of transplanted organs.

A politically riskier undertaking came at the initiative of Gore's wife, who convinced the senator to focus congressional attention on rock music lyrics. Tipper Gore, along with a group of influential Washington wives that included the spouse of Treasury Secretary James Baker, founded the Parents' Music Resource Center in 1985. The group launched a series of attacks against musical and video presentations that they accused of glorifying casual sex, violence and satanic worship.

The Commerce Committee eventually held hearings on the subject. Various singing stars were invited to comment on a proposal to put warning labels on music products so that parents could monitor what their children were hearing.

But Tipper Gore quickly found herself the target of some virulent attacks from rock musicians such as Frank Zappa. He dubbed her a "cultural terrorist." And despite the brisk sales of her book, *Raising PG Kids in an X-Rated Society,* even some Democratic boosters grumbled that Gore's wife ought not to have been provided a senatorial forum for her campaign. Wrote the *New Republic*'s Hendrik Hertzberg: "The fuss over porn rock has turned his campaign into a Tipper-ware party."

Despite such predictions that his wife's controversial cause could ultimately prove damaging to his political future, others argued that Tipper was a plus for Gore's campaign. Her crusade against allegedly pornographic music played well with older, more conservative voters, while her master's degree in psychology enabled the vivacious mother of four to strike a professional and feminist tone that could appeal to the 18-to-34 set.

One trait that Tipper clearly shares with her husband is ambition. Asked about the couple, former Gore opponent Victor Ashe told the *Chicago Tribune*, "They are a determined team and know exactly where they're going: 1600 Pennsylvania Avenue."

Pursuing the Extreme Center

Gore revealed that determination just two years after entering the Senate. With Carthage as his backdrop, Gore declared his presidential candidacy in June 1987, articulating a regional appeal, a generational pitch and a global theme: He would run as a young Southern centrist who was knowledgeable about nuclear arms. With his father and wife on the platform, Gore portrayed himself as a "Son of the South" and added that he was the only candidate with both the vigor and expertise to match the negotiating prowess of Soviet leader Mikhail Gorbachev.

"The free world urgently needs a leader who can match him, test him, bargain with him and make the most of this possibly historic opportunity for a safer, saner world," said Gore.

With his Super Tuesday strategy, Gore repeatedly stressed his regional ties as the campaign proceeded. But, as events unfolded, his themes of foreign policy expertise and "new generation" leadership took on new and different contexts.

Stumping in Southern states, Gore would routinely compare his heritage and interests to Tennessee's. It was an effective connection in a region that prides itself on its distinct culture and history.

But a big question for Gore was the Southern electorate's reaction to the disclosure that he had smoked marijuana several times—while a student at Harvard, an Army reporter in Vietnam and a journalist in Nashville. Gore acknowledged his past drug use in the wake of the uproar over Supreme Court nominee Douglas H. Ginsburg's marijuana admission. Gore did emphasize that he had not smoked marijuana since he was 24 and that he regretted having used it then.

Some feeling arose that the admission might actually help liven up Gore's image among young voters who were turned off by his self-description as a "raging moderate" and by his wife's crusade against pornographic rock music. But others predicted that Gore's marijuana admission would weaken his standing among the older, conservative-minded voters whose votes he badly needed.

"Gore had things going his way until he started talking about smoking pot," said Atlanta pollster Claibourne Darden. "It took the fizz right off his momentum."

Gore got that fizz by using the numerous debates among the Democratic contenders to enunciate more hawkish positions than his rivals on a handful of defense and foreign policy issues. Gore cited a number of issues on which he claimed to differ from all or virtually all his Democratic rivals: support for the Reagan administration's 1983 invasion of Grenada and its policy of escorting ships in the Persian Gulf, giving non-military aid to the Nicaraguan "contras," flight-testing ballistic missiles and funding the Midgetman missile.

Gore was not shy about implying that his Democratic foes were soft on defense. "The politics of retreat, complacency and doubt may appeal to others, but it will not do for me, or for my country," he proclaimed.

Gore's opponents charged him with opportunism, complaining that he was refashioning a basically liberal voting record to make it palatable to hawkish Southern Democrats. They noted that he had supported the nuclear freeze and opposed military aid to the contras. "Maybe the next debate should be between the old Al Gore and the new Al Gore," remarked Missouri Democratic Rep. Richard A. Gephardt.

Gore's attacks, though, won him considerable attention. Various surveys showed that his message held potential appeal for moderate-to-conservative Southern voters. A poll sponsored by the Democratic Leadership Council before and after the group's Oct. 5 national security debate in Miami showed that Gore's effort to differentiate himself had been effective. The polls of several hundred Southern "swing" voters—individuals who had backed Ronald Reagan in 1980 or 1984, but supported a Democratic candidate for the Senate in 1986—showed that support for Gore more than tripled (increasing from 12 to 38 percent) as a result of his performance in the debate. Whether he could sustain such shifts, of course, became the $64,000 question.

Gore sought to deepen his message by proposing a list of six objectives for international cooperation on economic policy: agreements to reduce the U.S. budget deficit and expand those of Germany and Japan, stabilize exchange rates and lower interest rates, increase regulation over surpluses and subsidies in world commodity trade, and convince various other wealthy countries to at least pitch in on U.S. aid to poorer countries—if not to the provision of military assistance.

On the central issue of the budget deficit, Gore would not categorically reject new taxes. But he endorsed no specific revenue measures, instead pledging a negotiating adeptness born of his congressional experience. He advocated more spending on education, AIDS research and low-income housing construction, but he claimed there would be no major new federal expenditures if he were elected president.

Back to the Future

From the day he first announced for political office, Gore convinced nearly everyone watching him that he would have a brilliant future in politics. His career so far has proven that assessment correct. But his jump for the White House as a freshman senator provoked some comments that he seemed more at home in the future than in the present.

On the career ladder, the next rung up has always seemed to beckon. He left law school to run for the House at age 28; he left the House to run for the Senate at age 36; and, after barely two years there and still shy of 40, he started running for president.

But dismissing Gore as a publicity hound with a short attention span would be unwise. In the same way that he devoted himself to learning about nuclear arms so he could become a serious contributor in that policy area, Gore now is applying himself to the task of winning over frustrated Southern voters such as Alabama state House Speaker Jimmy Clark, who told the *Tennessean*, "I believe the Washington, New York, New England axis has destroyed the Democratic party. We need to bring the Southern way of thinking back into national politics."

If Clark and others like him decided that Gore represented that "Southern way of thinking," a spot on the ticket as vice president—or perhaps even the presidential nomination itself—could be within the senator's grasp.

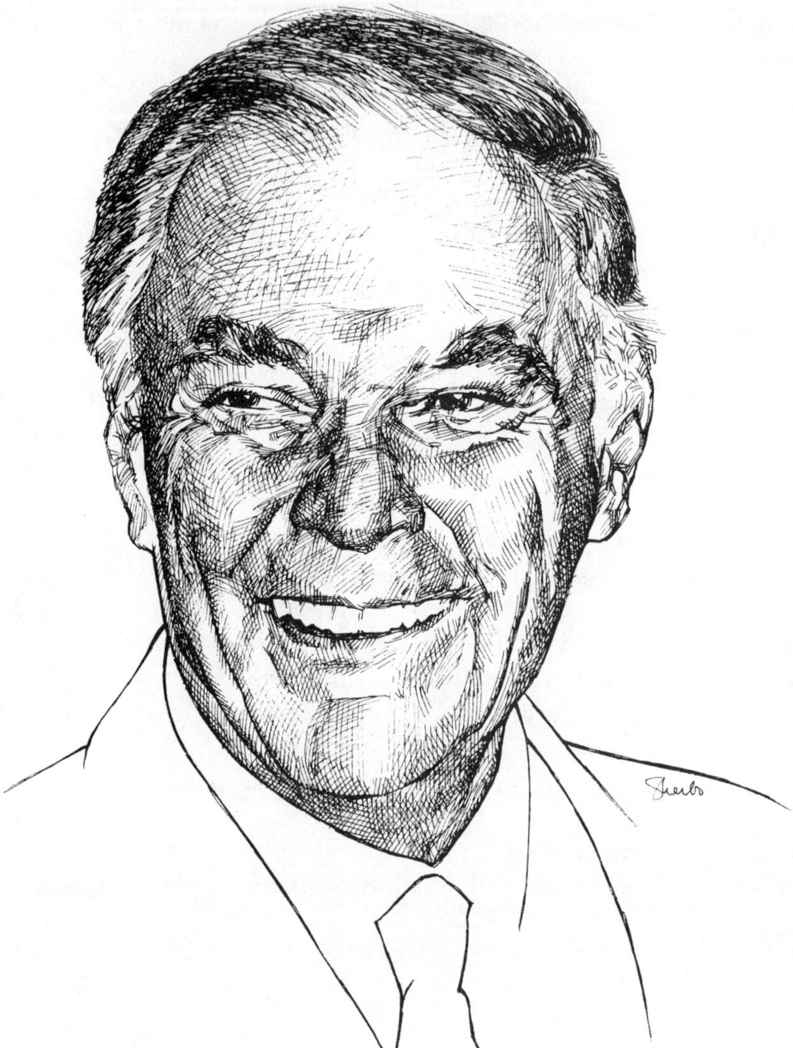
Sherbo

ALEXANDER M. HAIG JR.

From Soldier to Secretary of State After a Fast Climb in the Military

Unlike most of the other contenders for the 1988 Republican presidential nomination, Alexander Haig has never held an elected public office. On the other hand, perhaps none of his competitors could lay claim to an equal breadth of experience within the top levels of commerce, government and the military. Even before he became first secretary of state in the Reagan administration, Haig had been touted by some as having a background of presidential stature.

Indeed, when "the General" retired from NATO in 1979, a small group of supporters actually began organizing a Haig-for-President committee. But it was not to be. While he was one of the most politically skilled military figures of his generation, Haig had difficulty mounting a campaign once back in the United States. The same character traits that had served him so well in his rise to the top echelons of both the Pentagon and White House were not deemed assets by many members of the electorate.

It was at that point in late 1979, convinced that his candidacy was going nowhere, that Haig accepted a position as president of United Technologies. As with so many of the moves throughout his career, however, this first flirtation with the private sector would be short-lived. Just one year later, Haig left United Technologies to become Ronald Reagan's first secretary of state.

Yet again, the shift was fleeting. It was not a match made in heaven. Haig resigned from the Reagan administration in June 1982. He turned again to business, establishing his own consulting firm called Worldwide Associates Inc. and became a wealthy man in the process. It was from that position, in the summer of 1986, that Haig once again decided to mount a campaign for the presidency.

Although his business venture was financially successful, Haig's

Alexander Meigs Haig Jr.

Profession: Business executive; Army general (ret.).
Born: Dec. 2, 1924, Philadelphia, Pa.
Home: McLean, Va.
Religion: Roman Catholic.
Education: Attended University of Notre Dame, 1943; U.S. Military Academy, West Point, B.S., 1947; Georgetown University, M.A., 1961.
Military: Army, 1947-79.
Family: Wife, Patricia Fox; three children.
Political and Military Career: Deputy assistant, National Security Council, 1970-73; Army vice chief of staff, 1973; White House chief of staff, 1973-74; NATO commander, 1974-79; secretary of state, 1981-82.

announcement for the 1988 nomination indicates that he missed the drama and exhilaration of political life. Realizing how much work lay ahead of him, Haig threw his hat in the presidential ring early, declaring in the summer of 1986. He formally announced his candidacy on March 24, 1987, after public opinion polls showed that he enjoyed high name recognition among voters. However, little organizational money or national attention were to come his way. On the eve of 1988's first presidential primaries, he continued to trail the Republicans' two main contenders, George Bush and Robert Dole, by considerable margins.

In January Haig withdrew from the Iowa caucuses to concentrate on the New Hampshire primary. The candidate hoped to fare respectably enough in the Granite State to continue his race. Just a third-place finish would please him well and give him some impetus to head into the "Super Tuesday" primaries in the South in March.

Haig's campaign staff felt that his conservative, military background would stand Haig in good stead in the South, particularly if either Bush or Dole were to falter. On the other hand, a poor showing in New Hampshire would likely spell the end to his campaign, as it has for so many others.

Barbed Questions, Clear Positions

Despite his military and foreign policy expertise, Haig was to attract the most attention during the pre-primary debates by directing barbed questions at Bush about the Iran-contra affair. He also, however, was to take clear positions on a number of important and controversial issues.

Like the other contenders, Haig sees the federal deficit as a major problem, and he pledges to reduce it. However, he also says he does not want defense to be made the "whipping boy" for "excessive spending in the domestic sector." Rather, he calls for a presidential line-item veto and policies that would allow for a "safe glidepath"—thus permitting the country to balance the budget by the mid-1990s.

Haig, of course, is well known for his belief that the United States must stand up to the Soviet Union. To cut off aid to the contras, he feels, would only demonstrate America's continuing lack of will, something that will permit the Soviets to increase their presence in this hemisphere. In negotiations with the Soviets, Haig believes that the United States should bring pressure to bear to halt their "meddling" in Angola, Afghanistan and Kampuchea.

Haig is not blindly anti-communist, however. His support for the People's Republic of China dates from the early 1970s. In fact, belief in China's strategic importance was to cause him many difficulties in the Reagan administration.

Like some conservative Republicans, Haig does not favor the Intermediate Nuclear Forces (INF) arms treaty, which Reagan and Mikhail Gorbachev initialed at the December 1987 summit in Washington. Above all, Haig fears the treaty will harm deterrence because it does not address the more serious problem of the imbalance of conventional forces between NATO and the Warsaw Pact in central Europe.

Haig tries to position himself as the on-the-ground expert in such matters. Having served more than four years as NATO commander—and knowing European security matters well—the General claims credibility on this issue. Nevertheless, his stand was to face a wary reception among the electorate.

As for other foreign policy matters, Haig opposes economic sanctions in South Africa, believing they would harm the very people they are designed to help. He has called for Western nations to support moderate leaders while withholding support for the African National Congress, which he feels is "heavily Marxist and pro-Soviet."

Of firm Catholic upbringing, Haig opposes abortion, while generally supporting what are known as family values. One of the few domestic issues on which he has elaborated is education, for which he has detailed an extensive agenda. Here he advocates the re-establishment of basics and emphasis on foreign languages, math and computers. He also favors higher pay and higher standards for teachers, more parental involvement in schools and tuition credits for private schools and colleges.

Despite his education campaign and his overall record of public service, Haig still remains a somewhat uncomfortable figure to many Americans. For example, a recent *Time* article entitled "Why Is This Man Running?" was subtitled "Haig still yearns to be in control"—as if the desire to be president were not equally strong for the other candidates. The article cited a poll in which 46 percent of Republicans said they held an unfavorable impression of him, while only 26 percent were favorable.

In an era when many candidates spend as much time polishing their image as mastering complex issues, it is perhaps understandable that the General has been at a disadvantage. Some of this is attributable to his admittedly sharp-edged personality. But some of it may also be due to the country's continuing mistrust of the military, a legacy of Vietnam.

Early Career

Alexander Haig was born and raised in the Philadelphia suburb of Bala-Cynwyd. From an early age, he expressed interest in a military career.

When the boy was 10, his father, a lawyer, died. Although the family was helped by a well-to-do uncle, Haig worked a variety of jobs as a teenager to earn his way. Originally enrolled at Notre Dame, Haig won appointment to West Point on his second try. He graduated well down in his class and was commissioned as an armor officer in 1947.

Haig was first sent to Japan, where he served on Gen. Douglas MacArthur's staff with the Army of Occupation. In 1950 he married Patricia Fox, the daughter of MacArthur's deputy chief of staff. By then he had become an aide-de-camp to MacArthur. In a sense, a career pattern had already been established: diligent staff work and loyalty to the "right" superior would pay off.

During the Korean War, Haig participated in MacArthur's famous landing at Inchon and was afterward awarded a Silver Star. Later in the 1950s he was a staff officer at a tank battalion in Europe.

The early 1960s saw him reassigned to Washington. In 1962 he earned a master's degree in international relations at Georgetown University. From there Haig was sent to the Pentagon, where his first important job was on a task force monitoring Cuba in the wake of the Bay of Pigs disaster. It was here that Haig, now a lieutenant colonel, first made contacts with the CIA and covert activities in this hemisphere.

Although Haig's career had been on track from the beginning, it was at the Pentagon that he began to attract attention. A particularly effective briefer, one of his jobs was to prepare Secretary of Defense Robert McNamara for presentations to the president and the National Security Council (NSC). Among Haig's patrons were Army Secretary Cyrus Vance and Joseph Califano, then the Army's general counsel. When Califano was named McNamara's special assistant, Haig became his deputy.

Yet career advancement depended on distinguishing oneself in combat as well as performing staff duty. Haig went to Vietnam in 1966. As a combat officer with the First Division he participated in the battle

Alexander Haig believes his government experience qualifies him to be chief executive.

of Ap Gu, near the Cambodian border in 1967 and was awarded a Distinguished Service Cross. At the time, he was said to have been one of the youngest lieutenant colonels ever to have served as brigade commander.

Haig's next assignment was at West Point. Ironically, his superior there was Bernard Rogers, the man who would succeed him as NATO commander in 1979. While at West Point, Haig was promoted to full colonel.

Back to Government: The NSC

In early 1969 Henry Kissinger put Al Haig's career on the fast track when he selected him, upon the recommendation of Califano, to be his military adviser on the National Security Council staff. Respected for his sharp and often self-deprecating wit, as well as his stamina, Haig's first job was to prepare the NSC's daily intelligence summary.

Kissinger's NSC staff was made up of a number of young and ambitious men who would go on to important positions within the U.S. foreign policy community: Richard Allen, Lawrence Eagleburger, John Negroponte, Morton Halperin and Helmut Sonnenfeldt, among others.

From the beginning, the pace at the NSC was intense, as Kissinger reached out for primacy in the foreign policy arena of the Nixon administration. Perhaps the hardest worker on a staff of notoriously hard workers, Haig soon won the admiration of his ambitious chief.

Something of a liberal by Republican standards, Kissinger had hired several Democrats onto his staff. Anticipating criticism from the right, Kissinger's appointment of Haig was perhaps a sop to certain hard-liners. As a hard-liner himself, with combat experience, Haig helped solidify the NSC's conservative credentials. His knowledge of the Pentagon was useful to Kissinger, while military leaders, anxious to preserve their influence in Vietnam policy making, were only too glad to have a conduit to the NSC.

The NSC was soon bombarding the White House with situation reports on a vast number of projects, a great many of which Haig had worked on. But as Seymour Hersh says in his book *The Price of Power*, Haig also was soon demonstrating the "art of flattering a superior." Not above performing humble tasks for his chief, Haig simultaneously proved himself successful at outmaneuvering his rivals. Within a half-year, he had undermined Staff Secretary Richard Moose, in part because Moose had once worked for Arkansas Democrat J. William Fulbright, one of the Senate's leading opponents of the Vietnam War.

Haig used his increasing power to increasing advantage. Early in the Nixon administration, in an effort to halt a damaging series of leaks to the press, wiretaps secretly were authorized to be run on members of the NSC and various figures in the media. Although Kissinger was involved in the process, it was Haig who went to the FBI offices to read the printouts and report back on their findings. Knowledge of this kind of information, of course, gave Haig further ammunition in his own struggle to rise, while furnishing Kissinger vital information in his effort to limit the influence of Secretary of State William Rogers and Secretary of Defense Melvin Laird.

On the policy front, Haig was a strong supporter of the bombing of Cambodia, which began in secret in 1970. At the time many military officers believed such assaults would turn the tide of the Vietnam War against the Viet Cong. The idea also had the support of Kissinger—who knew the advantage of recommending to the president what the president wanted to hear.

Then, in 1970, Haig was appointed brigadier general and Kissinger's deputy, giving him control of staff issues. Within a short space of time Haig had succeeded in placing himself at the center of the NSC action, controlling the flow of information. Anyone seeking access to Kissinger had first to go through him.

Deeply involved in assessing the deteriorating situation in Vietnam, Haig came to the attention of Richard Nixon, despite Kissinger's attempts to isolate his staff from the White House. Haig increasingly was used as an intermediary between an occasionally jealous president and his highly visible national security adviser. Kissinger often relied on Haig to present his views to Nixon and report back to him what the president said and felt. At the same time Nixon often queried Haig as to what the peripatetic Kissinger was really up to.

Throughout all the intrigue, Haig's success at the NSC was based on his discretion and an ability to stay out of the limelight. He was not one to leak matters to the press when things did not go his way.

His work on the wiretaps led to involvement with the Daniel Ellsberg case, following the 1971 publication of the first of the Pentagon Papers, the hitherto secret history of U.S. military participation in Vietnam. Meanwhile, Haig was increasingly entrusted with matters of the highest state importance. In early January 1972 he was sent to China to complete preparations for Nixon's historic trip—which led the way to American recognition for the People's Republic and a major realignment of international relations.

In Beijing, Haig met with Chou En Lai. Previously a behind-the-scenes figure, the brigadier general suddenly encountered his first major publicity. In a profile of him in the *New York Times*, he was called "Kissinger's Kissinger" and cited for his hard-line views on Southeast Asia. Already he was on the list for promotion to major general.

As events in Southeast Asia and at the Paris peace talks progressed, Haig made numerous high-level trips to Saigon. Just prior to Nixon's re-election, he was sent to persuade South Vietnamese President Nguyen Van Thieu to drop his objections to the proposals made at the Paris talks.

In October 1972 Haig was promoted to four-star general, passing over the rank of lieutenant general entirely. In the process, he was jumped over the heads of some 240 officers, causing 25 higher-ranking generals to be retired. The effect was to cause a stir in the upper echelons of the Army. For some there was resentment over what was seen as a blatantly political appointment. No other four-star general in memory had ever had so little battlefield experience at the command level.

Practically without precedent, too, was the speed with which Haig had risen to the top: from colonel to four-star general in less than four years. Press accounts at the time claimed that only two other Army generals were thought to have risen so quickly: George Custer and George Marshall. On the other hand, many officers realized that Haig's association with the president could only help the military at a time when the Vietnam War was causing it to lose favor with much of the nation.

Haig's appointment to Army deputy chief of staff became effective January 1973. Kissinger reportedly was relieved to see his all-too-well-connected aide moved to the Pentagon. Despite the move, Haig remained in close contact with Nixon; reportedly he had a direct telephone line to the president's office.

White House Chief of Staff

In May 1973, as the Watergate scandal grew in significance, Haig was called to the White House to replace Nixon's chief of staff, H. R. "Bob" Haldeman. It is said that Haig did not want the job, fearing it would prevent his achieving the goal of becoming Army chief of staff.

But he felt he had no choice; it was his duty to accept a call from the commander-in-chief.

From the start, Haig was pressured to leave the Army by Ralph Nader and Democratic Sen. Stuart Symington of Missouri, who had uncovered a century-old law barring military officers from high civilian positions. New attorney general Elliot Richardson refused to accept the validity of the law, but Haig still left active duty on Aug. 1.

From the beginning, Haig took control of the White House apparatus. The staff, reeling from the effects of Watergate, was reassembled. Nixon's old-time faithfuls—Haldeman, John Ehrlichman, John Mitchell—were gone and disgraced. Melvin Laird was brought back as an inner adviser.

Under Haig's system, the senior staff, including figures such as Kissinger and Laird, met each morning for coffee. Haig controlled access to the president and determined which information would be placed before him. Although clearly serving "at the king's pleasure," before long he was being dubbed the "alternate president." With Nixon forced to deal with the stresses of the Watergate investigations, Haig was increasingly called upon to grease the wheels of government.

He also figured prominently in the halls of diplomacy. It was an era of détente, after all, and, partly because of the SALT I and ABM treaties of 1972, Haig came to spend a good deal of time with high Soviet officials: Andrei Gromyko, Alexei Kosygin, Leonid Brezhnev, Anatoly Dobrynin.

Despite being appointed in the wake of the initial Watergate break-in, Haig's high influence was to mark him for scrutiny as the scandal broke further. In November 1973 Haig was called to testify before the Senate concerning the famous 18-minute "Rose Mary Woods" gap in a White House tape. The following spring he was called to the stand again about a Howard Hughes contribution to the Nixon campaign. A few months later he testified on the wiretapping at the NSC.

Throughout his numerous appearances before Congress, Haig maintained his innocence, saying that the events of Watergate had occurred when he was not with the Nixon staff. Although charges frequently were raised against him, none ever was proved. Of all the officials who rose to prominence during the Nixon era, only Kissinger and Haig were to continue in high office after the resignation.

Indeed, when Gerald R. Ford became president in August 1974, he asked Haig to stay on as chief of staff. Some believe that Ford was indirectly obligated to Haig for having been brought on as vice president. Many more credit Haig for having been the one who convinced Nixon in the end that he must resign.

A Return to the Army: NATO Commander

Haig stayed with Ford for little over a month. The new president's team, once entrenched in the White House, saw Haig as a Nixon man and thus a threat to their efforts to create an independent image for their president. In September, Ford appointed Haig NATO commander. Haig did indeed show some Nixon loyalties in one of his last reported acts as chief of staff, asking Ford to name hard-line Nixon speechwriter Patrick Buchanan ambassador to South Africa.

Outside of Washington, not everyone was happy with Haig's appointment. The Dutch tried to block it. Many Europeans felt they were being assigned a Washington cast-off. Among those cool to Haig was his predecessor, Gen. Andrew Goodpaster, who had recommended him to Kissinger in the first place.

Yet, to the surprise of some, Haig earned high marks at NATO. He was still well connected in Washington, a fact that many felt helped to keep the U.S. commitment to NATO strong at a time when proposals such as the Mansfield Amendment (calling for reductions of American forces in Europe) were attracting attention.

As NATO commander, Haig expanded the scope of Allied maneuvers, bringing them more in line with combat realities. He pushed for better conventional equipment to combat the Warsaw Pact's numerical advantages, particularly in tanks. He urged stronger Allied coordination in weapons manufacturing. He also adjusted the deployment of NATO forces to strengthen a weakness in the central German front.

During Haig's tenure, NATO leaders pledged to increase their annual military spending by 3 percent in real terms. By the time of his retirement, Haig had established good relations with many European leaders, particularly with Helmut Schmidt and the West Germans. All in all, it made for wider acceptance, and Ford reappointed Haig to a second two-year term in late 1976. The decision was supported by Jimmy Carter when he took office.

In May 1976 the *Washington Post*, not usually considered a Haig supporter, described him as "one of the most articulate spokesmen

NATO has had." On the other side of the political fence, conservative columnists Rowland Evans and Robert Novak wrote that Haig had become "a Western symbol of will and determination." Haig was at the zenith of his career, his reputation high among leaders on both sides of the Atlantic.

With the support of Secretary of Defense Harold Brown, Carter reappointed Haig in 1978, despite the fact that Haig had threatened to resign when Carter opposed the anti-tank neutron bomb. A few months after accepting the appointment, however, Haig announced his resignation, effective June 30, 1979.

Retirement from the military allowed Haig to begin speaking his mind more directly on matters such as the SALT II treaty, which he felt did not sufficiently redress the nuclear imbalance in Europe. While considering various offers and testing the waters for political opportunities, Haig went to work for the Foreign Policy Research Institute in Philadelphia. Meanwhile, a Haig-for-President committee was founded by a small group of supporters.

A speech Haig gave at the Bohemian Grove Club in July 1979 attracted the attention of a number of prominent Republicans. Sounded out about being part of the Reagan team that August, Haig demurred for the time being, perhaps preoccupied by his own presidential ambitions.

After recognizing the hopelessness of his own presidential bid, Haig dropped out of the race in 1979. Just two days later came his appointment as president and chief operating officer of United Technologies, a company with important defense interests.

Haig claims to have been happy at United Technologies and out of politics. Whether he was healthy was another question; in early 1980 he underwent double bypass heart surgery in Houston. Later that year he accepted an invitation to address the Republican National Convention in Detroit. Afterwards, he says, he was told by Justin Dart, a close friend of Ronald Reagan, that he would be the next secretary of state.

Secretary of State

Haig had had little direct contact with Ronald Reagan before he was tapped to be the 59th secretary of state in December 1980. But the two men seemed united in their belief that détente with the Soviet Union had failed and that the United States must regain its military strength and the national will to stand up to Soviet "adventurism."

Haig had no easy time being confirmed. Democratic senators, led by Rhode Island's Claiborne Pell, steered the questioning toward allegations of Haig's involvement in the Watergate affair. After a record five-day hearing, however, only Senate Democrats Paul Sarbanes of Maryland and Paul Tsongas of Massachussetts voted against him in committee.

By his own account the new secretary of state's problems within the Reagan administration began almost immediately. Haig's frankness clashed with the "California" style of the inner circle. Particularly, presidential advisers Ed Meese and Michael Deaver felt from the beginning that the General was trying to grab power. Realizing his outsider status, Haig named William Clark, a long-time Reagan confidant, his deputy.

Brimming with energy and an assurance based on long involvement with foreign affairs, Haig found his term in office a continual frustration. From the outset, he lacked access to the president. The inner circle set the president's agenda, and domestic policy was to take the first seat.

As he would later write in *Caveat*, Haig believed that he had been given Reagan's backing—that he alone would be "the vicar," the one to articulate the president's foreign policy. The term was soon to haunt him, however. Despite assurances from the president, Haig saw his position undercut by other administration figures on a regular basis. Leaks in the Reagan administration "were not merely a problem," Haig would write, "they were a way of life."

Nonetheless, as secretary of state, Haig worked on a vast array of political problems. The first tough issue he faced was Central America. Two days after his inauguration, Reagan acted on Haig's advice and ended U.S. aid to Marxist Nicaragua, which had been given more than $150 million by the Carter administration since the triumph of the Sandinistas in July 1979.

The situation was even more delicate in El Salvador, where in late January the Farabundo Marti National Liberation (FMLN) movement launched its "final offensive," nearly toppling the government. At Haig's urging the U.S. ambassador to El Salvador, Robert White, was replaced; a policy of increased military support for the government was put in place.

Always a strong advocate of pressuring the Soviet Union, Haig lost his battle against resumption of grain sales to the USSR in the spring of

1981. Reagan's decision to honor his campaign promise to the Farm Belt would undercut American foreign policy goals later in the year, however, when the administration tried to prevent the Europeans from concluding a huge natural gas project with the Soviet Union.

The White House inner circle's resentment of Haig appeared to grow after a cover story in *Time* magazine appeared in March 1981, under the title "The 'Vicar' Takes Charge." It was in stories such as these that Haig's image as power-hungry took shape.

However, this was soon overshadowed by the events that surrounded the attempt on the president's life on March 30. Here too, Haig added to his own notoriety. His sharp profile on television and the statement that he was "in control here" in the White House has remained an enduring image of his career as secretary of state. Despite growing personality conflicts, however, Haig stayed on.

The administration's decision to sell early warning aircraft (AWACS) to Saudi Arabia soon involved Haig in a series of difficult Middle Eastern issues. He found himself battling with Israeli Prime Minister Menachem Begin when Israel bombed Iraq's nuclear reactor in June 1981. And only after a fierce battle in Congress did the administration finally secure the AWACS sale—though not without a corresponding loss in American influence over Israeli behavior.

In December 1981 Poland declared martial law and the independent trade union Solidarity was declared illegal. Reagan's inner circle was outraged; it was only with difficulty that Haig could convince them that there were limits to America's power in East Europe. "Russia did what it had to do," Haig wrote in his memoirs.

The administration's response to the Polish situation was complicated by the U.S. decision in late December to impose sanctions against European companies participating in the Soviet natural gas contract. Coupled with the unusually high value of the dollar, this brought some of the worst strains in a generation to trans-Atlantic relations. Given his strong association with Europe, Haig's prestige within the administration dropped further.

On March 19, 1982, a small detachment of Argentine soldiers landed on the obscure South Atlantic island of South Georgia. The Falklands War was about to start, causing a serious dilemma for American foreign policy. Under the sponsorship of UN ambassador Jeane Kirkpatrick, the United States had been moving toward closer relations with the military government of Argentina, and one of the manifestations of this new relationship was the clandestine training the Argentines were providing the embryonic "contra" guerrilla movement in Honduras. This improvement in relations would help fuel Argentina's mistaken belief that the United States would not side with the British in the event of war.

Late in March British Foreign Secretary Lord Carrington called Haig to ask for help. Haig instructed the ambassador to Buenos Aires, Harry Shlaudeman, to convey American displeasure. Shlaudeman's appeal was to have little effect. On April 1 the Argentines landed at Port Stanley, the capital of the Falklands. As the British prepared to respond, Haig undertook his own brand of "shuttle diplomacy," flying between London, Washington and Buenos Aires. One result of this effort was to elicit charges of "grandstanding" from others within the administration. Haig's failure to resolve the conflict, he believes, was the ultimate cause of his losing the president's confidence.

But it was the Israeli invasion of Lebanon that marked Haig's final chapter as secretary of state. On June 6, 1982, Israeli troops crossed the Lebanese border in an effort to drive the Palestinian Liberation Organization (PLO) from the country. Haig has written that he had been aware of Israeli intentions as far back as the previous fall, when he had spoken with Begin at Anwar Sadat's funeral.

Although Haig has repeatedly denied it, many press accounts have implied that he never sufficiently discouraged the Israelis from attacking. Yet it is far from certain that he had the power to do so, even had he wished. American ties to Israel had been badly strained by the AWACS sale as well as by the negative U.S. reaction to the formal annexation of the Golan Heights in December 1981.

So, even as he was directing U.S. efforts to contain the situation in Lebanon, Haig's resignation letter was sitting on President Reagan's desk. Finally, on June 25, 1982, the president accepted it, though he asked Haig to continue working on Lebanon until George Shultz took over.

At that point, the fiery and controversial public life of Alexander Haig appeared to have reached its conclusion. His successful turn to the private sector seemed to augur a rich, crowning achievement for the General. Conventional wisdom had it that the old soldier would fade away into the world of commerce. This, by early 1988, seemed a likely fate even after a full year and a half of presidential campaigning. While Haig hoped that the citizens of New Hampshire might provide him with one more round of political ammunition, the polls suggested otherwise.

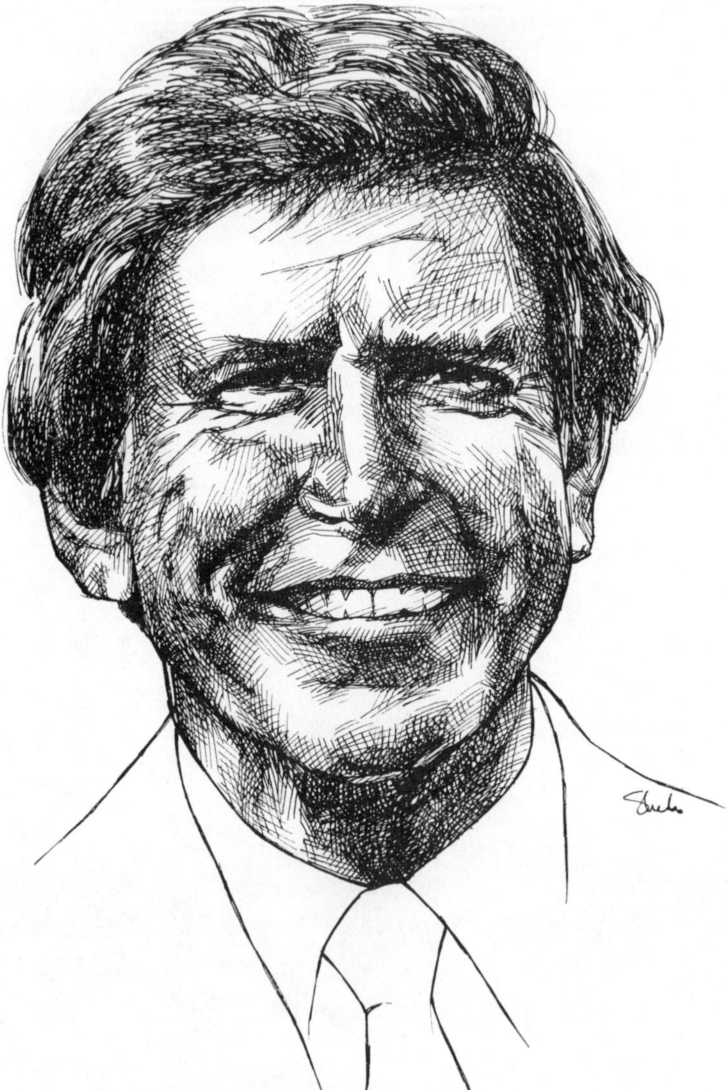

GARY HART

Offering 'New Ideas' to Fuel An On-Again, Off-Again Candidacy

"This will not be like any campaign you have ever seen," former senator Gary Hart of Colorado said late in 1987, as he launched his second 1988 presidential campaign. It is hard to imagine a more fitting statement coming from Hart, a politician in many respects unlike any other this country has ever seen.

Hart began his life in politics as an outsider, and he has never really seen fit to come in from the cold. In the 16 years since he first made a name for himself in political circles, Hart has made a career out of challenging the existing power structure and turning conventional wisdom on its head.

He did it first in 1972, when he took the reins of Sen. George McGovern's anti-establishment presidential campaign and mobilized scores of people who had never taken an active part in elections before.

Hart did it again as a two-term member of the Senate, winning election and re-election as a left-leaning Democrat in a conservative Western state. During his tenure, he became known as a cerebral loner whose impatient attempts to rethink traditional approaches to policy problems left him well outside the mainstream in the Senate's clubby, conformist environment.

When Hart decided to run for president in 1984, he again took to the outside track. Sounding the call for "new ideas" to replace what he branded the shopworn remedies of the past, Hart capitalized on dissatisfaction with establishment favorite Walter F. Mondale to make a surprisingly strong showing in the battle for the Democratic nomination.

As he began gearing up for another run at the White House in 1988, Hart found himself in alien territory. For once, he was the front-runner, the insider, the man to beat. That situation did not last long. His political position crumbled when allegations of sexual improprieties

Gary Warren Hart

Profession: Lawyer.
Born: Nov. 28, 1936, Ottawa, Kan.
Home: Troublesome Gulch, Colo.
Religion: Presbyterian.
Education: Bethany Nazarene College, B.A., 1958; Yale University, B.D., 1961; LL.B., 1964.
Political Career: U.S. Senate, 1975-87; sought Democratic nomination for president, 1984.
Military: Naval Reserve, 1981-present.
Family: Wife, Lee Ludwig; two children.
Senate Committees: Armed Services, 1975-87; Public Works, 1975-76; Environment and Public Works, 1977-87; Select Committee to Study Governmental Operations With Respect to Intelligence Activities, 1975-76; Select Committee on Intelligence, 1977-78; Budget, 1979-87.

overwhelmed his campaign, and he felt compelled to withdraw. But by December he was back, struggling to breathe life into the campaign he had abandoned just seven months earlier and registering his biggest shock yet to the American political system.

History will judge the wisdom of his actions. After an initial surge of enthusiasm following his re-entry, Hart has had to face up to the harsh realities of a campaign still saddled with concern about his character, allegations about improper fund-raising activities, a hostile party hierarchy and acute shortages of money and organization. Should Hart somehow survive those daunting odds and make a respectable showing in the 1988 race for the Democratic nomination, he will be able to claim a Lazarus-like ascent from electoral purgatory.

A Conservative Forge

The man whose political iconoclasm and unorthodox image have made him a national enigma emerged from a rather staid, conservative, religious forge. Born in the east Kansas farm town of Ottawa, Hart was raised as a member of the Church of the Nazarene, a conservative Methodist sect espousing strict and austere morality.

Hart's father, whose last name was Hartpence, worked as a rancher before going into the farm machinery business. His mother was a housewife active in church affairs. They voted Republican, and Hart, who shortened the family name in college, has recalled growing up with an admiration for a fellow Kansan, President Dwight D. Eisenhower.

Hart carried his religion with him into college, graduating from Bethany Nazarene College, a tiny church-related school near Oklahoma City, Okla. He then enrolled in Yale Divinity School, where he plotted an academic career in religion and philosophy. Those plans were scuttled, however, after he received his baptism in the world of electoral politics —his volunteer service in Massachusetts Sen. John F. Kennedy's 1960 presidential campaign.

"I'd never really considered any alternative profession," Hart would tell journalist David Broder years later. "But the 1960 campaign opened up the possibility of public service as a reasonably attractive avenue to pursue, and it ultimately led me to switch to law school."

To pursue his legal education, he returned to Yale, then went to work as a lawyer in the Justice Department. He subsequently signed on as a special assistant to Interior Secretary Stewart L. Udall, investigating problems with Western oil shale leases. Hart fueled his interest in politics by working for Sen. Robert F. Kennedy during the 1968 presidential primaries.

Of Three-by-Five Cards and Canvassing

At the end of the Johnson administration, Hart moved to Denver and began practicing law. But it was not long before he was back in the political arena—this time for good. In 1969 he met Sen. McGovern, who had stepped in as a substitute presidential candidate the previous year after Robert Kennedy's assassination. McGovern impressed Hart with his intelligence, and the young attorney decided the South Dakota Democrat was presidential material.

Hart agreed to coordinate the West for McGovern's 1972 presidential campaign but soon assumed a more central role: national campaign director. It was in that role that Hart developed his reputation for grassroots organizing. He mastered the complex rules of the Democratic nominating process (rules McGovern himself had helped rewrite) as well as the world of three-by-five cards, phone banks and door-to-door canvassing. Hart helped engineer a coalition of liberals and anti-war Democrats that enabled McGovern to secure the nomination during the primary season.

That coalition was drowned out in a torrent of Republican votes that fall. But Hart emerged with his whiz-kid image intact, and with a desire to put his tools to work in a campaign of his own. Returning home to Denver, he set about writing *Right from the Start*, a chronicle of the 1972 effort, and began laying plans to run for the Senate in 1974.

Underdog Senate Campaign

He began his bid for the Democratic senatorial nomination as a distinct underdog. Former state senator Herrick S. Roth, a past president of the Colorado AFL-CIO, began the campaign as the front-runner; although Roth had been ousted from his presidential post, he commanded enough residual labor support to win the top-line primary ballot listing at the state Democratic convention. Roth also benefited from exposure he had gained as a Denver talk show host.

But Roth had not reckoned with Hart's organizational skills. Transferring his grass-roots mobilizing abilities from the national to the state level, Hart deployed some 3,000 workers across Colorado. He wound up with a 14,000-vote victory on Primary Day.

According to some veteran Colorado politicians, Hart built his victory by bringing a new generation of voters into the campaign fray. "Hart got into the race in 1974 by virtue of having organized new people, not the party regulars," recalled Mark Hogan, a former lieutenant governor and Colorado Democratic Party chairman who served as Hart's national campaign coordinator in 1984. "It wasn't a kids' crusade . . . but he found people who had not been all that active in party politics."

In the fall, Hart faced off with Republican Sen. Peter H. Dominick (1963-75), who had some major weaknesses. One was his health; plagued by back problems, Dominick was in obvious pain much of the time during the general election campaign.

Dominick's role as chairman of the Republican Senatorial Campaign Committee proved another major vulnerability. Hart accused the incumbent of having "laundered" donations from a dairy cooperative in 1972 and funneled them to President Richard Nixon's re-election committee. Dominick protested that he had done nothing illegal, but the issue kept him on the defensive in a year in which Watergate made any ethical controversy a serious liability.

Dominick launched a counteroffensive, seeking to pin a liberal label on Hart. But he had difficulty making it stick. Despite his past affiliation with McGovern, Hart had no public record of his own to defend and thus was free to sound more conservative themes. He spoke out against public housing, busing, unconditional amnesty for draft resisters and gun control, showing an instinct for Western political attitudes that evidently struck a resonant chord. Hart finished with 57 percent of the vote statewide.

The advantages Hart reaped as a challenger in a strong Democratic year were largely erased the next time he stepped into the electoral ring, running for re-election in 1980. Hart found himself consistently rated as one of the most vulnerable Democratic incumbents in the country.

His problems were compounded by the fact that he faced a GOP challenger whose rocky road to the Republican nomination had given her a strong personal appeal.

Secretary of State Mary Estill Buchanan had a moderate bent that did not sit well among the conservatives who dominated the Colorado

On Dec. 15, Gary Hart announced he was re-entering the presidential race.

GOP. She failed to muster sufficient support at the state Republican convention to secure a spot on the ballot. But she fought her way onto the ticket, going over the heads of party leaders to petition for a ballot slot and then staving off legal challenges to her candidacy. Enthusiastic support from a core moderate minority enabled Buchanan to capture 30 percent of the vote, barely enough to clinch the GOP nomination.

Buchanan's moderate politics appealed to some of Colorado's Democratic electorate, and she began the fall campaign substantially ahead of Hart. But Buchanan lost momentum when she showed herself to be ill-informed on many national issues. She also erred in launching attacks on Hart that the incumbent was well prepared to defend. He turned aside her charges of liberalism by reminding voters of his push for construction of new military facilities in the state. And he played up testimonials from several more conservative colleagues in the Senate, including Arizona GOP Sen. Barry Goldwater.

Ronald Reagan's coattails helped Buchanan come close. But in the end, Hart's always efficient organization helped him clinch a 19,000-vote victory.

Thinking Man's Alternative

During his 12 years in the Senate, Hart established a reputation as an apostle of new ideas. He painstakingly sought to reassess conventional wisdom and fed his colleagues a steady diet of proposals on subjects ranging from military preparedness and environmental policy to taxation and job creation.

His affinity for puzzling out new ideas gave him an image as the thinking man's alternative to politicians prone to tired rhetoric. In striving to translate his notions into law, he was interesting more often than he was successful—but he was also universally regarded as a senator worth hearing.

Pondering seemed to be Hart's favorite part of his Senate job. "He likes to be out among witnesses, trying to foment the idea," Republican Sen. Alan K. Simpson of Wyoming said of Hart during the days when the two served together on the Environment and Public Works Committee. "He likes the question and answer, so he can show his creativity and thought."

But if Hart seemed to thrive on shaping ideas, he was less interested in selling them to his colleagues. A man who demonstrated little warmth for his fellow senators, he sometimes appeared to view the social requirements of his job as an unwelcome chore.

"Hart is the furthest thing from a 'wheeler-dealer,' " said Democratic Sen. J. James Exon of Nebraska, who sat with Hart on the Armed Services Committee. "That doesn't mean that he's not an effective U.S. senator.... But he is an idealist. It's very hard for a fairly pure idealist to get something done over in this pen."

Hart himself recognized that his personality seemed mismatched to the clubby requirements of legislative life. "I'm a disciple of the school that says a lot of people in public life are really shy, reticent people," he once said.

'Third Options'

Hart traces the origins of his new-ideas philosophy to skepticism about the continuing viability of Franklin D. Roosevelt's New Deal. He has sought to distance himself from the statist solutions to policy problems he felt were engendered by years of Democratic reliance on Roosevelt's liberalism.

"The New Deal has run its course," Hart once proclaimed. "The party is over. The pie cannot continue to expand forever."

Arguing that the challenges facing American government have outstripped the traditional means of treating them, Hart says he sought out new ground bypassing old-line liberal and conservative distinctions. "What I have tried to do," he has argued, "is create third options between the left and the right—in defense, in the environment, in the economy."

New approaches to defense policy occupied most of Sen. Hart's time and energy. To his way of thinking, decades of debate about defense have been improperly focused. "Time and again, the most effective military has not necessarily been the most expensive military," Hart said in a 1982 position paper. "How the money was spent has usually proven more important than how *much* was spent."

Founder of the bipartisan, bicameral Military Reform Caucus, Hart urged a shift in conventional warfare policy toward what he termed "maneuver warfare"—in which the military would concentrate on disrupting the enemy's ability to coordinate its forces, rather than trying to destroy it tank-by-tank and plane-by-plane.

Though he came from a landlocked state, Hart made himself into an expert in naval operations; he even joined the Naval Reserve in 1981. He sought to convince the Navy to shift away from the construction of huge, multibillion-dollar aircraft carriers—which he felt would be easy prey in the event of an enemy attack—toward a greater number of smaller, more mobile and much less expensive ships. He also wanted to equip those ships with vertical-takeoff (V/STOL) jets to help maximize their strategic utility.

Hart's efforts met with only limited legislative success, however. He managed to win approval in 1979 of funding to begin design of several carriers equipped to handle V/STOL technology. But he never managed to block procurement of large carriers.

Yet even his critics praised his persistence. "After a while it becomes pro forma," said one Senate aide familiar with defense issues. "You know, 'Oh no, here comes Hart with another carrier amendment.' He goes through his routine, the opposition goes through its routine, and then everybody votes as they have in the past. But he deserves some credit for that. He's still carrying the torch in an environment that's still dark."

Hart also established himself as one of the Senate's leading experts on the details of arms control. He welcomed the nuclear freeze movement of 1982 but raised questions about verification of such an agreement and worried that countries other than the United States and the Soviet Union would not be bound by it.

From his post on the Armed Services Committee, Hart opposed the MX missile, the B-1 bomber, nerve gas weapons known as binary munitions and some other new weapons systems. Yet he was never really part of the group of hard-core Pentagon critics in his party who routinely supported cuts in defense budgets on the Senate floor. He stood up for increases in military pay; in 1980, for example, he argued in favor of a comprehensive pay and benefits bill costing some $790 million.

"The Democratic Party can't be the party that just recommends defense cuts," Hart once said. "If we do, we will lose election after election."

Three Mile Island and Oil Import Fees

On environmental issues, Hart tended to follow a middle course between environmentalists and business groups. Early in his Senate career he lashed out at fellow members of the Public Works Committee for giv-

Hart's Interest Group Ratings

Vote ratings by interest groups help to give a picture of Gary Hart's orientation during his Senate career. This table shows how often Hart voted on key legislative issues in accordance with the positions of groups chosen to represent liberal, labor, business and conservative viewpoints. They are the Americans for Democratic Action (ADA), AFL-CIO, Chamber of Commerce of the United States (CCUS) and Americans for Constitutional Action (ACA) or American Conservative Union (ACU).

	ADA	AFL-CIO	CCUS	ACA	ACU
1975	94	82	6	11	—
1976	75	84	0	8	—
1977	90	75	11	4	—
1978	65	78	22	17	—
1979	58	89	9/27 [1]	15	—
1980	61	47	39	36	—
1981	95	82	11	17	—
1982	95	88	40	15	—
1983	80	93	29	7	—
1984	60	100	25	0	—
1985	100	95	18	—	0
1986	95	87	21	—	14 [2]

[1] In 1979 there were two Chamber of Commerce scores for members of the Senate. The CCUS originally calculated scores based on 11 votes and excluded several procedural votes. Subsequently, the chamber revised its ratings, using 16 votes instead of 11. Revised score follows orginal score.
[2] Congressional Quarterly began publishing ACU ratings in 1985.

ing too much credence to industry claims that stricter environmental standards would cut into their profits and hurt the economy.

Hart was still an ally of environmentalists during the debate on renewal of the Clean Air Act in the 97th Congress (1981-83). But by then his tone had changed. As chairman of the National Commission on Air Quality, Hart helped prepare a 1981 report that drew criticism from environmentalists and industry spokesmen alike. He warned the former against holding unrealistic expectations.

"If you start all over again, you're going to lose your shirts," Hart told his critics. "It's a question of realizing and accepting the political realities, understanding the makeup of Congress and understanding how large the anti-regulatory wave is that's crossing the country."

A former chairman of the Environment Committee's Nuclear Regulation Subcommittee, Hart led the Senate's investigation into the 1979 Three Mile Island nuclear power plant accident. While he unsuccessfully sought a six-month moratorium on the licensing of new reactors pending a study of safety measures in all plants, he never advocated abandoning nuclear power altogether. He argued that no viable alternative to nuclear energy had been proposed to cover the next 25 years; he recommended instead improved safety precautions and a permanent solution to the disposal of nuclear wastes. In 1982 he supported a long-term nuclear-waste planning bill that became law.

An early advocate of policies to reduce U.S. dependence on imported oil, Hart in 1980 was one of just 10 senators who stood in support of President Jimmy Carter's effort to impose an oil import fee. He was also one of just eight Democrats to vote against Carter's windfall profits tax. Hart argued that the tax would quell incentives to explore for and produce new oil. In its place Hart supported a stiff severance tax on already-discovered "old" oil—a move that pleased Colorado's independent oil companies, which deal primarily in new oil.

While Hart also served on the Budget Committee during his Senate tenure, he did not make much of a mark there. Proposals offered as floor amendments—such as his plan to scale back tax deductions for business lunches, with the savings to be spent on the school lunch program—did not meet with much success.

But he did manage to advance some novel proposals. Hart suggested converting the federal income tax system into a tax on consumption, covering only income not saved or invested. He also argued that government should be involved in encouraging growth in high technology industries and helping to retrain workers for jobs in such fields.

'New Ideas' a Mixed Blessing

Hart made his image as a new-ideas guru the basis of his 1984 presidential campaign. While the strategy initially proved an enormous asset—

propelling Hart from virtual anonymity into the role of serious contender for the Democratic nomination—it ultimately proved his undoing.

Hart began the race as one of the darkest horses in the eight-man Democratic field. He lacked money, and his loner's role in the Senate had left him with relatively poor name recognition nationwide. Mondale, by contrast, had regularly received national coverage as vice president under Jimmy Carter. Armed further with a wide array of endorsements and the advantages of having spent some two years on the campaign trail, the Minnesotan was almost universally favored to win the nomination going away.

It did not work out so smoothly. Mondale's assets became something of a liability as he struggled unsuccessfully against critics' characterizations of him as a tool of the special interest groups that had endorsed him. And Hart, whose new-ideas strategy was beginning to catch on with voters disenchanted with Mondale's old-line liberalism and staid style, was well positioned to take advantage of the front-runner's problems. Concentrating his organizational efforts in the early caucus and primary states, Hart was able to muster an upset victory in the New Hampshire primary—gaining much-needed visibility and momentum overnight.

But with the increased exposure came increased scrutiny of Hart's character and his strategy. Reporters discovered that he had changed his name years earlier, and that he had sometimes misrepresented his age during the campaign—revelations that, when combined with Hart's natural reluctance to talk about himself, made it seem as though "there was something missing there," in the words of one political consultant.

Critics also began arguing that Hart's "new ideas" essentially consisted of "newness" for its own sake. Mondale found an effective way to tap concern about Hart's platform and personality by uttering one simple phrase, taken from an advertisement for a fast-food hamburger chain: "Where's the beef?"

Stung by the criticisms, Hart sought to be more specific about his proposals for economic and military reform as the spring primary season wore on. But the more specific Hart got, the more difficulty he seemed to have generating enthusiasm. He went on to capture several key primary victories, most notably in Massachusetts, Wisconsin, Ohio and California. But Hart's wins tended to come in states where delegates were divided proportionally among the candidates, making for a smaller payoff for victory. Mondale, by contrast, chose the locations of his primary victories carefully. He carried states in which the winner took all—or at least a large percentage—of the delegates at stake. Aided further by his overall strength in state caucuses, Mondale staved off Hart's surge to emerge with his predicted nomination victory intact.

Campaign 1988

Hart's unexpectedly strong showing in 1984 whetted his appetite for another run, and he wasted little time preparing for 1988. Buoyed by the exposure he gained in his first campaign, he began the race as the early front-runner. But from the very outset, that status was somewhat shaky.

Consultants, party spokesmen and reporters all debated whether Hart had emerged from the 1984 race with a core of loyal supporters—or whether he was simply the lucky beneficiary of dissatisfaction with Mondale and the Democratic establishment. Critics continued to complain that his new-ideas strategy lacked substance, and that he did not project a strong sense of identity.

Hart sought to address the complaints about substance by issuing major statements on education, trade, the economy, defense and foreign policy. To show his sense of roots, he distributed an autobiographical essay about the history of his family and upbringing shortly before making a widely publicized trip home to Ottawa, Kan.

But his efforts were undermined in early May when, less than a month after he made his official entrance into the race, the *Miami Herald* reported that Hart had been alone in his Washington, D.C., townhouse with an attractive, 29-year-old actress and model named Donna Rice.

Hart angrily denied the *Herald* account, criticizing the surveillance and contending that Rice had departed the townhouse through a back door, unnoticed by the reporters. But the story soon took on a life of its own, fueled by subsequent reports that Hart had taken an overnight ocean cruise to Bimini with Rice in April.

Hart soon started trying to downplay the incident, but, when that tack failed, he tried addressing the issue head on. In a May 6 press conference held in Hanover, N. H., he opened himself up to a number of intensely personal questions—including whether he had ever committed adultery. "I don't have to answer that question," he replied.

With polls showing Hart's popular support to be plummeting, it was clear his campaign was on the ropes. When the *Washington Post* presented a top Hart aide with allegations about another Hart liaison, this one with a Washington woman, the candidate decided that the campaign had been too hard-hit to recover. "I refuse to subject my family and my friends and innocent people and myself to further rumors and gossip," Hart said in announcing his withdrawal in Denver on May 8. ". . . Under the present circumstances, this campaign cannot go on."

His departure did not end speculation about his political future, however; stories continually cropped up suggesting Hart might be interested in returning to the race. Hart's closest confidants sometimes seemed to fuel the rumor mill. During the summer several aides hinted that Hart might be considering coming back into the campaign. But the rumors met with a critical response, and shortly thereafter Hart debunked the rumors.

Not content with a spot along the sidelines, Hart sought to keep his hand in national affairs by lecturing around the country and writing articles. In September, he appeared on the ABC-TV news program "Nightline," ruling out plans to re-enter the race, apologizing to friends and supporters and acknowledging that his association with Rice had been "a very, very bad mistake."

The "Nightline" appearance caused a calm on the Hart watch for a time. But just when it seemed the talk had finally died down, Hart brought himself back to the fore. On Dec. 15, a blustery winter day, he announced in Concord, N.H., that he was reviving his candidacy.

"I don't have a national headquarters or staff," he said. "I don't have any money. I don't have pollsters or consultants or media advisers or political endorsements. But I have something even better. I have the power of ideas, and I can govern this country. . . . Let's let the people decide. I'm back in the race."

Not surprisingly, Hart's return met with negative reactions from the national Democratic hierarchy. Many of his fellow Democratic contenders also took umbrage at Hart's suggestion that he had returned to the race only because no national leaders had entered and adopted his ideas.

For his part, Hart said he re-entered the race with the intention of winning. He pledged in a television interview that he would not "perpetuate a campaign that's not going anywhere." But he also acknowledged that he could make a contribution even if his bid ended without a nomination victory. If he could finish the race with enough delegates to influence the policy positions adopted at the Democrats' national convention, he said, "that would be a major achievement."

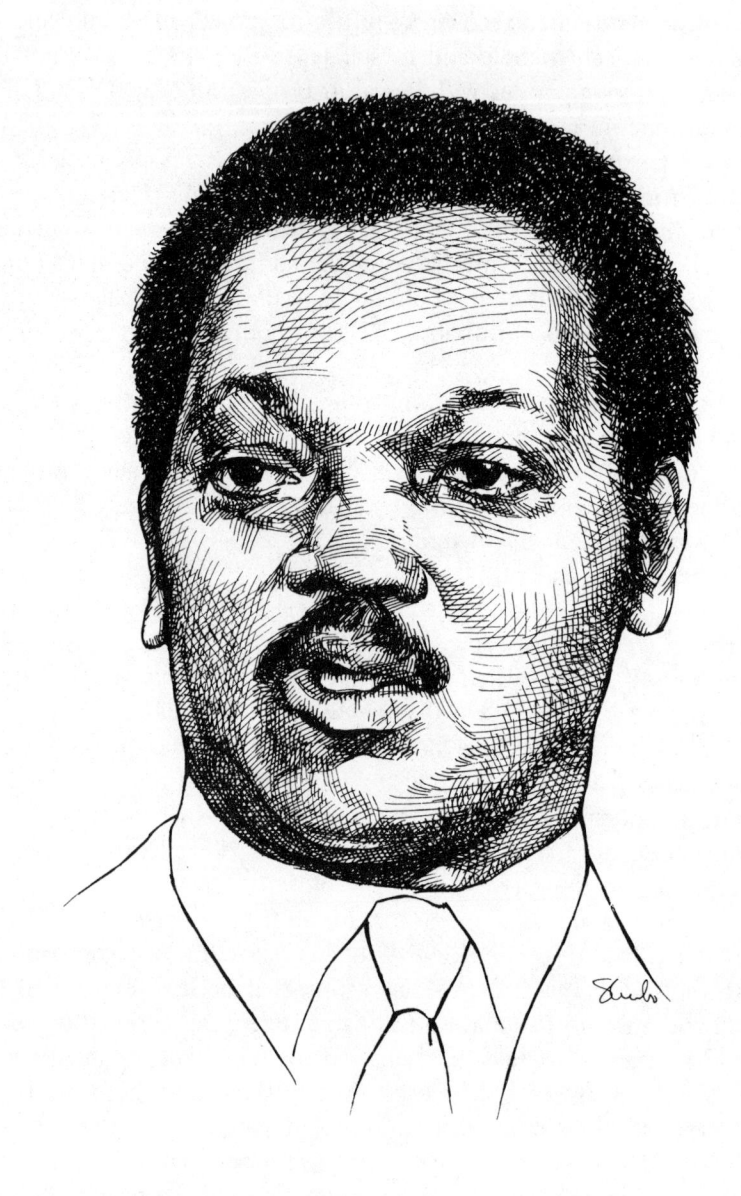

JESSE JACKSON

Working Within the Party
For Stronger White Support

The Rev. Jesse Jackson, now waging his second consecutive bid for the presidency, is a significantly different kind of candidate this time around.

Gone is the man who once depended almost exclusively on his fellow blacks to spark his campaign. The Baptist preacher has hardly forsaken the black Democrats who formed his core constituency in 1984. But Jackson has taken great pains in 1988 to add other colors to his "rainbow coalition," refashioning his rhetoric and revising his campaign schedule to reach out—with some demonstrable success—for more white support.

Gone, too, is the embittered candidate who bristled at the rules governing the nomination process, badmouthed the Democratic Party and threatened to walk out to form one of his own. The Jackson on display in 1988 has adopted a comparatively conciliatory tone, touting party loyalty and stepping forward to referee whenever his Democratic rivals grow too hostile toward each other in debate.

What has not changed very much are the odds on Jackson's winning. Those odds are heavily influenced by racial considerations.

"This country is not ready to nominate a black man or woman for the presidency," former Democratic Party chairman Robert Strauss said in 1987. "It's not fair, and I'm not proud of it, but it's the real world." Many would decry the state of affairs Strauss describes, but relatively few would disagree.

But if Jackson is unlikely to reach the winner's circle, he is in little danger of falling to the back of the pack. A commanding presence capable of igniting large crowds with his rhythmic and impassioned oratory, he began his campaign with an intense and committed base of support that his opponents have struggled to match.

Jesse Louis Jackson

Profession: Clergyman; civil rights activist.
Born: Oct. 8, 1941, Greenville, S.C.
Home: Chicago, Ill.
Religion: Baptist.
Education: Attended University of Illinois, 1959-60; North Carolina Agricultural and Technical State University, B.A., 1964; attended Chicago Theological Seminary.
Career: Ordained Baptist minister, 1968; founder and national director, Southern Christian Leadership Conference's Operation Breadbasket, 1966-71; founder and executive director, People United to Serve Humanity (PUSH), 1971-present (currently on leave); sought Democratic nomination for president, 1984.
Family: Wife, Jacqueline Lavinia Brown; five children.

Further, he enjoys remarkably high visibility in a field crowded with candidates who are hardly household names. Many American voters do not like Jackson or agree with him, but almost everybody knows who he is.

Jackson's political strengths make it seem all but certain that he will return to speak at the Democratic National Convention as he did four years ago and play perhaps an even more significant role there.

Jackson has attained his political heights without ever holding public office, as his critics are fond of pointing out. He has spent most of his life, however, involved in a political cause: civil rights.

Jackson was born and raised in Greenville, S.C., a town that embraced segregation but escaped the most violent forms of racism found in other parts of the South. The young Jackson bore more than just the scars of segregation, however. His mother was not married when he was born, and he suffered humiliation in his childhood because of his illegitimate birth. That pain was eased somewhat when his mother married Charles Jackson, a janitor whose salary helped keep the family out of dire poverty.

"I had to fight just for personal dignity," Jesse Jackson has said about his past. " . . . Fighting for my dignity was the first phase. Now I fight for the dignity of others."

Jackson became active in the civil rights struggle during college in the early 1960s. He originally wanted to attend the University of Illinois, but he later claimed that the school was bigoted and that the coaches of the Illinois football team would not permit him to play quarterback because of the color of his skin. So he turned instead to North Carolina Agricultural and Technical (A & T) State University, traditionally a heavily black school. He quickly established himself as a leader in the civil rights movement on campus, leading sit-ins and other demonstrations. It did not take long before Jackson was president of a statewide civil rights student organization.

He also attracted attention at A & T in other ways. He assumed the job of quarterback he had coveted at Illinois and served as student body president.

After graduation, Jackson moved back to Illinois to attend the Chicago Theological Seminary. The move proved crucial to his career. It led him to become ordained as a Baptist minister in 1968 and brought him to Chicago, which has been his home and main battleground ever since.

It was during his stay at the seminary that Jackson joined up with the Rev. Dr. Martin Luther King Jr. and the Southern Christian Leadership Conference (SCLC). When King led a march in Selma, Ala., in 1965, Jackson organized a group of fellow students to make the trip south. There he began to attract attention from King and others as a potentially potent force in the movement.

"He immediately took charge," said Atlanta Mayor Andrew Young, who served as one of King's top lieutenants. "It was almost like he came in and, while people were lining up, he wouldn't get in line. He would start lining people up."

Jackson's efforts began to stir some resentment among King's top aides—resentment that, among some, lingers until this day—but he won the confidence of King, who decided to enlist Jackson in his attack on economic inequality in the North. In 1966 King named Jackson head of the Chicago chapter of Operation Breadbasket, a program intended to encourage economic self-help for blacks. Jackson used his position to help wage a militant fight against housing segregation in and around the city.

After Memphis

King's assassination at a Memphis motel in 1968 marked the beginning of a new phase in Jackson's career, bringing him more attention from the national media and increased enmity from some followers of the slain civil rights leader.

Jackson's actions in the immediate aftermath of the slaying are largely responsible for that enmity. He said, or was reported to have said, that he was on the motel balcony when King was shot, and that he cradled the dying civil rights leader in his arms. Others on the scene have disputed that account, and Jackson has since denied making that statement. But he has never been able to shake completely free of the controversy. The fact that Jackson was the only member of King's entourage who made himself available to the press after the murder fueled further criticism that Jackson was overly interested in self-promotion.

Jackson only made matters worse when, upon his return to Chicago a few days after the shooting, he made television appearances and delivered an address to the City Council wearing a garment he claimed was smeared with King's blood.

The media was soon pointing to Jackson as King's successor in the civil rights movement, a gesture that did not sit well with King's lieutenants. The Rev. Ralph David Abernathy was King's annointed successor but received far less attention than Jackson.

For the next few years relations between Jackson and Abernathy soured, and Jackson finally split with the SCLC in 1971. Things came to a head in a fight between the two over funds from a black trade fair in Chicago dubbed "Black Expo." Jackson, who was suspended from the SCLC for 60 days, quit to form his own civil rights operation, People United to Save Humanity (PUSH). The organization was later renamed People United to Serve Humanity.

Abernathy is now one of the few from King's inner circle to support Jackson's presidential campaign. But he has been less than enthusiastic about his endorsement of Jackson at times. Referring to Jackson and the events that followed King's death, Abernathy has said: "I hope God has forgiven him. He has had time to pray. He is a different man now. It would be wrong to hold it against him."

Like Operation Breadbasket, Operation PUSH was intended to attack economic inequality, first in Chicago, and later on a national scale.

Jackson maintained that what blacks and other economically disadvantaged groups needed was not another government program, but a role in the economy that more accurately reflected their numbers. If a group in society accounted for a certain percentage of a company's sales, say 15 percent, then they should also account for 15 percent of the company's executives, 15 percent of the company's wholesalers, and so on.

PUSH has never been considered a particularly well-organized operation, but Jackson's leadership role has helped guarantee that it would receive considerable attention. Jackson himself has been criticized for not doing the detail work necessary to ensure that his initiatives are fully implemented. He has acknowledged his weaknesses as a hands-on manager but says his most important role with PUSH is to motivate people to do good work. "I am a tree shaker, not a jam maker," he often says.

Jackson first began shaking trees locally. Aided by local black

Jesse Jackson addressing the 1984 Democratic National Convention.

clergy, Operation Breadbasket organized effective boycotts against grocery stores in Chicago ghettos that sold inferior merchandise or hired few black employees. Jackson soon began employing the boycott tactic in a variety of other fights. If he felt a store did not sell enough products made in the black community, Jackson would try to dissuade black shoppers from patronizing the store. He met with considerable success.

Operation Breadbasket's first national effort was against the A & P food chain. When A & P refused to meet Jackson's demands to hire more blacks and display the products of black-owned firms, the group launched a boycott and engaged in picketing. The company eventually signed an agreement with Jackson to promote more blacks into high-level positions.

Jackson continued such tactics with Operation PUSH, conducting national campaigns against major corporations such as Coca-Cola, Philip Morris and Heublein. In many cases, his efforts resulted in millions of dollars in business for blacks. But his tactics have not always been embraced by the black community. When he challenged Anheuser-Busch brewery in 1982, for example, he was denounced by some local black business owners in St. Louis, who had been satisfied with the Missouri-based company's own campaign to hire more blacks.

PUSH has also received considerable attention for its self-help program intended to motivate students—PUSH for Excellence (PUSH-EXCEL). Touring the nation, Jackson has impressed numerous school audiences—students, teachers and administrators—with his charm and charisma. On many occasions he has brought students to the point of tears, chanting, "I am somebody." He calls upon students, teachers, administrators and parents alike to work harder to improve the quality of education.

That message has proven as pleasing to some of Jackson's more conservative critics as it has to his most ardent supporters. Still, the PUSH-EXCEL program has not been entirely free of controversy. The Carter administration began funding the program in 1977, after PUSH-EXCEL received favorable attention on national television. But some critics wondered aloud about whether the funding was used properly, and others questioned whether the program could have any lasting impact.

Joseph A. Califano Jr., who served as secretary of health, education and welfare under Jimmy Carter and helped channel funds to PUSH, later wrote in a book that "the problem with Jackson's program was his inability to sustain its momentum when he was not present." In 1981 the Reagan administration cut funds to the point that PUSH-EXCEL stopped seeking federal money altogether.

Chicago Politics

Jackson's involvement with the PUSH programs gave him entrée into the world of Chicago politics, ruled for 21 years by Mayor Richard J. Daley's iron fist.

Jackson and Daley had their share of confrontations. One of their first clashes came in 1970, when Jackson was in the middle of an anti-hunger campaign. Jackson pushed the state government to spend more on food programs and then called on the City Council in Chicago to spend $35 million to fight hunger. Daley easily blocked Jackson's proposition.

The following year Jackson decided to challenge "Pharaoh Daley" for re-election. His entrance into the race effectively pre-empted any other opposition to the mayor, but Jackson did not always seem committed to his challenge. Daley wound up winning a fifth term easily after Jackson's name was thrown from the ballot.

Not long after, Jackson began making forays into national politics. In 1972 he started a brief and unsuccessful effort to form a Liberation Party to support a black presidential candidate. But his prime interest remained Chicago. At the Democratic National Convention that same year, Jackson managed a measure of revenge against Daley. Teaming with a liberal white alderman from the city's North Side, Jackson challenged the state's delegation to the convention on the grounds that Daley's machine had improperly picked the delegates. Daley lost out on a narrow convention vote, and the group supported by Jackson was seated.

After Daley's death, Jackson's stature in Chicago seemed to grow. He received considerable media attention in 1983 when the city elected a black mayor named Harold Washington, even though Jackson had not played a key role in Washington's campaign.

Late in 1987, however, Jackson's image as a city power broker suffered a setback when Washington died suddenly of a heart attack. When the City Council met to choose an acting mayor to serve out the remainder of Washington's term, Jackson threw his weight behind black Alderman Timothy Evans. A majority of the Council members supported another black alderman, Eugene Sawyer. The turmoil in Chicago might affect Jackson's presidential campaign. Before Washington's death, Jackson was expected to arrive at the convention with a strong ally influencing the Illinois delegation. The man now leading Chicago is a man Jackson tried to defeat.

'I'm a Third World Person'

Although Jackson's 1988 campaign is decidedly more mainstream and populist in tone than his 1984 bid, he has still staked out positions to the left of his rivals in the Democratic field.

At a time when "fiscal conservative" appears to be the most popular label to wear, Jackson unabashedly bears the banner of increased federal spending. Few Democrats go near the term "industrial policy" that was bantered about a few years ago, but Jackson urges the creation of a national investment bank to rebuild the country's infrastructure.

His program also calls for a shift in economic priorities. "The Japanese are making Hondas and Toyotas and Sony and Panasonic VCRs [video cassette recorders]," Jackson argues. "President Reagan is making B-1 bombers. We're making what the world is not buying."

On matters of trade Jackson seems to take a different approach than most of his competitors. While many concentrate on steps that can be taken against the nation's trading partners to reduce the trade deficit, Jackson is quick to argue that part of the problem lies not with foreign governments, but with U.S.-based multinational corporations. "The number-one exporter from Taiwan," he says, "is General Electric."

Jackson is also at odds with most of his Democratic competition on foreign policy. While East-West relations tend to dominate the others' discussion, Jackson pays particular attention to North-South relations, calling, for example, for a massive effort to help develop Latin America. "I'm a Third World person," Jackson has said. "I grew up in an occupied zone [Greenville, S.C.] and had to negotiate with the superpower, really the colonial power."

Jackson's attitude toward Israel is perhaps his most controversial foreign policy stand. Jackson insists that he supports "Israel's right to exist within secure boundaries," but he also says that "there can be no peace in Israel unless there is justice for Palestinians." Jackson is one of the few national politicians who talk about creating a Palestinian homeland.

Jackson's stance on Israel has alienated Jewish voters, who represent a potent Democratic constituency. Many of them still remember his reference to New York City as "Hymie Town" during the 1984 campaign—a remark that gave him an image as an anti-Semite. Jackson's refusal to disavow the support of Muslim leader Louis Farrakhan—who enraged Jews by branding Judaism as a "gutter religion" and offering praise for Adolph Hitler—did little to improve his standing in the American Jewish community. Actually, many Jewish leaders were wary of Jackson's attitude toward Israel even before the previous campaign. Jackson angered many Jews when he took a well-publicized tour of the Middle East in 1979. During that trip, Jackson met with Arab leaders, such as Syrian President Hafez Assad, and voiced complaints about Israeli policies. The image that many remember from that trip is of Jackson embracing Yasir Arafat, leader of the Palestinian Liberation Organization (PLO).

Since that trip to the Middle East, Jackson has become something of a self-appointed world ambassador. While many of his critics say his trips amount to nothing more than opportunities for self-promotion, his efforts have nonetheless earned him some favorable reviews. On his trip to Reykjavik, Iceland, in 1986, Jackson was able to force a brief dialogue with Soviet leader Mikhail S. Gorbachev about the plight of Soviet Jews.

Perhaps Jackson's most memorable international journey came late in 1983, when he traveled to Syria to help secure the release of captured U.S. airman Lt. Robert O. Goodman.

Jackson, who has never held a public office, can boast that he has met with more living world leaders than any of his rivals. If deceased leaders are counted, he quipped at one debate in 1987, then Vice President George Bush may have surpassed him.

Campaign Strategy

By polling some 18 percent of the 18.2 million Democratic primary votes cast in the 1984 race for his party's nomination, Jackson ensured himself a place as an influential spokesman for blacks within the Democratic Party. His success in improving upon that performance and enhancing his influence will depend heavily on his ability to re-energize his core black constituency. That may not be so easy as it might seem.

Jackson did not enjoy monolithic support in the black community in his first campaign. By the time he got his late-starting effort off the ground, many influential black leaders had already signed on with the

Democratic front-runner, former vice president Walter F. Mondale. In early Democratic primary states such as Alabama and Georgia, Jackson drew no better than a bare majority of the black vote. But his message of black pride eventually took hold, and by the end of the primary season he was regularly pulling in 80 to 90 percent of the black vote.

Jackson's performance convinced many black leaders of his credibility; aided further by the fact that the 1988 Democratic field does not contain a white candidate with Mondale's strong links to the civil rights movement, Jackson began this campaign with most of the black political hierarchy in his corner. Still, some have remained unconvinced.

Jackson has long been criticized in civil rights circles for having an excessive ego, and some leaders still feel that Jackson is more interested in promoting himself than in promoting a cause. Still others refuse to support him because they do not think he has the ability to win or the qualifications to serve as president.

"I have said that I don't believe he can win because I believe the rainbow [coalition] is a myth," said Mayor Coleman Young of Detroit. "I think there is no substantial group of white people who are supporting Jesse. It's various shades of black, that's the rainbow he's talking about."

Atlanta Mayor Andrew Young says that there is "a major difference" between running for office and running a movement. "I think Jesse can legitimately say he's run movements."

Jackson also has to worry about the possibility that there will be less enthusiasm for his candidacy among his core constituency than in 1984, both because his message of protest has been toned down, and because those voters may feel they sent their "message" in the last campaign.

"You can only run the first major black presidential campaign once," says Thomas E. Cavanaugh, a former analyst with the Joint Center for Political Studies, a Washington, D.C.-based black political think tank.

It is clear that if that enthusiasm wanes, it will have an important impact. Blacks make up 12 percent of the nation's population, but they cast 18 percent of the Democratic primary ballots in 1984, according to a study by the *New York Times*. Those record-setting numbers were no doubt inspired by Jackson.

For his part, Jackson recognizes the potential for sag in his black support and urges black voters to "do what the papers say you won't do."

Beyond building up his core constituency, Jackson has made a major effort to court white support. The *New York Times* study of the 1984 primary results showed that Jackson won the support of more than three of every four blacks who voted, but only one in 20 white votes. In general, he ran well in areas where there was a sizable black population—in the South and in urban centers such as Chicago, New York, Philadelphia and Washington. In the more rural American heartland, he fared poorly.

To improve upon that showing he has expanded his message of black empowerment to include the economically depressed of all races. "The purpose of the campaign in 1984 was to empower blacks both nationally and within the Democratic Party," says Cavanaugh. "This time his campaign has a more populist theme."

In his stump speeches Jackson argues that "yesterday's fights" against "racial violence" have been largely won. Because such violence is illegal, he says, it can be dealt with. "But economic violence is legal," he argues. "Foreclosing farms: legal. Closing plants: legal. Bringing in products from countries ruled by right-wing dictators and made by sweatshop labor working for slave wages: legal."

Jackson has tried to take his message directly to a new audience—the "victims" of "economic violence." Since the 1984 election, Jackson has been a familiar figure at farm and labor rallies. It was not terribly surprising that Jackson indicated he would undertake another presidential campaign at a Labor Day rally in impoverished coal and steel country in western Pennsylvania.

"When they close down the plant and lock the gates the lights go out," he told one group of striking mill workers in 1987. "And when the lights go out, we all look amazingly similar in the dark."

Jackson has also changed the tone of his rhetoric in the 1988 election, an alteration that may further aid him in attracting white votes. In his first presidential bid, Jackson campaigned as an outsider, registering harsh criticisms of the Democratic Party. He was particularly displeased with the Democrats' delegate-selection rules, which gave considerable influence to "insiders"—the party and elected officials, known as "superdelegates," who went strongly for Mondale—and set primary and caucus vote thresholds that Jackson felt robbed him of his fair delegate share.

Now Jackson sounds like more of an insider. "I want the party to win," he has said. "We need to heal the wounds of the party, to maximize what we have in common." When Democratic candidates began criticizing one another at several debates, it was Jackson who spoke up and told them to concentrate on the issues facing the country.

The less-critical tone that Jackson has taken on may be aimed at reducing the high negative rating he receives in many polls, but it is also probably true that he has less reason to be critical of the nominating process in 1988 than in 1984. Rather than dwell on rules that hurt him last time—which have been left largely untouched—Jackson has tended to revel in changes in the primary and caucus calendar that could benefit him enormously. Most importantly, Jackson stands to gain from changes that left the South, his strongest region, voting en masse on March 8, known as "Super Tuesday." The Southern bloc vote was viewed as a potential boon to Jackson from the moment Super Tuesday was conceived, because it could catapult him into the front of the Democratic pack in the delegate count, giving him both attention and momentum.

Even if Jackson receives the same votes he received in 1984, he will be in a strong position, particularly if a handful of candidates split the white vote. In Mississippi, for example, Jackson won 30 percent of the delegates in 1984; competing against several candidates, he could have won the state. And the same is true in other areas. In Maryland he won 23 percent of the delegates in 1984; in Georgia he won 24 percent.

Personality Is Key

Jackson has made several other changes in his approach for the 1988 campaign. Learning from the last outing, when he had a virtually nonexistent campaign apparatus, he has tightened his organization. Jackson has also revamped his fund raising, replacing his 1984 emphasis on passing the hat in black churches with the more sophisticated and efficient technique of direct mail.

He has also sought to soothe key constituent groups—such as Jews—whose feathers he ruffled last time around. Jackson has addressed Jewish forums, talked with editors of Jewish publications and actively sought to involve Jewish activists in his campaign. Those efforts may help him blunt some of the criticism he faced in the Jewish community.

Still, personality rather than organization is likely to be the crucial factor for Jackson. "I think Jesse is the campaign," said Bert Lance, a Jackson adviser who worked as budget director in the Carter administration.

How Jackson is dealt with is of great concern within the party for several reasons. The most obvious is the need to win black votes in November. Democrats also have to wonder what lies ahead for Jackson if his second effort fails. Jackson could campaign again, but a third try could relegate him to the status of a perennial candidate. Without another campaign, though, would he be able to find a suitable platform within the party to promote his views?

But in the long run, how Jackson fares in 1988 may be judged more critically by his peers than by Jackson himself. He views this contest as part of a broader crusade. "This isn't just a campaign," he said in 1987. "It's a mission. My future doesn't depend upon what happens in one state, or two states, or even one election. In a real sense, I'm running every day, every year."

But what Jackson will ask, and what others in the party will be willing to listen to, are very much matters of speculation. Jackson's candidacy has been criticized, even by blacks, for actually weakening the position of black voters in the party, because, it is argued, other candidates will not even attempt to woo a bloc they feel is already lost to Jackson. But there is little doubt that other candidates could be convinced to woo Jackson.

Jackson gains an additional advantage from the configuration of the 1988 Democratic field. And without the emergence of a clear-cut front-runner, the vote could be split to Jackson's advantage. The more the vote is splintered, the better chance Jackson has of wielding influence.

In a season dominated by questions about character, Jackson, like Gary Hart, has been confronted with rumors of extramarital affairs. But many observers say that the national press is unwilling to level harsh criticisms at Jackson because they fear they will be accused of racism.

Jackson, for his part, has responded to such questions by saying that matters of faithfulness are "between the candidate, his or her family, their conscience and their God."

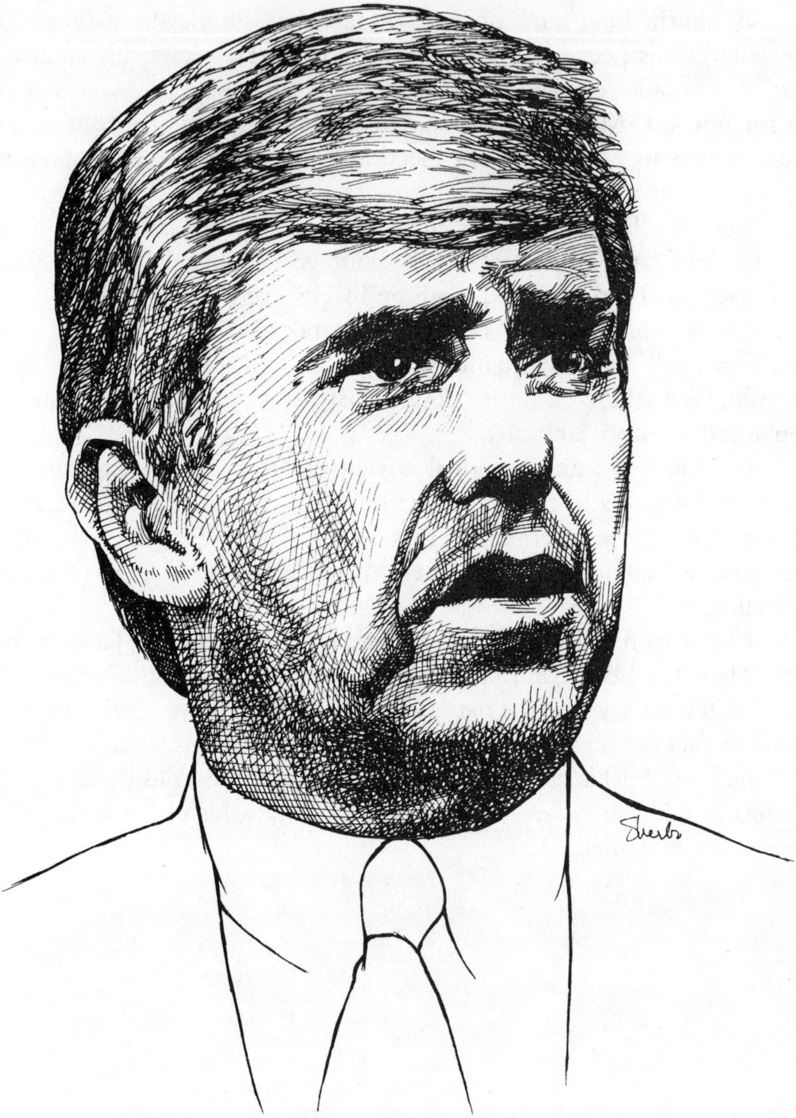

JACK KEMP

Opening the Party And Moving It Right

Republican Rep. Jack F. Kemp of New York has a tricky balancing act on his hands. In seeking the GOP nomination for the presidency in 1988, Kemp has sought to portray himself as the heir apparent to Ronald Reagan: He hopes to revivify the coalition of conservatives that helped nominate Reagan in 1980 and played a vital part in his two nationwide victories.

At the same time, however, Kemp wants to build beyond the core Reagan constituency, broadening the base of the Republican Party to include blue-collar workers, minorities and others who have generally been considered off limits to conservative candidates since the New Deal. "I don't want the Republican Party to be an all-white party, an all-white-collar party, a business party or a middle-class party," Kemp said on one of his stops along the 1988 presidential trail.

The two-pronged strategy that Kemp is employing in his White House bid has also marked his 17-year House career. Kemp has always fit in comfortably with colleagues who see the Soviet Union as an evil empire, swear allegiance to the space-based anti-missile system and support increased federal spending for the military. But he has never been a leader on most of the key questions of social policy so important to the hard-right conservative constituency. And his crusade on behalf of supply-side economics—the issue that vaulted him from back-bench anonymity in the House onto the national stage—is an all-out affront to traditional conservative economic orthodoxy.

Kemp's swipes at conservative articles of faith and his efforts to cater to traditionally Democratic voters have earned him attention as a politician who does not fall readily into set categories. But those tendencies have also left him in a bit of a bind politically. Whether he likes it or not, the Republican primary and caucus electorate that stands

Jack French Kemp

Profession: Professional football player; radio and television commentator.
Born: July 13, 1935, Los Angeles, Calif.
Home: Hamburg, N.Y.
Religion: Presbyterian.
Education: Occidental College, B.A., 1957.
Political Career: U.S. House of Representatives, 1971-present.
Military: Army Reserve, 1958-62.
Family: Wife, Joanne Main; four children.
House Committees: Education and Labor, 1971-75; Select Committee on Small Business, 1973-75; Appropriations, 1975-present; Budget, 1981-87; Select Committee on Children, Youth and Families, 1987-present.

to judge his presidential candidacy is still a predominantly white, white-collar, middle-class, business-oriented group, and those people have not embraced Kemp's forays off the reservation all that warmly. As a result, Kemp has found himself well behind the GOP front-runners, Vice President George Bush and Senate Minority Leader Robert Dole, despite nearly two years of active (if undeclared) campaigning.

Kemp may yet catch fire. Even some of the front-runners' staunchest supporters acknowledge that Kemp could move into the breach should either one of those two candidates stumble and fall. Many Republicans are loath to discount the chances of a man who has never lost an election before.

But whatever fate befalls Kemp's candidacy, one thing is certain: It will not lack for enthusiasm. A former star quarterback for professional football's Buffalo Bills, Kemp pursues politics with an athletic intensity that suggests he never really left professional sports. As more than one Kemp observer has noted, it sometimes appears as though the feisty 52-year-old gets a physical "high" from competitive debating. "It's not that he just believes," a longtime Kemp aide once said. "It's that he truly wants the beliefs he has to win out over other beliefs."

A Well-Armed Dove

Kemp makes no bones about his bid for the support of Reagan conservatives. "I am the only Republican running who was for Ronald Reagan in 1980," he has said. "I am the only Republican running who helped author the platform upon which Ronald Reagan ran in 1980 and 1984."

And in some respects, Kemp is well positioned to cater to the GOP's most conservative wing. His views on defense and foreign policy, for example, place him firmly in the conservative tradition. Although he did little in the way of serious committee work on defense and foreign policy matters throughout much of his House career, Kemp has argued consistently for higher levels of military spending as a member of the Appropriations Committee.

"They say I'm a hawk, but I'm a dove, a heavily armed dove," Kemp once said. In 1980, when President Carter began to take a tougher line on U.S.-Soviet relations, Kemp dismissed the president's actions as "the most dangerous kind of international posturing; the making of an empty threat."

In 1981, during the height of his influence on tax policy, Kemp took over as ranking Republican on the Appropriations subcommittee dealing with foreign aid. Surprising critics who figured Kemp would shun the tedious work of the subcommittee and leave the serious decisions to somebody else, he proved adept at working out compromises to protect administration-requested funding for military aid. Kemp got Democrats to accept those funding levels in exchange for support of international development programs.

Perhaps his most vocal role on foreign aid has been as a defender of Reagan's policies in Central America. A congressional adviser to the Kissinger Commission, he fought hard throughout the 98th Congress (1983-85) for the administration's requested level of military aid for El Salvador. The Appropriations Committee in 1984 rejected his amendment to provide the full level of Central America funding, but he eventually won much of that back on the House floor.

During debate over the fiscal 1986 foreign aid budget, which was contained within an omnibus spending bill, Kemp grumbled about budget cutters who put a halt to President Reagan's four-year buildup of military assistance to friendly countries overseas. "We have a lot of allies we have to be concerned about," Kemp said. "Cutting security assistance undercuts our own interests around the world. I don't think isolationism is the answer to saving the budget."

Not surprisingly, Kemp was a big supporter of Lt. Col. Oliver L. North, the National Security Council officer who took charge of the Iran-contra arms-for-hostages deal. "In six days," Kemp said, following North's testimony before the special congressional committees convened to investigate the Iran-contra affair, "he did more to build support for democracy in our hemisphere than the State Department and the Congress have done in six years." In the wake of North's testimony before the congressional committees, Kemp called upon President Reagan to double his request for additional aid to the anti-government rebels in Nicaragua.

Later in 1987 Kemp voiced sharp criticism of the Central American peace plan put forward by Costa Rican President Oscar Arias. Kemp said the plan lacked the teeth necessary to pressure the Sandinistas into carrying out fundamental changes in Nicaragua. Specifically, Kemp urged that any regional peace plan should include an assurance that Soviet military support for the Sandinistas would end.

Kemp also delivered a veiled threat to Arias, saying that it would be "very difficult" to justify U.S. economic aid to Costa Rica if that country was seen to be lobbying against American aid to the contras.

Kemp took a hard-line approach to the U.S.-Soviet treaty banning intermediate-range nuclear forces, which Reagan and Soviet leader Mikhail Gorbachev signed in December 1987. Kemp complained that the Reagan administration, along with other North Atlantic Treaty Organization (NATO) governments, had painted itself into a corner. "We have exaggerated the virtues of arms control to calm the voices of domestic dissent," Kemp said in a speech given at the Heritage Foundation, a conservative think-tank in Washington. "And now the Soviets are calling our bluff."

Echoing a fundamental conservative concern, Kemp also warned that agreement on a treaty might lull the Western public into a false sense of security in the face of a Soviet military threat. He asked: "How are the democracies to sustain the political basis for correcting military disparities and repairing our defense shortcomings in a climate of treaty-signing ceremonies, summit handshakes and self-congratulatory smiles?"

But Kemp saves his strongest rhetoric for the Strategic Defense Initiative (SDI), the Reagan administration's plan to erect a shield to protect the United States against attack from Soviet missiles. "The

Strategic Defense Initiative is the greatest peace initiative of our time," Kemp said in his presidential campaign announcement speech. He has also said that "the central drama of our time is the struggle between democracy and totalitarianism, but the central dilemma of our day is that we lie defenseless against Soviet missiles."

Early in 1987 Kemp took part in a skirmish over the interpretation of SDI. He joined a group of conservatives who voiced concern that the costly program would be doomed politically unless the administration demonstrated that some defenses—necessarily limited in scope—could be deployed within the next several years. The group urged Reagan to carry the battle for SDI funding to the public, before support for the program began to slip away.

Social Agenda

In the realm of social policy, Kemp also bears some important conservative earmarks. He supports school prayer, opposes the Equal

Jack Kemp has campaigned as a champion of supply-side economics.

Rights Amendment and forced busing, and urges handgun owners to take political action to ward off efforts by the "anti-gun lobby" to compromise the right to keep and bear firearms.

Kemp is a staunch foe of abortion, and over the past several years he has teamed with GOP Sen. Orrin G. Hatch of Utah to promote legislation denying federal family planning funds to clinics that provide abortion counseling or referrals. Kemp and Hatch have sought to attach that measure to legislation reauthorizing Title X of the Public Health Service Act. Kemp also worked to ensure that there would be an anti-abortion plank in the 1984 Republican platform.

Further, Kemp has sought to discourage abortion practices overseas. In 1985 he won passage of an amendment to the fiscal 1986 foreign aid authorization bill that barred U.S. contributions to any international agency that "supports or participates in the management of programs of coercive abortion or involuntary sterilization." Originally included in the fiscal 1985 supplemental appropriations bill, the measure was used by the Reagan administration to block U.S. support of the United Nations Fund for Population Activities because of that agency's alleged ties to China's mandatory family-planning programs.

Kemp has made his opposition to abortion a staple of his campaign, calling for a constitutional amendment to ban the practice. "I am consistently pro-life," he has said in stump speeches. "I believe that we need to recognize the dignity of all human beings born and unborn."

Path to Majority

But Kemp has seldom made the litmus-test social issues so important to the conservative movement his first priority. "In an economically healthy society," he has said, "a lot of the social problems conservatives worry about wouldn't be problems any more."

One reason Kemp has not made more of social issues during his congressional career is that he sees them as distractions in the effort to build a national Republican majority with the aid of working-class voters. He apparently feels that goal cannot be accomplished by pursuing some of the traditional strategies of conservatives in the GOP.

That much shows through in his attitude towards organized labor, a constituency of some significance in and around his Buffalo-area congressional district. While many conservatives are quick to denigrate the captains of the labor movement, Kemp urges caution. "This business of always calling labor 'big labor' or 'labor bosses' is wrong," he said in 1978. "We should have more respect for the American labor movement."

He was saying similar things during the early days of the Reagan administration, arguing against efforts to dismantle the Occupational Safety and Health Administration and telling an audience of conservatives that "attacking the New Deal is a mistake for us."

In 1984 Kemp made headlines back home when he refused to cross a picket line in Buffalo. A local building trades union was picketing to protest the use of scab labor in renovating the building that housed the Erie County Republican Executive Committee.

Another indication of Kemp's willingness to challenge conservative tradition is his habit of occasionally joining forces with liberals viewed as anathema by most members of the GOP's right wing.

He forged one such alliance with fellow New Yorker Robert Garcia, a liberal Democrat of Puerto Rican background who represents the blighted Bronx in the House. Kemp and Garcia teamed to push legislation promoting urban "enterprise zones," an idea Kemp borrowed from a pair of British economists. The bill would encourage development in impoverished urban areas by declaring tax moratoriums and easing regulatory restrictions. Kemp helped earn President Reagan's general support for the idea, but it has never really taken off in Congress. Although the Senate has passed a version of the proposal twice, the idea has never gone anywhere in the House.

Kemp also wants to aid the poor by encouraging their aspirations to home ownership. Toward that end, he has sponsored legislation to permit public housing tenant groups to join together to buy their dwellings from the federal government.

At a time when many conservatives find themselves at arms' length from black political leaders, Kemp stands out. "He's worked with me on the Ethiopian situation and has been very constructive on African aid," Democratic Rep. Julian C. Dixon, former chairman of the Congressional Black Caucus, told the *Washington Post*. "He is sensitive to the concerns of black members of Congress."

Off the Reservation

But it is Kemp's unyielding support for supply-side economics that marks probably his most radical departure from Republican tradition. While many old-line Republicans continued to preach the need to avoid deficit spending and balance the federal budget above all else, Kemp was veering off in a radical direction, arguing that across-the-board cuts in marginal tax rates would lead to economic expansion and ultimately bring in additional tax revenue. Despite criticism from the old guard, Kemp persuaded himself of the core assumptions of supply-side economics beyond the slightest doubt and converted the idea into a national crusade.

Specialists have been skeptical of Kemp's economic understanding ever since he began championing supply-side, even though he talks at a level of sophistication unusual for anyone in public office. By late 1987 even some of the conservative movement's most visible leaders were beginning to question Kemp's unflinching confidence in his economic prescription. "You don't get conservatives' juices flowing by saying you can eat three hot fudge sundaes a day and still lose weight," said conservative direct-mail specialist Richard Viguerie.

But Kemp has not let such grumbling sway him. He continues to profess faith in his crusade, sidestepping his critics like the tackle-dodging quarterback he used to be. In announcing his presidential candidacy, Kemp lashed out at those who "look to the future with such anxiety and such pessimism that they can only think of ideas which would impose austerity and pain...." He has also hit his opponents for the GOP nomination, accusing them of harboring an economic philosophy that is akin to "bitter pills and bitter medicine."

Swept by the Tide

It was not always that way. When Kemp first started out in politics, he recalls, he adhered firmly to the very philosophy he now holds in such contempt. "I was a traditional Republican when I started. I favored a balanced budget at all costs." He described his outlook as "a green-eyeshade mentality."

His ideas began to change, however, in the mid-1970s. The motor of change: his Buffalo-area district's slide into economic morass. "With unemployment at 14 to 15 percent in my area," Kemp said, "being a Republican talking about balancing the budget was bad politics and was, frankly, bad economics."

As a response to the situation in his House district, Kemp began taking a greater interest in legislative initiatives aimed at creating new jobs. He also developed an interest in the economic legacy of President

Kemp's Interest Group Ratings

Vote ratings by interest groups help to give a picture of Jack Kemp's orientation during his House career. This chart shows how often Kemp voted on key legislative issues in accordance with the positions of groups chosen to represent liberal, labor, business and conservative viewpoints. They are the Americans for Democratic Action (ADA), AFL-CIO, Chamber of Commerce of the United States (CCUS) and Americans for Constitutional Action (ACA) or American Conservative Union (ACU).

	ADA	AFL-CIO	CCUS	ACA	ACU
1971	16	18	—[1]	85	—
1972	25	36	89	70	—
1973	12	33	67	80	—
1974	17	30	50	79	—
1975	5	14	94	93	—
1976	5	22	82	85	—
1977	10	17	94	96	—
1978	15	15	88	96	—
1979	11	16	88	92	—
1980	6	12	75	86	—
1981	10	7	100	82	—
1982	15	25	74	78	—
1983	10	7	89	89	—
1984	10	15	87	75	—
1985	10	12	79	—	81[2]
1986	15	31	58	—	89
1987	4	11	100	—	94

[1] *CCUS did not compile vote records in some years.*
[2] *Congressional Quarterly began publishing ACU ratings in 1985.*

John F. Kennedy. Kemp touted Kennedy's 1963 tax cut and began borrowing from Kennedy's rhetoric as well. The phrase "a rising tide lifts all boats" still appears frequently in Kemp's writings and speeches.

But Kemp did not become a true believer in the curative powers of a massive cut in personal income taxes until one day in 1975, when *Wall Street Journal* columnist Jude Wanniski dropped by his office for a morning interview that finally ended in Kemp's dining room at midnight. Having undergone an almost religious conversion, Kemp began pursuing the low-tax, high-growth philosophy with a cheerleader's enthusiasm.

He wasted little time in trying to pitch it to the top leaders of his party. Kemp went to the Republican national convention in Kansas City with an offer for Ronald Reagan, who was then challenging President Gerald R. Ford for the GOP nomination. According to reports published later, Kemp and Wanniski pledged "four or five" additional delegates if Reagan would endorse the tax cut being sponsored by Kemp and GOP Sen. William V. Roth Jr. of Delaware. The plan reportedly was never actually taken to Reagan.

But a few months later Kemp's notion began showing up in Reagan's syndicated newspaper column. Kemp spent much of 1977 taking his idea on the road; it brought so much publicity that by the spring of 1978 the national press was full of reports about the former pro quarterback and his seemingly boundless supply-side zeal.

Still, Kemp would have to wait awhile before the idea came to legislative or political fruition. A modified version of Kemp's bill—offered by the Democrats—made it through the Senate in 1978 but went no further. The tax cut also came to a vote in the House but was defeated on a 240-178 party-line vote.

Also in 1978 the tax cut became the centerpiece campaign theme for the Republican Party. It met with less than spectacular results. GOP candidates around the country found the idea difficult to defend in debate, as Democrats scored points by arguing that the tax cut would enlarge the federal deficit, not shrivel it.

By 1980 the tide began to turn. Reagan endorsed the full-scale tax cut—30 percent over three years—and placed Kemp's name on a list of potential running mates. When Reagan won the White House that fall, several Kemp protégés were given top-level jobs in the Treasury Department.

The first year of Ronald Reagan's presidency was an extraordinary triumph for Kemp. For the first time, he had the opportunity to take to the inside track the ideas he had been pushing for from the outside.

"It was important for me to stop being a bomb-thrower, or an idea-thrower," Kemp told the *Washington Post*. "The things I had been fighting for were in the Reagan agenda. Now it was important for me to come in and be on the team and help move it into reality." Kemp sought and won the chairmanship of the House Republican Conference shortly after the 1980 elections.

Though he was without a senior position on any committee that handled the budget or tax-cut measures, he was clearly the single most important congressional force in their passage. New York Republican Rep. Barber B. Conable Jr. was the nominal GOP sponsor of the 1981 tax cut bill, but he simply offered what had been drafted at the White House. Kemp was in on the drafting.

At the end of July, when Congress cleared the bill cutting taxes by 25 percent over three years, he could claim a unique personal triumph. "Name any bill that ever went through like that," Kemp boasted shortly afterward. "No one has ever done it who wasn't on the Ways and Means Committee."

Six months later, when Reagan proposed a budget that preserved all the tax cuts despite a projected deficit of more than $100 billion, Kemp initially praised Reagan for his courage. "We don't worship at the altar of a balanced budget," he said repeatedly. He urged Reagan to move up the 1982 and 1983 reductions six months, from July to January.

Parting Ways

But as the administration began to ponder selective tax increases to keep the deficit down, Kemp began staking out an independent role. As a member of the House Budget Committee in 1982, he called the Reagan deficit projections "phony," breaking with Budget Director David A. Stockman, his ally in drafting the economic changes the year before. He proposed an amendment in committee to make a "baseline adjustment" that would assume faster economic growth and thus lower deficits. The amendment lost, 21-8.

The major break, however, was yet to come. In the spring of 1982 Reagan swallowed hard and agreed to support $98 billion worth of tax increases over three years to lower the deficit. Kemp's basic reductions in the personal tax rate were left intact, but many of the specialized business cuts were proposed for elimination.

Kemp wasted no time making himself the leader of the opposition. "The country simply cannot stand up to such a dramatic tax increase in its depressed condition," he said. He launched a national campaign of public speeches and newspaper articles against the tax bill and insisted that Reagan would not be crippled politically by a defeat on one issue.

Other Republicans, however, did not see it that way. Sen. Paul Laxalt of Nevada, one of Reagan's closest political confidants, accused Kemp of a "lack of loyalty." Sen. Robert Dole of Kansas—now one of Kemp's rivals for the Republican presidential nomination—accused Kemp of "Vietnamizing" the Reagan presidency. Dole had a special reason for feeling the sting of Kemp's criticism; his Finance Committee had drafted the bill.

But Kemp stood his ground, arguing that it would have been "cowardly to believe so strongly and not say anything." He and his coalition of supply-side loyalists ultimately gained the support of House Republicans, although many of those were more concerned about the political implications of an election-year tax boost than about the effects of the bill on economic policy. In any case, 103 Republicans stuck with Reagan and the bill passed easily.

In the months after the 1982 tax fight, Kemp was as aggressive as ever in defending his supply-side beliefs and arguing that the tight money policies of the Federal Reserve Board were stifling economic recovery. He said, "I don't think we ought to stop cutting taxes until the tax rate is down to 15 percent or 20 percent and the bottom rate on the poor is down to 5 percent or 6 percent."

If Kemp lost friends at the White House by fighting the tax bill, he seemed to gain new respect among members of the Republican right, who regarded the 1982 bill as a lamentable departure from Reagan's campaign platform. To many on the right, Kemp's crusade against the tax bill made more of an impression than his vote later in the year against a constitutional amendment to balance the federal budget. Kemp was one of only 20 House Republicans to oppose that measure.

Not content with promoting his tax-cutting philosophy on the domestic front, Kemp in the mid-1980s began to talk of fighting the battles abroad. He inveighed against the Reagan administration's attempts to require other countries to raise taxes as part of an economic austerity plan. In 1984 Congress approved a Kemp amendment barring the administration from withholding U.S. aid to enforce tax increases and other conditions mandated by the International Monetary Fund as a condition for receiving short-term loans.

Kemp did not play so clear-cut a role in the 1986 tax overhaul as he had in enacting the supply-side tax cuts. But he was instrumental in drumming up Republican support, and he was the House sponsor of one of the most prominent early revisions of the tax code.

He initially distanced himself from elements of President Reagan's proposal—saying, for example, that the 35 percent top tax rate was too high—but he helped get the bill through the House at a critical moment.

In late 1985 Kemp and most other House Republicans initially opposed the Democratic-drafted tax revision bill reported from the Ways and Means Committee, and they were successful in blocking the first effort to bring it up on the floor. Responding to Reagan's plea that the House GOP support the bill, Kemp dropped his opposition and parted with most Republican leaders after extracting a promise from Reagan that he would veto the final product if the biggest GOP complaints were not eventually addressed. In the end, after a conference committee produced a version that modified some of the House provisions and yielded a top individual tax rate of 28 percent, Kemp voted for it.

When he is not tangling with the tax code, Kemp often as not is airing his views about American monetary policy. He favors a return to the gold standard, arguing that it would help ensure low inflation and interest rates over the long term. A sharp critic of the policies of the Federal Reserve Board, Kemp has sponsored legislation to require the board to publicize its decisions when they are made.

Kemp's heavy focus on economic issues has obviously been a political boon for him; it enabled him to rise virtually overnight from obscurity in the House minority to a position of national stature, thereby paving the way for his presidential campaign.

But the economic emphasis has not come without cost. Kemp has had to struggle to show critics that he has command of a broader array of issues—and that he is not, as his detractors often claim, a "Jackie-One-Note."

Pursuing a Dream

While visions of the Oval Office have occupied Kemp's mind in recent years, he had a very different dream as a boy. Growing up in west Los Angeles, Kemp knew very early on that he wanted to make his future in the game of football.

"Some little boys want to be cowboys or firemen," Kemp once told a reporter. "I wanted to be a National Football League quarterback."

He found encouragement in the Kemp household. His father was an entrepreneur who started his own delivery truck company. His mother was a social worker, fluent in Spanish and armed with a degree in education from the University of California at Berkeley. Kemp recalls his parents as being "small-business-oriented Republicans." They raised their children as Christian Scientists, instilled in them conservative values and placed a premium on athletic competition.

Kemp received B's and C's in high school; he says he preferred sports to academics. When it came time to choose a college, he selected Occidental, a small liberal arts school in California. One major reason: He liked the T-formation offense employed by Occidental's football team.

Kemp majored in physical education at Occidental—taking a number of history courses as well—and established himself as one of the top small-school quarterbacks in the country. He also met his future wife, a cheerleader, one night at a fraternity party dance.

As some of his college acquaintances recall him, Kemp had a politician's concern for appearances and reputations long before he actually entered the political ring. "Jack was always concerned about his image, his reputation, doing things the right way," former Occidental roommate Jim Mora told a reporter for *Esquire* magazine. "It was important to him how he looked, his personal grooming, how he dressed."

Following college, Kemp was drafted in the 16th round by the Detroit Lions of the National Football League (NFL). But success did not come immediately. He bounced around from team to team for several years, hanging, in his words, "on the bottom rung of the NFL ladder."

It was only a temporary stay. Kemp hit his stride with the old Los Angeles Chargers, winning the league's most valuable player award in 1960. Five years later he again won most valuable player designation, this time as quarterback for the Buffalo Bills in the American Football League (AFL). Kemp led the Bills to two AFL championships.

Like any professional football player, Kemp suffered his share of injuries. He broke both ankles and suffered "12 or 13" concussions, according to Kemp's count. An injured shoulder kept Kemp from joining his Army Reserve unit when the reserves were called to Berlin, West Germany, in 1961; his doctors issued him a medical exemption (Kemp has said that he never asked for the exemption, and would have served if called). In 1962 a lineman stepped on his throwing hand, doing severe damage to his second finger. When doctors told Kemp they would have to set the finger permanently in one position, the story goes, he asked them to make sure it would conform to the contours of a football.

A New Field of Interest

Meanwhile, Kemp was slowly but surely developing an interest in politics. It began in earnest while he was taking some graduate school courses toward a master's degree in political science, which he never completed. Kemp found himself attracted to the conservative, ardently free-market economic philosophy of Friedrich von Hayek and Ludwig von Mises.

He got his baptism in real-world politics in the conservative forge of southern California. Kemp volunteered in Richard Nixon's presidential campaign in 1960, and in Nixon's unsuccessful bid for the California governorship in 1962. He also worked on Barry Goldwater's 1964 bid for the presidency, and Ronald Reagan's 1966 gubernatorial campaign.

During the 1960s Kemp met up with Herb Klein, editor of the *San Diego Union* and a conservative compadre of Nixon. Klein hired Kemp to write part time for the paper during the off season and introduced him into the California GOP's social circles. By the late 1960s Kemp was working during the spring and summer as an assistant to Gov. Reagan's chief of staff.

After leaving California for the Buffalo Bills, Kemp showed himself capable of taking a leadership role by co-founding the American Football League's Players Association; he served as that body's president from 1965 to 1970. At the end of his tenure, he decided to try his hand at a political campaign of his own.

In 1970 Erie County Republicans were looking for a strong candidate to recapture the suburban Buffalo congressional district that the party had lost in 1964. The incumbent, Richard "Max" McCarthy, was a candidate for the Senate. Kemp agreed to run for McCarthy's House seat.

Democrats charged that Kemp was a know-nothing football player without the background or knowledge to be an effective congressman. But he had instant appeal in Buffalo and wound up winning by a narrow margin. Two years later, aided by his own hard spadework and Nixon's presidential re-election landslide, Kemp clinched a second term by an overwhelming margin. After that re-election became a routine affair; he only once dropped below 70 percent of the vote districtwide.

As the years wore on Kemp's star rose within the New York Republican Party and many urged Kemp to consider running statewide. He considered seeking a Senate seat in 1980 but decided against it when Republican incumbent Jacob K. Javits announced for another term. Kemp was reluctant to challenge the popular Javits head on in a primary.

Two years later Kemp had another promising statewide opportunity. Democratic Gov. Hugh L. Carey had decided against seeking another term. But Kemp again demurred, leaving the path to the GOP nomination clear for his supply-side soul mate, Lew Lehrman. In 1986, when Kemp was cited yet again as a potential statewide candidate—this time as a challenger to Democratic Gov. Mario M. Cuomo—the Republican moved to quiet such talk once and for all. "I rule out running for governor of New York," Kemp said. "I don't aspire to be governor. The action for me is in Washington."

A number of GOP activists around the country agreed with that assessment and urged Kemp to take up residence at 1600 Pennsylvania Avenue. As early as 1980 conservative newspaper columnist James J. Kilpatrick was mentioning Kemp's name as a potential nominee; Reagan-Kemp signs appeared on the floor of the Republican convention that year before Reagan chose George Bush as his running mate. "Kemp in 1988" placards littered the convention hall in Dallas in 1984.

The opportunity to run in 1988 was too strong to resist, and Kemp began laying the groundwork for his presidential candidacy early on. In 1984, according to the *Wall Street Journal,* Kemp delivered speeches on behalf of some 97 Republican congressional candidates; his political action committee, dubbed the Campaign for Prosperity, dispensed roughly $300,000 to Republicans along the way. By 1985 his calendar was filling up with appearances in some of 1988's key GOP primary and caucus states.

That start was a little too early, in the eyes of the Democrat who challenged Kemp for re-election to his House seat in 1986. The Democrat was Buffalo City Councilman James P. Keane, a feisty, 40-year-old former firefighter who came from a family long active in area politics and whose name was well known. An indefatigable campaigner, Keane crisscrossed the district arguing that Kemp had played too much to the national spotlight, forsaking his Buffalo-area constituency.

Few expected Keane to oust the incumbent Republican, but the

Democrat did force Kemp to scale back his presidential politicking somewhat and stay a little closer to home. The final result—a comfortable 57-42 percentage point GOP victory—demonstrated that Kemp still retained widespread affection in the 31st despite his larger political ambitions. Still, it was the worst showing Kemp made since initially capturing his House seat—despite his expenditure of more than $2 million, the biggest outlay by any House candidate in the 1986 elections, according to Common Cause.

Bucking the Odds

As a House member seeking the presidency, Kemp is bumping up against some daunting historical odds. The only sitting House member ever to win election to the White House was James A. Garfield, who notched his victory in 1880. Garfield's reign did not last long; he was assassinated during his first year in office. Throughout the 20th century, no House member has even managed to capture a major party nomination for the presidency.

In attempting to rally support among GOP primary voters nationwide, Kemp soon felt frustration. He found himself mired at 10 percent—or slightly less—in a variety of public opinion polls measuring voter preferences for the 1988 GOP nomination. He was not low enough in the polls to be a genuine dark horse who could make a breakthrough by exceeding expectations in the pivotal early voting in Iowa and New Hampshire. And he was not quite high enough in the polls to be accorded the seriousness given heavyweights such as Bush and Dole.

Kemp knows that he faces long odds in his bid for the presidency. But, drawing on the lessons he learned as the man who calls the plays in the football huddle, he prefers to shut out talk that his effort might fail and concentrate on honing a winning attitude.

"Some people can tell you why you won't win," he said in an interview with the *Washington Post*. "Some people can tell you why what you are doing won't work, why the nation is going into a recession, why the sky is falling. If you are a quarterback calling a play, you've got to believe in it, make your team believe in it."

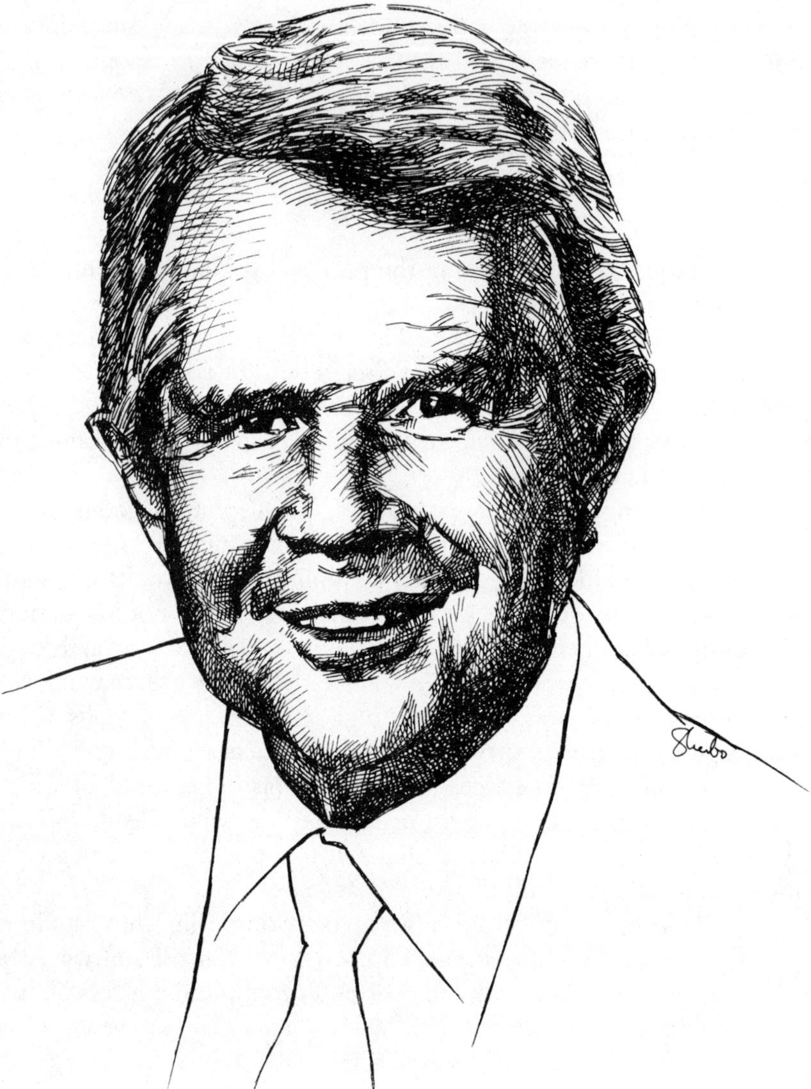

PAT ROBERTSON

Recruiting an 'Invisible Army' To Fight for 'Traditional Values'

If Ronald Reagan's presidency had turned out exactly as his critics eight years ago warned it would, there would have been no cause for Pat Robertson to leave his television ministry and try for the White House in 1988.

But contrary to many predictions at the beginning of the decade, the Reagan era did not bring about wholesale change in the law of the land as it affects an array of social policies. The call for a return to "traditional values" was an important facet of Reagan's rhetoric in both his 1980 and 1984 presidential campaigns, and from the White House he has periodically issued pronouncements urging Congress to abolish abortion and permit prayer in public schools. But throughout Reagan's years these and other priorities on the traditional-values agenda took a back seat to the administration's goal of revamping the federal government's taxing and spending policies. Even though Reagan's three Supreme Court appointments clearly shifted the high court to the right, the 1980s have left many strongly religious conservatives with an empty feeling, a feeling of promises unfulfilled.

Among the candidates running for the presidency in 1988, Robertson is the man who gives voice to those frustrations. He may have made a concerted effort to refashion his public image and broaden his appeal; shortly before formally launching his campaign in October 1987 he resigned as minister of the Southern Baptist Church and as head of his Christian Broadcasting Network (CBN), and he asked the media to call him a businessman and former religious broadcaster, not a "TV evangelist."

But none of that positioning changed the fact that Robertson draws his support from devoutly Christian conservatives who believe that the two national parties are paying too little attention to halting America's declining "moral strength."

> ## Marion Gordon 'Pat' Robertson
>
> **Profession:** Religious broadcaster; businessman.
> **Born:** March 22, 1930, Lexington, Va.
> **Home:** Virginia Beach, Va.
> **Religion:** Southern Baptist.
> **Education:** Washington and Lee University, B.A., 1950; Yale University, J.D., 1955; New York Theological Seminary, M.Div., 1959.
> **Career:** Minister, Southern Baptist Church, and religious broadcaster, 1959-87; founder, Christian Broadcasting Network, 1960.
> **Military:** Marine Corps, 1950-52.
> **Family:** Wife, Adelia "Dede" Elmer; four children.

The Early Years

Given his background, Robertson seems an unlikely champion for "movement conservatives" who chafe at their lack of influence within the Republican Party and vow to shake up the party establishment. There was nothing of the underdog in Robertson's upbringing, and nothing Republican. He was born in 1930 into a Virginia family of great status and power; his father, A. Willis Robertson, served 34 years in Congress, first as a House member and then in the Senate. He was part of the rural political machine of Harry F. Byrd Sr., the all-powerful Democratic juggernaut that ruled the Commonwealth of Virginia virtually unchallenged for a half-century.

Robertson was raised in Lexington, Va., a genteel Southern town whose personality was, and still is, shaped by its two tradition-revering institutions of higher learning: the Virginia Military Institute, which fancies itself the South's West Point and was a conduit for Confederate military talent in the Civil War; and Washington and Lee University, a private and historically all-male school whose stately campus exudes an air of satisfaction with the status quo.

Perhaps in reaction against all the rigid responsibility of his home town, his family and his prep school training at the elite McCallie School in Chattanooga, Tenn., Robertson showed a wild side as a college student, and even as a young adult. He never lacked for brains; he graduated magna cum laude from Washington and Lee in 1950 and was Phi Beta Kappa. But, as the saying goes, he never let studying get in the way of his education. The man who later in life would lead a presidential campaign aimed at rejuvenating "traditional morality" enjoyed drinking, gambling and womanizing in a way that some of his intellectually less able classmates could not afford.

Controversy in the Marine Corps

After graduating from college Robertson spent two years in the Marine Corps during the Korean War. That brief chapter in his life has been analyzed as much as any other, because when he claimed in later years to have served as a "combat officer" in Korea, some who served in the military with him stepped forward to object. They said he was not a front-line fighter, and that, in fact, he was best-known at the time as a "liquor supply officer" who drew the plum assignment of making frequent trips to Tokyo on "official business."

In the fall of 1987 Robertson took steps to defuse charges that he had padded his résumé, deleting the controversial "combat officer" reference. But well into 1988 he was still embroiled in a nasty legal fight with Pete McCloskey, a former House member from California who served with Robertson in Korea. McCloskey claimed to have proof that Robertson was exempted from hazardous duty thanks to the intercession of his father, the influential senator. Robertson strenuously denied that he had sought any sort of special treatment and, for months, he and McCloskey traded insults in the media as their lawyers prepared to litigate a suit that Robertson filed against McCloskey, and a counter-suit filed by McCloskey. Some campaign aides counseled Robertson to drop the matter, saying that it was detracting from his larger message, but Robertson seemed determined to have his day in court.

Unfortunately for Robertson, a rather uncooperative judge set that date for March 8—the day of the "Super Tuesday" primary voting in many Southern states where Robertson believed his campaign would fare well. Recognizing the impracticality of devoting time to a judicial grudge match on such a landmark political occasion, Robertson decided to drop his suit. McCloskey, however, demanded that he be compensated for the expenses incurred in his counter-suit, and he got his way. In the headlines, it was an embarrassing defeat for Robertson on the eve of Super Tuesday.

Heading for a Turning Point

Robertson settled back into his old ways following his stint in the military. When he returned from Korea and entered Yale Law School he behaved much as he had at Washington and Lee—blending a judicious amount of studying with gentlemanly extracurricular diversions such as card-playing.

He also did another gentlemanly thing in his final year of law school: He married a Yale nursing student named Adelia "Dede" Elmer about 10 weeks before she gave birth to their child, a boy. At first Robertson did not seem to be a doting husband and father; many law school classmates were not even aware he was married, much less a parent.

But in later years Robertson was more concerned about appearances and he placed the date of his wedding as March 1954, instead of August, as had been the case. Résumé-checkers in the media pounced on the discrepancy, but the disclosure did not diminish the zeal of Robertson's loyal supporters. They accepted his explanation that the premarital indiscretion—and the several other off-color aspects of his younger years—should not count against him because they occurred before he underwent the religious conversion that changed the course of his life.

That "born-again" experience came in 1957 while Robertson was living and working in New York and pursuing what he has described as an acquisitive, pleasure-seeking life style devoid of deeper meaning. He enrolled in New York Theological Seminary and took a master of divinity degree there in 1959. Before long he had relocated to Virginia Beach, Va., and bought a down-and-out television station there for a bargain-basement price.

Robertson says that he was told by God to get into the TV business. While that claim is difficult to verify, it is not difficult to see that the business venture was blessed with tremendous success. Driven by the popularity of the "700 Club" talk show—a sort of Johnny Carson show for the religious TV viewer, with Robertson as the host—the Christian Broadcasting Network blossomed into a major media force and branched out into several other operations, including a university. Robertson wrote three books on his religious views and gained a wider audience for them by discussing them on the "700 Club."

Thanks to the success of CBN, Robertson earned wide exposure as a religious leader and credibility as a successful businessman. The latter became an important part of Robertson's presidential campaign strategy, as he sought to broaden his appeal beyond his core supporters.

A New Crusade

Robertson indicated on Sept. 17, 1986, that he would seek the Republican presidential nomination if, in a year's time, he could collect the signatures of three million people urging him to run. On Sept. 15, 1987, in Chesapeake, Va., he declared his intention to run, showing a stack of petitions that he claimed contained the signatures of 3.3 million Americans encouraging his candidacy. "I feel like somebody strapped on a couple of jet engines on my back and we're ready to take off," he declared, setting Oct. 1 as the date for his formal announcement speech.

Pat Robertson announces his candidacy in front of supporters' petitions.

Candidates '88

Robertson had reason to be optimistic. He scored a surprise victory in a Sept. 12 straw poll conducted by Iowa Republicans at a large fund-raising event in Ames. Robertson's well-organized effort gave some much-needed credibility to his campaign, while denting the image of invincibility being erected by strategists for the GOP front-runner, Vice President George Bush.

Bush had finished first in a similar straw vote eight years earlier, en route to winning the 1980 precinct caucuses. This time, he finished third in the balloting behind Robertson (who won 34 percent of the roughly 3,800 ballots cast) and Kansas Sen. Robert Dole (25 percent). Bush drew a relatively anemic 22 percent. Robertson also got another boost just before his announcement in Chesapeake. On Sept. 15 he had solidified his position in Michigan, another key early state on the 1988 Republican delegate selection calendar. Michigan planned its delegate selection for the weekend of Jan. 29-30, a full week before Iowa's caucuses.

Michigan Republicans began their delegate-selection process in August 1986 with the election of roughly 9,000 precinct delegates, who were to meet in county conventions in mid-January of 1988. They, in turn, were to select roughly 1,800 delegates to the state convention, where Michigan's national convention delegates would be chosen.

Bush, Robertson and New York Rep. Jack F. Kemp all competed in 1986 for precinct delegates, and most media accounts of the complicated election seemed to put Bush ahead of his rivals. But followers of Robertson and Kemp joined forces, and in early 1987 they won control of the state party apparatus. At a Sept. 15 meeting of the state committee they exercised their power, blocking a proposal favored by the Bush camp to give automatic seats at the county conventions to roughly 1,500 county and state legislative officeholders and recent nominees—a group regarded as pro-Bush. The Robertson-Kemp forces treated the proposal as a "sour-grapes" attempt to change the rules of the game. The Bush forces argued that state law directed that the additional delegates be seated.

Challenging Task

Despite his huge list of names, his well-oiled, CBN-spawned fund-raising operation and his 1987 success in Michigan and Iowa, Robertson faced formidable odds in his bid for the presidency.

Even though he resigned from the ministry and from his executive positions with CBN just before formally launching his White House campaign, Robertson had trouble convincing the media and the voters to look beyond their image of him as a television preacher. In campaign releases he pointedly referred to himself as an educator, author, lecturer, broadcaster—anything but that dread phrase "TV evangelist"—partly because the prestige of that profession plummeted after the 1987 sex scandal involving Jim Bakker, whose "PTL Club" and attendant TV empire bore some resemblance to Robertson's operation.

Since Robertson had no record in public office that journalists could scrutinize, the media quite naturally focused on what he had said and done during his long tenure on the airwaves as host of the "700 Club." The Robertson revealed on those airwaves conducted faith-healing sessions in the studio and took credit for turning away a hurricane from Virginia Beach because he led his followers in a prayer drive to spare the city.

Robertson's issue positions also made good copy for reporters. He tends to speak his mind plainly, drawing the sort of "good-versus-evil" contrasts that have been a facet of Reagan's rhetoric. A sampling of headlines from newspapers around the country explains why Robertson's views are regarded by many as a bit out of the mainstream, even for the conservative GOP: "Robertson Calls Abortion Holocaust"; "Robertson Assails Iran-Contra Hearings as 'Star Chamber' "; "Robertson Proposes Voluntary Urban Aid" (to replace most federal urban aid programs); "Robertson Urges Private Pension Plan" (to initiate the process of privatizing the Social Security system); "Robertson Disputes Doctors on AIDS" (he says the disease can be transmitted by breathing). Taken together, these and other positions strike many voters as a bit extreme.

Robertson began his presidential bid much lower in the polls than the other man of the cloth in the campaign, the Rev. Jesse Jackson. Robertson was favored by just 8 percent of Republicans and Republican-leaning independents in a Gallup Poll completed in early September 1987 (compared with 40 percent for Bush and 19 percent for Dole). But his capacity to become a factor in the nominating contest was never doubted, because of the potential clout of the conservative church-going community. That feeling was strengthened by the suspicion that many in that community do not show up in presidential preference polls.

As Gary Jarmin, a political consultant with clients in the Christian Right, put it, the church is "the ideal political unit. The people are already there, and they have the most intense ideological glue that holds people together—faith." The churches Robertson planned to rely on were scattered throughout the large and amorphous evangelical movement. The sheer number of evangelicals—estimates range from 50 million to 70 million Americans, depending on how the term is defined—gave birth to the notion that Robertson might be able to mobilize an "invisible army" of religious conservatives who had little if any previous involvement in politics.

But some observers recognized that uniting even a segment of the evangelical community would be a chore. The evangelical label takes in a wide range of Christians who believe the Bible is the infallible word of God, but who vary in their interpretations of it. Fundamentalists, such as TV evangelist Jerry Falwell, practice a more formal, strictly Bible-based brand of religion and tend to frown upon Pentecostals and charismatics, whom they view as overly emotional. Charismatics, such as Robertson, hold to a belief that God supplements his biblical message by way of "gifts" bestowed upon believers. The ability to perform faith-healing and to speak in tongues are counted among such gifts by charismatics.

Charismatics are estimated to account for perhaps 10 million voters across the country, but the group's political preferences are not well-charted. Many evangelicals had not even been involved in presidential politics until 1976, when born-again Southern Democrat Jimmy Carter caught their eye. But in 1980 and 1984 Reagan drew much of the evangelical vote.

Whatever the size and political preference of the larger evangelical community, it was clear as soon as Robertson started talking about running for president that he had assembled a loyal grass-roots following of some size by skillfully using his television network and the political arm of his organization, called the Freedom Council.

Robertson's confidence in the grass-roots network led him to dismiss the significance of public opinion polls, which consistently showed him with little mass appeal. "I don't need the party structure to win the nomination," he told the *Des Moines Register* in 1987. "I need about 15 to 20 percent of my [evangelical] base and I'll win the Republican nomination."

Robertson was correct in claiming that it would not take all that many votes to become the GOP nominee. While 100 million Americans may vote in the general election for president in November of 1988, no more than 15 million voters participated in the previous competitive GOP nominating contest, held in 1980. That year Reagan swept the primaries with fewer than eight million votes. In that context, Robertson's ability to attract more than three million people to sign his candidate petitions made him seem a very formidable contender.

To maximize their candidate's potential, Robertson's strategists focused their efforts on caucus states, where voter turnout is lower than in primary states and organizational expertise is the key to success. In primary states they planned a special effort to win delegates in predominantly Democratic congressional districts, areas where the Republican Party did not boast a particularly strong or well-organized establishment. The strategists figured that in such places a few hundred votes could make the difference, enabling their candidate to sweep the bloc of GOP delegates at stake.

But even Robertson's most die-hard supporters know that winning the presidency on the first try is a very, very difficult task. If he fails in 1988 another test of his long-term impact on the political process will be the 1990 congressional elections. If many GOP candidates connected with Robertson file for the House or Senate that year, it could be a sign that Robertson's people are spreading through the system, lying in wait for 1992 and another campaign from their famous leader.

Adding fervor to Robertson's personal campaign effort is the feeling among many of his supporters that they are engaged not only in a fight for a presidential nomination, but also in a high-stakes battle for control of the Republican Party. Now that members of the religious right have become key foot soldiers in the GOP in many states, they want to play a major role in party leadership.

"In a sense, Robertson is saying, 'We have a right to have a voice ourselves,' " says David Edwin Harrell Jr., a historian and the author of a Robertson biography. "Republicans may have gotten more than they bargained for in getting the religious vote."

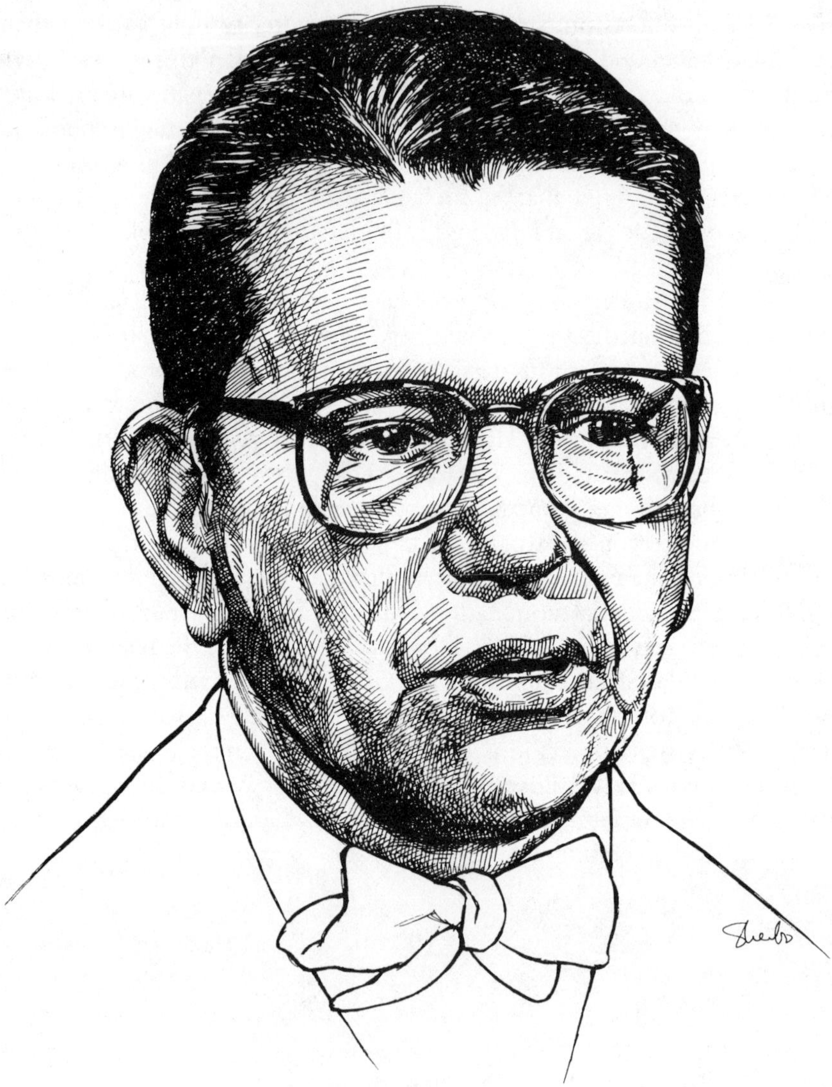

PAUL SIMON

Running for President
The Old-Fashioned Way

Four years ago, a senator from Colorado named Gary Hart vaulted from the murky anonymity of the Democratic presidential nominating process by casting himself as the candidate of "new ideas." In 1988, Sen. Paul Simon of Illinois is hoping to enjoy a similar kind of success by taking the opposite tack.

"Old-fashioned ideas" is the all-but-spoken motto of Simon's presidential campaign. From his old-line liberal philosophy to his bow-tied, horn-rimmed appearance, Simon is the embodiment of another political age, one more in tune with the tenets of Franklin Delano Roosevelt's New Deal than with those of Ronald Reagan's conservative climate of austerity. Voters can be forgiven if they sometimes feel they are watching a man who was frozen in 1940, only to be thawed out in time to file this year for the presidency.

Simon's left-leaning politics and clean-cut image have brought him sustained success in Illinois. First elected to the state Legislature in 1954, he served there for 15 years before winning the post of lieutenant governor in 1968. He went on to spend a decade in the U.S. House, then moved to the Senate by registering an upset over three-term GOP Sen. Charles H. Percy in 1984. In over 30 years in public life, Simon has lost an election only once: a failed bid for the governorship in 1972.

And his political persona proved to be a valuable asset during the early stages of the 1988 presidential nominating campaign. When several other Democratic contenders were forced to bow out of the race under clouds of controversy, Simon, at age 59 the oldest candidate in the field, attracted increased attention because of his squeaky-clean character and image of integrity.

It is unclear whether Simon will be able to convert this attention into sustained success in the primaries and caucuses. What is clear,

Paul Martin Simon

Profession: Author; newspaper publisher.
Born: Nov. 29, 1928, Eugene, Ore.
Home: Makanda, Ill.
Religion: Lutheran.
Education: Attended University of Oregon, 1945-46; Dana College, 1946-48.
Political Career: Illinois House of Representatives, 1955-63; Illinois Senate, 1963-69; Illinois lieutenant governor, 1969-73; sought Democratic gubernatorial nomination, 1972; U.S. House of Representatives, 1975-85; U.S. Senate, 1985-present.
Military: Army, 1951-53.
Family: Wife, Jeanne Hurley; two children.
Committees: (House) Post Office and Civil Service, 1975-77; Education and Labor, 1975-85; Budget, 1977-83; Science and Technology, 1983-85; (Senate) Rules and Administration (1985-87); Judiciary, 1985-present; Labor and Human Resources, 1985-present; Budget, 1987-present; Foreign Relations, 1987-present.

however, is that Simon is loath to alter his political perspective or his physical appearance in pursuit of his goal. If he succeeds in his quest for the Oval Office, it will be because he refused suggestions from allies and adversaries alike to change his ways.

"To become fashionable, some people tell me to get rid of my bow tie and my horn-rimmed glasses and, most of all, to change my views," he said at Southern Illinois University in Carbondale, Ill., in announcing his presidential candidacy. "Well, Harry Truman wore a bow tie and horn-rimmed glasses, and he didn't knuckle under to pressure to change his views. Nineteen eighty-eight is not going to be the year for a candidate slickly packaged like some new soft drink."

Back to the Tried and True

Simon has made an effort to set himself off from the rest of the

Democratic pack by appealing to the party's traditions—tacitly deriding his rivals as revisionists who have strayed too far afield. "I am not a neo-anything," he said bluntly during his announcement speech. "I am a Democrat."

To Simon, being a Democrat means harking back to the days of the New Deal and the Great Society. Like his political heroes, Paul H. Douglas and Hubert H. Humphrey, he believes that the federal government should be active in providing social services at home, but restrained in its military activities abroad. In Simon's lexicon, "spending" is not necessarily a dirty word.

That much is clear from some of the programs he has put forward in the campaign. He has called for increased federal aid to education, for example, in hopes of improving American knowledge of foreign languages and eradicating illiteracy. He would also like to extend Medicare benefits to include the costs of long-term health care for the chronically ill. And he touts a six-cent-per-gallon increase in federal gasoline taxes, to help generate revenues to repair and rebuild the nation's roads.

Perhaps the most dramatic—and the most controversial—plank in Simon's platform is his jobs program. Modeled after Roosevelt's Works Progress Administration, Simon's plan would ensure that every American citizen who wants a job can get one.

"The nation's highest commitment—our most important national goal—must be to guarantee a job opportunity for everyone who wants to work," Simon has said.

The program would be open to anyone who had been unemployed for five weeks or more and who had unsuccessfully sought work in the private sector. Those eligible would be awarded a government-sponsored job paying the minimum wage, and would put in a four-day work week, with time off on the fifth day to look for permanent, private-sector employment. The jobs, arranged by local boards, would range from helping at day-care centers and teaching the illiterate to read to planting trees and cleaning up graffiti.

Simon feels that his plan would be a more effective way to get at the problem of unemployment than the web of welfare and other assistance programs currently in place.

"There is a host of things that need to be done in our society, but instead of doing them we are paying people to sit home and do nothing," he said. "Not good for them, and not good for our country."

The jobs program would cost an estimated $8 billion annually, which Simon says could be defrayed in large part via savings on welfare and other unemployment assistance programs.

Accounting for His Ideas

Despite his plans for such new federal expenditures, Simon still contends that he has a strong streak of fiscal conservatism. He is fond of billing himself in stump speeches as a "pay-as-you-go" Democrat and touts his support for a constitutional amendment to balance the federal budget. He argues that he could erase the federal deficit within three years of taking up residence at 1600 Pennsylvania Avenue.

Simon envisions squeezing some savings out of the massive defense budget, arguing that cuts can be made without compromising national security. He also might save on foreign aid; he opposes sending aid to the "contras," the anti-government rebels in Nicaragua. He is banking on the jobs created by his employment plan to generate new revenue, and he says he will levy new taxes only as "a last resort." If taxes do have to be raised, Simon says he would increase the levy only on the wealthiest Americans, those who he says have benefited most from Reaganomics.

His critics, of course, find Simon maddeningly short on specifics. The increases in outlays he has supported and his promise to curb budget deficits, they argue, simply cannot be reconciled. "Senator Simon says he is pay-as-you-go," said former Arizona Gov. Bruce Babbitt, one of Simon's rivals for the Democratic presidential nomination, in late 1987. "But he has a tendency to drive past the toll booth without paying anything in." Echoed an aide to another Democratic candidate, "You can't be the darling of the New Deal Democratic constituents and at the same time be for Ronald Reagan's pet fiscal theory."

Even some disinterested observers have cast doubt on Simon's ability to retire the national debt in three years. "In my view no candidate, not even one as committed to reducing the deficit as Paul Simon, could achieve that goal," Robert Greenstein, director of the Center on Budget and Policy Priorities, told the *New York Times*.

Education Is Job One

Simon's campaign proposals reflect the kind of stance he has taken throughout most of his 13-year congressional career. He has been a strong supporter of increased federal activism on a number of domestic issues, but he occasionally breaks with liberal Democratic orthodoxy.

His predominant interest during his House tenure was federal aid to education. He fought for generous funding in the multi-year higher education bill that became law in 1980; in 1981, he worked to forestall the drastic retrenchment in education funds proposed by President Reagan.

Also in the early 1980s, Simon vehemently opposed Reagan's plan to require a means test for student loan recipients, claiming a million students would lose loans. Congress eventually placed a means test on student borrowers with family incomes above $30,000.

In 1982, Simon started a counterattack, adding education funds to three major budget proposals. The budget eventually adopted did not fund those programs at a level Simon could accept. But he also sponsored legislation, which Congress passed, blocking the Education Department from making further cuts in aid programs through the regulatory process.

He tried again in 1984, introducing a proposal to expand student aid substantially, especially to those at the low end of the income scale.

Paul Simon and wife, Jeanne, greeting supporters in New Hampshire, 1988.

But the cost worried Simon's colleagues, and they convinced him to withdraw his bill.

At once defending student aid and opposing draft registration, Simon was one of the few House voices objecting to student aid cuts for those who fail to register. Simon tried in 1982 to offer an exemption for anyone who notified the Selective Service in writing that he had religious or moral objections to registration. His amendment was first modified, then killed. Simon also spoke out against a similar ban on job training funds for draft resisters; that ban was passed by voice vote.

Simon also involved himself in the fight to overturn the Supreme Court's *Grove City* ruling. That decision held that the anti-discrimination laws passed in 1972 did not apply to an entire school or college just because one of its programs received federal money. Working with colleagues on the Education and Labor Committee and on the Judiciary Committee, Simon sponsored a bill to extend the non-discrimination laws to entire institutions. They steered the measure through the House, but it died in the Senate.

Early in 1983, Simon helped push through a bill to improve math and science education, which was one of the first major pieces of legislation to be passed in the 98th Congress. To that bill he added funds for another pet priority—foreign language education. Earlier, he amended a military spending bill to ask for a study of the feasibility of requiring foreign language instruction in military academies.

Moving to the Senate in 1985, Simon kept up his interest in educational issues. When the Senate Labor and Human Resources Committee debated a bill to reauthorize the Higher Education Act in the 99th Congress, Simon promoted a number of causes, including aid to historically black colleges and a new limited program of federal support for graduate students. The final education bill gave a special funding preference to historically black colleges, but concerns about cost ruled out grants to graduate students.

Simon seized an opportunity to vent his frustration over the Reagan administration's education policy after his party took control of the Senate in 1986. When Massachusetts Democrat Edward M. Kennedy took the Labor and Human Resources Committee chair and held hearings exploring policy initiatives, Simon lashed out at Education Secretary William J. Bennett.

Comparing Bennett unfavorably with his predecessor, Terrel H. Bell, Simon said that "He fought for every dollar he could get for education. I don't hear that fight from the secretary of education today.... You're leading the retreat instead of the charge."

In another social area, consumer protection, Simon has advocated federal action to prevent insurance industry price-fixing.

Labor Loyalist

In general, Simon has been a close ally of organized labor. Through 1986 his AFL-CIO approval rating averaged 85 percent.

In the late 1970s labor found favor with his defense of Comprehensive Employment and Training Act (CETA) public jobs, which were under attack from a variety of critics. In 1982 Simon supported a job training bill designed to replace the much-maligned CETA program, defending that bill, too, from fiscal attacks. When some members proposed leaving the funding level to the budget process, Simon objected. "This bill is so far from what we ought to be doing in this nation at this time that it is pathetic," he said.

Simon also has earned praise from organized labor for his support of the Humphrey-Hawkins full employment bill, which served as an inspiration for his own jobs program. Sponsored by the late Sen. Hubert Humphrey (D-Minn.) and Democratic Rep. Augustus Hawkins of California, the bill, like Simon's proposal, sought to guarantee a job for every American willing to work. When the bill was diluted on the House floor to add unrelated anti-inflation and farm parity goals, his voice was one of the loudest raised in opposition.

In 1984 he sided with the unions by proposing legislation requiring companies to prove they were insolvent before they could void labor contracts under Chapter 11 of the bankruptcy code. That strategy by troubled companies had just been upheld by the Supreme Court.

On at least one issue of interest to labor's leadership, however, Simon has broken ranks. He embraced the idea of a subminimum wage for teenagers early on in his House career, even though it is one of the economic proposals that labor has historically opposed most militantly.

Simon has shown a traditional liberal bent, however, on the issue of federal aid to the handicapped. In 1980 he fought to preserve strict federal requirements that communities equip all mass transit vehicles with access for the handicapped. When the House adopted a compromise allowing alternatives such as special jitney buses, Simon branded the chamber's action "a backward step."

The Penny-Pinching Side

In his congressional career as in his presidential campaign, Simon has sought to leaven his liberal instincts with a dose of fiscal restraint. While his parsimonious side sometimes surprises his left-leaning colleagues, Simon's supporters insist it is in character with a man who got his start in business running a small-town Midwestern newspaper.

Doing nothing in the face of mounting deficits, Simon once wrote, is "a policy of folly," similar to 1920s policies that led to the Great Depression.

In 1986, Simon put his principles into practice by joining Republican Sen. Strom Thurmond of South Carolina and other conservatives in support of a constitutional amendment to balance the federal budget. Before throwing in with the conservatives, though, Simon won their reluctant assent to include language specifying that a tax increase to erase the deficit could be approved by a simple majority vote in each chamber.

Subsequently, Simon added a provision requiring the president to submit a balanced budget to Congress, something Reagan has failed to do. Those "sweeteners" persuaded a number of skeptical Democrats to support the amendment, but it fell one vote short of achieving the two-thirds majority required for Senate approval.

Simon voted against two of the landmark pieces of economic legislation of this decade: the tax cuts of 1981 and the 1986 tax revision bill. He is particularly proud of his vote against the latter bill, which passed the Senate by a vote of 97-3 en route to becoming law.

"I don't know of a single organization that was against it," Simon has said. "I was one of three votes against that bill in the Senate, and that was one of the best votes I ever cast." He claimed the bill added to the federal deficit and mainly benefited the rich.

As a member of the House Budget Committee for three terms, Simon argued for changes in the consumer price index that would slow the growth in federal programs keyed to the cost of living. He also suggested that federal retirees should have benefits adjusted for inflation only once a year, not twice. As it turned out, neither idea proved very popular.

Like many of his colleagues, Simon found the budget process frustrating. "We are in the process of moving from a time in the history of the House when committees had too much power . . . and we have moved to a point where the floor itself becomes a large, unwieldy committee," he said in 1978. "We are legislating by whim rather than really doing the substantial job that ought to be done."

Defense, Foreign Priorities

One of Simon's favorite targets for savings has been the defense budget.

He has been a vigorous opponent of the MX missile system, offering an amendment in 1980 to cut some $500 million from a $1.6 billion MX authorization. Simon lost that vote, 152-250.

He fared a little better in 1981, when he convinced the House to defer MX spending at least until the whole program could be restudied. "Without SALT II," he said, "this whole thing is worthless."

By the end of 1982, the House seemed to agree with him. It passed an amendment, sponsored by New York Democrat Joseph P. Addabbo, cutting off money for building President Reagan's proposed "dense pack" basing mode for the MX. But Simon did not abandon his crusade. In 1983, he proposed cutting off funds for research into an interim MX basing mode.

In the realm of foreign affairs, Simon's chief interest over the years has been world hunger, an issue he inherited from Sen. Humphrey. In 1982, Simon successfully sponsored an amendment to a stopgap funding bill requiring that 50 percent of development aid money go toward those living in "absolute poverty." Conferees later lowered that figure to 40 percent.

In 1987, Simon joined Democratic Rep. Howard Wolpe of Michigan in proposing a plan to authorize a five-year commitment in economic development aid for Africa, offering African countries incentives to make reforms aimed at protecting the environment and encouraging agricultural and industrial production.

Where Do Nice Guys Finish?

Throughout his career, Simon has displayed courteous and conciliatory instincts that seemed more in keeping with the congresses of 50 years ago than the more rough-and-tumble climate that often marks chamber politics today.

He demonstrated those instincts in the late 1970s, when the Carter administration turned down his bid to have a new St. Louis airport

Simon's Interest Group Ratings

Vote ratings by interest groups help to give a picture of Paul Simon's orientation during his career in the House and Senate. This table shows how often Simon voted on key legislative issues in accordance with the positions of groups chosen to represent liberal, labor, business and conservative viewpoints. They are the Americans for Democratic Action (ADA), AFL-CIO, Chamber of Commerce of the United States (CCUS) and Americans for Constitutional Action (ACA) or American Conservative Union (ACU).

	ADA	AFL-CIO	CCUS	ACA	ACU
House Service					
1975	89	91	12	18	—
1976	80	81	13	0	—
1977	85	73	24	0	—
1978	65	84	22	10	—
1979	74	72	17	0	—
1980	78	72	59	24	—
1981	75	79	12	0	—
1982	75	95	15	25	—
1983	70	100	18	9	—
1984	45	100	33	13	—
Senate Service					
1985	85	95	34	—	5 [1]
1986	80	80	32	—	9
1987	35	40	13	—	0

[1] *Congressional Quarterly began publishing ACU ratings in 1985.*

located across the Mississippi River in Illinois.

The Illinois site would have helped bring jobs to some depressed areas around his House district. But Simon greeted news that Carter Transportation Secretary Brock Adams had decided against the site philosophically. "I could have fumed and fussed and protested with statements issued to the press," Simon wrote in a letter to his constituents. "But the facts are that while I wish Brock Adams had rendered a different decision . . . I respect his judgment . . . and I know that the most foolish thing anyone could do . . . is to fail to recognize the facts."

Sometimes Simon also demonstrates a journalistic penchant for seeking both sides of a story. This trait, added to his natural politeness, has occasionally prompted exasperated colleagues to express dissatisfaction with his leadership skills.

In 1986, Simon was chastised by liberals for not opposing Reagan's nomination of Sidney A. Fitzwater to be a federal district judge, even though Fitzwater once had posted signs in black-majority wards warning voters they could be prosecuted for election fraud. Liberals saw him as insensitive to minorities, and they expected help blocking his nomination from Simon, who had been designated by Judiciary Committee Democrats as the point man for monitoring the fitness of judicial nominees.

Simon called the sign-posting a mistake, but said he saw no "pattern of racism" in Fitzwater's record. With such a well-known liberal backing the nominee, many squeamish moderates felt they could go along.

"He gives a lot of people cover," one civil rights lobbyist complained.

Fitzwater won Senate approval by a vote of 52-42.

Similar concern about Simon's lack of aggressiveness as a leader arose during his 1980 bid as a House member to chair the chamber's Budget Committee. Simon drew only 39 votes in the Democratic Caucus, finishing a distant third to David R. Obey of Wisconsin and Oklahoma's James R. Jones, the eventual winner. Many members attributed Simon's poor showing to colleagues' feeling that he was "almost too nice" a man for the job.

Plunging in with Zeal

While Simon's political base is in the heartland, his roots are in the West. He was born and raised in Eugene, Oregon, where his father ran a Lutheran ministry and his mother worked in a local cannery. To help with the family finances, Simon and his younger brother sometimes gathered fruits and vegetables at harvest time.

Religion played a significant part in Simon's upbringing. In addition to ministering to his congregation, Simon's father published Lutheran periodicals. He also encouraged his son to follow him into the ministry, but Simon says he abandoned that course after a brief stint at a Lutheran prep school. (Simon's brother did become a member of the clergy, however.)

Hoping to improve the fortunes of the religious printing business, Simon's father moved his family to Highland, Ill., in 1946. It was there that Simon chose a career. While still in college—he attended both the University of Oregon and Dana College, located in Blair, Neb.—he received word from his father that civic activists in Troy, Ill., were searching for someone to assume ownership of the local newspaper. Simon dropped out of Dana and moved to Troy to take the reins at the tender age of 19.

Simon soon made a name for himself in southern Illinois, crusading against vice and political corruption in Madison and St. Clair counties. His zeal attracted attention—he was invited to testify before a special U.S. Senate subcommittee investigating crime—and raised a few local eyebrows. As the Troy postmaster recalled recently in a round of Simon presidential campaign ads, "everybody gave him credit for having courage but wondered whether he was being a little bit foolhardy."

Critics of the young owner of the *Troy Tribune* branded his paper "a Democratic rag." But Simon was hardly a down-the-line Democratic partisan. In the 1948 presidential race, he endorsed Republican Thomas E. Dewey, spurning Harry S Truman—the plain-spoken, bow-tied Missourian whose name Simon often invokes on the 1988 presidential trail.

Simon set his journalistic sights high—"I wanted to be the Walter Lippmann of my generation," he once told the *Washington Post*—and his business flourished. He soon assembled a chain of 14 weekly newspapers in the area.

He also acquired an interest in running for public office. Following a two-year tour of duty in the Army, he returned to southern Illinois to launch a bid for the state House in 1954. It was in that campaign that a reporter first noted Simon was wearing a bow tie. Mindful of the attention, he has worn one ever since.

Aided by an intensive door-to-door effort, Simon outpolled two organization-backed incumbents in the Democratic primary, and went on to capture a seat. Eight years later, he moved to the state Senate. During that time, he met his wife, who was also a member of the Illinois Assembly; they became the first husband-wife team of legislators in the history of that body.

Simon established impeccable reform credentials in the Legislature, filing detailed financial disclosure reports and receiving the "best legislator" award from the Independent Voters of Illinois seven times, more than anyone else in the history of the state at that time.

His reform tendencies did not always sit well with some of his old-line organization colleagues from Chicago, however. When Simon helped write a magazine article about corruption in the state Capitol, he received a "Benedict Arnold" award from his fellow legislators.

Defeat, Recovery and a Scare

In 1968, state Democratic leaders picked Simon as their candidate for lieutenant governor, hoping that his reform reputation would help a state ticket struggling against reported scandal and an expected Republican tide. The gubernatorial and Senate candidates lost, but Simon prevailed, and immediately became the premier Democratic officeholder in the state and heir apparent to the gubernatorial nomination in 1972.

But things did not work out quite that smoothly. A wealthy corporate lawyer named Daniel Walker challenged him in the gubernatorial primary, offering a populist pitch. Walker sought to paint Simon as a tool of Mayor Richard J. Daley's Chicago Democrats—even though, in reality, the Daley machine was clinging to Simon, rather than the other way around. Walker also seized on Simon's statement that tax increases might be necessary to improve state social services.

Walker won by 40,000 votes and went on to serve a single term as governor before being defeated for renomination. Simon taught political science for two years at a college in Springfield.

But his hiatus from politics was short-lived. When Democratic Rep. Kenneth Gray announced he was giving up the 24th District, Simon decided to run for it. Although the district was located a bit south of his old home base, Simon was favored from the start. His primary loss to Walker had not diminished his popularity, and only added to his name recognition. His Republican opponent, former Harrisburg Mayor Val Oshel, tried to tar him as a carpetbagger, but voters in the 24th District— which had grown increasingly Democratic—ignored the charges. Simon won easily, and strolled to re-election in 1976 and 1978.

He remained significantly to the left of many of his constituents, however, and the disparity seemed destined to catch up with him eventually. In 1980, the problem came home to roost.

During the campaign, Simon sought to point out signs that he was fiscally conservative, reminding constituents of his criticism of federal budget deficits and his support for enhancing tax incentives for savings. But his decision to endorse Massachusetts Democrat Edward M. Kennedy for president damaged that effort. Underfinanced Republican challenger John T. Anderson (no relation to the presidential candidate) came within 2,000 votes of an upset, aided by Ronald Reagan's strong showing in the district.

Senate Race: Nasty Business

By 1984, Simon was again ready to test his fortunes statewide. His target was Republican Sen. Charles H. Percy, who, despite three terms in the Senate, entered the election year on somewhat shaky ground.

Percy had always had an image problem in Illinois; many voters felt the aristocratic-looking business executive was aloof from their home-state concerns.

But that problem grew worse after 1981, when Percy became chairman of the Senate Foreign Relations Committee. Critics joked that he spent more time on the problems of Cairo, Egypt, than those of Cairo, Illinois.

Further, Percy found himself buffeted by crosscurrents of opposition: from liberals and moderate Republicans who found him too supportive of President Reagan's foreign policy, and from conservatives who complained he was not supportive enough.

Percy drew a conservative primary challenge from GOP Rep. Tom Corcoran; he also faced a sizable independent expenditure campaign launched by a disgruntled Californian. The incumbent survived, but the assault left him limping into the general election campaign.

Simon was not without problems of his own. Although he was the best-known of the four Democrats who filed for Percy's seat, he was slow to organize, and for a time he seemed in danger. State Senate President Philip J. Rock sewed up the support of both the state and the Cook County (Chicago) Democratic organizations, and State Comptroller Roland W. Burris showed strong support in the black community, closing off a crucial part of the liberal electorate. A third candidate,

Chicago lawyer Alex Seith, ran a barrage of media advertisements that cut into Simon's advantage in name recognition.

But Simon pulled through, aided by his strong support from organized labor, especially in the downstate counties. Buoyed further by the backing of Chicago's liberal lakefront wards, he clinched the Democratic nomination with 35 percent of the primary vote.

The fall matchup proved one of the most vituperative campaigns in the country. Soon after Democratic presidential nominee Walter F. Mondale began warning of the need for higher taxes, Percy aired ads claiming that Simon wanted even higher taxes than Mondale. "If you think you're not paying enough taxes," an announcer said, "Paul Simon's your man." Percy forces also accused Simon of being soft on Iran's militant Islamic leader, the Ayatollah Ruhollah Khomeini.

Simon, mindful of the charges he left unanswered during his failed gubernatorial primary campaign, hit back. He accused Percy of distortion, and aired his own advertisements branding Percy a conservative in league with the likes of the Rev. Jerry Falwell.

In the end, though, what the candidates said about each other may have been less important than what Percy said about himself. Breaking with a history of centrist campaign politics, the incumbent sought to cast himself as a conservative defender of the Reagan administration. That message met with a lukewarm response among many Illinois conservatives, who felt Percy had spent too many years as a leader in moderate GOP politics to stake that claim.

Percy's conservative stance also alienated many of the blacks and independents who had supported him in the past, and Simon was well-positioned to capture the defectors. Aided by racial controversy in Chicago city politics that helped produce a heavy black vote and a good showing in his downstate base, Simon overcame Percy's strength in the suburbs and Reagan's re-election coattails to post a 50 to 48 percent victory.

Going National

Simon maintained a relatively low profile during his first year in the Senate, but by 1986, he became more visible. He talked confidently about the need for liberals to "show the flag," even if that meant proposing ambitious new federal programs sure to meet defeat.

"Unless we start talking about these things, they will never happen," Simon said. "The danger is we all start fighting for the status quo, when in fact there is no such thing as the status quo—you're either making progress or slipping back."

He also began moving into a more visible role in national politics. He formed a political action committee to contribute money to Democratic congressional candidates around the country, and took an active interest in the development of the 1988 Democratic presidential field.

Ironically, Simon was not his own first choice as a presidential contender. He initially sought to persuade Sen. Dale Bumpers of Arkansas, a moderate-to-liberal Southerner, to seek the nomination. It was only after Bumpers decided against a campaign that Simon entered the race himself. He was no doubt spurred on by the interest of a small group of House Democrats, who circulated a letter touting Simon as presidential material and urging him to run.

The ground did not shake upon his entrance into the race; Simon began his campaign little-known outside of Illinois. But the events of the summer and fall of 1987 seemed to play in his favor. As Washington reeled from disclosures about the Reagan administration's arms-for-hostages deal, Gary Hart's personal life and incidents of plagiarism attributed to Sen. Joseph R. Biden Jr. of Delaware, Simon began receiving increased media attention. His old-fashioned politics and avuncular appearance seemed a welcome remedy for the season's turmoil and controversy.

Simon soon saw some of his favorable reviews turn into harsh scrutiny, as reporters began probing the economic consequences of his traditional, liberal views.

Strategy for 1988

Simon devised a strategy centered on the early caucuses in Iowa, which borders his home state. He hoped that some patterns of support that helped make his 1984 Senate victory possible would work to his benefit in the presidential caucusing.

Simon's 1984 victory was built by melding his base in rural, downstate Illinois with a solid minority and labor vote from Chicago. A similar combination of urban and rural appeal, Simon reasoned, would help him capture at least a second-place finish in Iowa. And that kind of showing would sustain him in New England and give him a much-needed burst of momentum in the South on delegate-rich "Super

Tuesday." Having survived those contests in good shape, he would then head into Illinois and other industrial states, where his traditional liberalism has more natural appeal.

The viability of Simon's strategy is questionable. Recent liberal candidates, including Mondale, have shown little appeal in rural areas outside their own states. And the Rev. Jesse L. Jackson has great appeal among black voters who might otherwise be attracted to Simon's left-leaning candidacy.

Simon's electability is another question. National Democratic leaders are mindful of the fact that the GOP has won four of the last five presidential elections, and they are very anxious to avoid extending that streak. Some in the party fear that Simon fits too easily into the mold of fellow Midwesterner Mondale, whose traditional liberal politics contributed to a 49-state Republican victory.

"There is a burden on every Democratic candidate to demonstrate he can be competitive," Democratic National Committee member Mark Siegel told the *Wall Street Journal* late in 1987. "Simon hasn't made that case yet."

Simon isn't worried. He feels strongly that the same personal qualities and issue positions that have brought him political success to date will help carry him to victory.

"What I stand for is decent jobs for Americans, quality education for our kids, long-term care for our parents and grandparents, and sensible restraint in the arms race," Simon has said. "The American people want these things."

OTHER CANDIDATES

Two Perennials
And a First-Timer

The following three candidates formally declared their candidacies for the 1988 presidential nominations of the Democratic or Republican parties:

Lyndon H. LaRouche Jr.

Perennial Democratic candidate Lyndon H. LaRouche Jr. has sped across the political spectrum from the Far Left to the Far Right. Charismatic but reclusive, the controversial LaRouche has backed thousands of candidates for public and party office over the last decade, first through the U.S. Labor Party, then within the Democratic Party.

LaRouche and his supporters have long baffled politicians with their hard-to-label philosophy and style of belligerent confrontation. His views include support for a laser defense system, advocacy of quarantining victims of acquired immune deficiency syndrome (AIDS) and belief in an international drug-trafficking conspiracy run out of England's Buckingham Palace.

LaRouche followers were considered little more than a nuisance to Democratic officials until 1986, when two of their candidates recorded the group's first statewide primary victories—for Illinois lieutenant governor and secretary of state.

Since then LaRouche and his supporters have been unable to expand their political base and the group has faced numerous legal difficulties. In 1987, following charges that LaRouche's supporters committed credit card fraud in funding his 1984 presidential campaign, LaRouche and six of his followers stood trial for allegedly trying to obstruct a criminal investigation of the groups' activities. If convicted, LaRouche could receive up to five years in jail and a $250,000 fine. His legal problems have forced LaRouche to spend more time in court than on the campaign trail.

Profession: Political party executive.
Born: Sept. 8, 1922; Rochester, N.H.
Home: Leesburg, Va.
Education: Attended Northeastern University.
Career: Management consultant, L. H. LaRouche Research, 1953-66; founder and contributing editor, *Executive Intelligence Review*, 1975-present; chair, advisory committee, National Democratic Policy Committee, 1980-present; member, National Caucus of Labor Committees; chair, International Caucus of Labor Committees; member, Fusion Energy Foundation, Club of Life.
Military: Army, 1944-46.
Family: Wife, Helga Zepp; divorced from first marriage and common law marriage dissolved; one son.

Harold Stassen

With his ninth run for the White House, 80-year-old Harold Stassen, the Don Quixote of American politics, has again placed his hallmark on the presidential nomination process. But his 1988 campaign is a far cry from those of the 1940s when Stassen, a Republican, was the "boy wonder" of American politics and his future seemed to hold unlimited possibilities.

Stassen was elected governor of Minnesota at the age of 31, keynoted the 1940 Republican National Convention at the age of 33 and was the youngest delegate participating in the drafting of the United Nations Charter in 1945.

A major contender for the Republican presidential nomination in 1948 along with New York Gov. Thomas E. Dewey and Ohio Sen. Robert A. Taft, Stassen won four presidential primaries that year but lost the crucial Oregon primary to Dewey.

In 1948 Stassen moved his political base to Pennsylvania where he served as president of the University of Pennsylvania from 1948 to 1953. In 1952 he again entered the presidential lists but threw his support to Dwight D. Eisenhower at the Republican convention.

He served in top positions under President Eisenhower—in charge of the foreign aid program from 1953 to 1955 and as a special assistant to

Other Candidates

the president with Cabinet rank for disarmament questions from 1955 to 1958. In 1956 he unsuccessfully tried to lead a movement to get Vice President Richard Nixon off the ticket.

Over the next 31 years Stassen slowly became transformed into a standard political joke as he ran losing races for public office time after time. He lost bids for the Pennsylvania Republican gubernatorial nomination in 1958 and 1966 and for Philadelphia mayor in 1959. In recent years his main activity has been a law practice with the Philadelphia firm of Stassen, Kostos and Mason.

Stassen has sought the Republican presidential nomination in every election since 1948, except when Republican Presidents Eisenhower and Nixon were seeking renomination (1956 and 1972).

Through all his political meanderings, Stassen has achieved something that very few perennial candidates manage—he has kept his dignity and his sense of humor. A good public speaker, he promotes a moderate Republican position.

Profession: Lawyer.
Born: April 13, 1907; West St. Paul, Minn.
Home: Philadelphia.
Religion: Baptist.
Education: University of Minnesota, B.A., 1923; LL.B., 1929.
Career: Dakota County, Minn., attorney, 1930-38; Minnesota governor, 1939-43; U. S. delegate to the San Francisco Conference, 1945; president, University of Pennsylvania, 1948-53; vice president and founder, National Council of Churches, 1951-52; director, Foreign Operations Administration, 1953-55; special assistant to the president for disarmament, 1955-58; member, National Security Council, 1953-58; president, Division of Christian Education of the National Council of Churches, 1953-present.
Military: Navy, 1943-45.
Family: Wife, Esther Glewwe; two children.

James A. Traficant Jr.

A self-described populist, James A. Traficant Jr. was a drug-busting Ohio county sheriff before winning election to Congress as a Democrat in 1984. He has been described by the *New York Times* as "an iconoclast who favors cowboy boots and four-letter expletives." In his presidential campaign, Traficant is appealing to blue-collar workers by advocating a platform that calls for revitalization of American industry.

In his first term in Congress, Traficant waged a one-man "Buy America" crusade, seeking to use virtually any spending bill as a vehicle for his plan to force the federal government to purchase supplies and equipment made in U. S. factories. Sometimes he was ruled out of order; sometimes he was shouted down. But occasionally he made his presence felt. In 1986 the House passed his amendment requiring the Pentagon to give preference to American contractors if they could come within 5 percent of matching a foreign bid. The amendment died in conference.

Subtlety is not Traficant's strong point, whether the topic is jobs or the intricacies of U. S. foreign policy. In one speech he urged President Reagan to "either use one of his $600 toilet seats or get off the pot and give Congress some facts" on the situation in Nicaragua. Traficant is a strong opponent of American military aid to the "contra" forces there.

Traficant's forceful personality, combined with voter unrest over local economic conditions, helped make him the only Democratic challenger anywhere in the nation in 1984 to defeat a Republican incumbent untouched by scandal. But few incumbents have had to compete with a local legend like Traficant. An intense loner, a brilliant public speaker with a flair for publicity and a fiery populist style, Traficant made his mark in the 17th District long before he ran for Congress.

A former football star at the University of Pittsburgh, Traficant ran a drug-abuse program in Mahoning County before being elected sheriff in 1980. He continued his anti-drug campaign in office, claiming credit for record drug busts through undercover operations.

But Traficant quickly made even bigger enemies than local drug dealers. Within two years he had alienated virtually every government official in the area, claiming that most were controlled by organized crime. He feuded with the FBI, the local Democratic Party, the Internal Revenue Service, the mayor of Youngstown and even some of his own deputies. He became a hero to the district's economically hard-hit factory workers, spending three days in jail at one point for refusing to process home mortgage foreclosures.

Traficant's bravado peaked when he went on trial for accepting a bribe from organized-crime figures; he maintained that he took the money to gain evidence. Though he has no legal training, Traficant defended himself, and the publicity surrounding his courtroom performance and acquittal helped him take the district from GOP hands in 1984.

Profession: Public official.
Born: May 8, 1941, Youngstown, Ohio.
Home: Poland, Ohio.
Religion: Roman Catholic.
Education: University of Pittsburgh, B.S., 1963; Youngstown State University, M.S., 1973; M.S., 1976.
Political Career: Consumer finance director, Youngstown Community Action Program; director, Mahoning County Drug Program, 1971-81; sheriff, Mahoning County, 1981-85; U.S. House of Representatives, 1985-present.
Family: Wife, Patricia Choppa; two children.
House Committees: Public Works and Transportation, 1986-present; Science, Space and Technology, 1986-present; Narcotics Abuse and Control, 1987-present.
Group Ratings: Following are Traficant's group ratings from the Americans for Democratic Action (ADA), AFL-CIO, Chamber of Commerce of the United States (CCUS) and the American Conservative Union (ACU):

	ADA	AFL-CIO	CCUS	ACU
1985	95	100	28	0
1986	95	100	27	9

CANDIDATES' PREVIOUS ELECTIONS RESULTS

Bruce Babbitt

Governor (Arizona)

1982	Babbitt (D)	453,795	62.5%
	Leo Corbet (R)	235,877	32.5
1978	Babbitt (D)	282,605	52.5
	Evan Mecham (R)	241,093	44.8

Bill Bradley

Senator (New Jersey)

1984	Bradley (D)	1,986,644	64.2%
	Mary V. Mochary (R)	1,080,100	34.9
1978	Bradley (D)	1,082,960	55.3
	Jeffrey Bell (R)	844,200	43.1

George Bush

President/Vice President

1984	Reagan/Bush (R)	54,455,075	58.8%
	Mondale/Ferraro (D)	37,577,185	40.6
1980	Reagan/Bush (R)	43,904,153	50.7
	Carter/Mondale (D)	35,483,883	41.0

Senator (Texas)

1970	Lloyd Bentsen (D)	1,194,069	53.5
	Bush (R)	1,035,794	46.4
1964	Ralph Yarborough (D)	1,463,958	56.2
	Bush (R)	1,134,337	43.6

Representative (Texas—7th District)

1968	Bush (R)	110,455	100.0
1966	Bush (R)	53,756	57.1
	Frank Briscoe (D)	39,958	42.4

Mario Cuomo

Governor (New York)

1986	Cuomo (D)	2,775,229	64.6%
	Andrew P. O'Rourke (R)	1,363,810	31.8
1982	Cuomo (D)	2,675,213	50.9
	Lew Lehrman (R)	2,494,827	47.5

Robert Dole

President/Vice President

1976	Carter/Mondale (D)	40,830,763	50.1%
	Ford/Dole (R)	39,147,793	48.0

Senator (Kansas)

1986	Dole (R)	576,902	70.0
	Guy MacDonald (D)	246,664	30.0
1980	Dole (R)	598,686	63.8
	John Simpson (D)	340,271	36.2
1974	Dole (R)	403,983	50.9
	Roy Williams (D)	390,451	49.1
1968	Dole (R)	490,911	60.1
	William I. Robinson (D)	315,911	38.7

Representative (Kansas—1st District)

1966	Dole (R)	97,487	68.6
	Bernie Henkel (D)	44,569	31.4
1964	Dole (R)	113,212	51.2
	Bill Bork (D)	108,086	48.8

Previous Elections Results

1962	Dole (R)	102,499	55.8
	Floyd J. Breeding (D)	81,092	44.2
1960	Dole (R)	62,335	59.3
	William A. Davis (D)	42,869	40.7

Michael S. Dukakis

Governor (Massachusetts)

1986	Dukakis (D)	1,157,786	68.7%
	George Kariotis (R)	525,364	31.2
1982	Dukakis (D)	1,219,109	59.5
	John W. Sears (R)	749,679	36.6
1974	Dukakis (D)	992,284	53.5
	Francis W. Sargent (R)	784,353	42.3

Pierre S. 'Pete' du Pont IV

Governor (Delaware)

1980	du Pont (R)	159,004	70.6%
	William J. Gordy (D)	64,217	28.5
1976	du Pont (R)	130,531	56.9
	Sherman W. Tribbitt (D)	97,480	42.5

Representative (Delaware—At Large)

1974	du Pont (R)	93,826	58.5
	James Soles (D)	63,490	39.6
1972	du Pont (R)	141,237	62.5
	Norma Handloff (D)	83,230	36.9
1970	du Pont (R)	86,125	53.7
	John D. Daniello (D)	83,230	44.6

Richard A. Gephardt

Representative (Missouri—3rd District)

1986	Gephardt (D)	116,403	69.0%
	Roy C. Amelung (R)	52,382	31.0

Candidates '88

1984	Gephardt (D)	193,537	100.0
1982	Gephardt (D)	131,566	77.9
	Richard Foristel (R)	37,388	22.1
1980	Gephardt (D)	143,132	77.6
	Robert A. Cedarburg (R)	41,277	22.4
1978	Gephardt (D)	121,565	81.9
	Lee Buchschacher (R)	26,881	18.1
1976	Gephardt (D)	115,109	63.7
	Joseph L. Badaracco (R)	65,623	36.3

Albert Gore Jr.

Senator (Tennessee)

| 1984 | Gore (D) | 1,000,607 | 60.7% |
| | Victor Ashe (R) | 557,016 | 33.8 |

Representative (Tennessee—4th District)

1982	Gore (D)	104,105	100.0
1980	Gore (D)	137,612	79.3
	James B. Seigneur (R)	35,954	20.7
1978	Gore (D)	108,695	100.0
1976	Gore (D)	115,392	94.0

Gary Hart

Senator (Colorado)

1980	Hart (D)	590,501	50.0%
	Mary Buchanan (R)	571,295	49.0
1974	Hart (D)	471,691	57.2
	Peter H. Dominick (R)	325,508	39.5

Jack Kemp

Representative (New York—38th District)

| 1986 | Kemp (R) | 92,508 | 57.5% |
| | James P. Keane (D) | 67,574 | 42.0 |

Previous Elections Results

1984	Kemp (R)	168,332	75.0
	Peter J. Martinelli (D)	56,156	25.0
1982	Kemp (R)	133,462	75.3
	James A. Martin (D)	43,843	24.7
1980	Kemp (R)	167,434	81.6
	Gale A. Denn (D)	37,875	18.4
1978	Kemp (R)	113,928	94.8
1976	Kemp (R)	165,702	78.2
	Peter J. Geraci (D)	46,307	21.8
1974	Kemp (R)	126,687	72.1
	Barbara L. Wicks (D)	48,929	27.9
1972	Kemp (R)	156,967	73.2
	Anthony P. Lorusso (D)	57,585	26.8

Representative (New York—39th District)

1970	Kemp (R)	96,898	51.6
	Thomas P. Flaherty (D)	90,949	48.4

Paul Simon

Senator (Illinois)

1984	Simon (D)	2,397,303	50.1%
	Charles H. Percy (R)	2,308,039	48.2

Representative (Illinois—22nd District)

1982	Simon (D)	123,693	66.2
	Peter G. Prineas (R)	63,279	33.8

Representative (Illinois—24th District)

1980	Simon (D)	112,134	49.1
	John T. Anderson (R)	110,176	48.3
1978	Simon (D)	110,298	65.6
	John T. Anderson (R)	57,763	34.4
1976	Simon (D)	152,344	67.4
	Peter G. Prineas (R)	73,766	32.6
1974	Simon (D)	108,417	59.6
	Val Oshel (R)	73,634	40.4

INDEX

Abernathy, Ralph David, 204
Abortion, 134, 149, 174, 220, 233
Adams, Brock, 252-253
Advertisements, negative, 11
Agnew, Spiro, 59
Agricultural policy
  Du Pont, 131-132
  Dukakis, 112-113
AIDS, 134, 239, 261
Allen, Robert, 25, 26
Anderson, Jack, 57
Anderson, John T., 256
Anderson, Richard, 25
Anderson, Warren M., 77
Andrus, Cecil, 29
Arafat, Yasir, 209
Arias, Oscar, 218
Arizona Health Care Cost Containment System, 29-30
Armstrong, William L., 35-36
Ashe, Victor H., 164, 165, 167
Askew, Reubin, 158
Aspin, Les, 164
Assad, Hafez, 209
Avery, William H., 92
AWACS sale, 183

Babbitt, Bruce E.
  attorney general, 26-27
  background, 18, 24-26
  campaign, 8-9, 14, 19-20, 31, 129
  governor, 21-23, 27-31
  policy stands, 17-19, 23, 31, 32
  previous elections results, 267
  Simon, 246
  taxes, 17-19

  water management plan, 22-23, 28-29
Badaracco, Joseph L., 142
Baker, Howard H. Jr., 62, 100
Bakker, Jim, 239
Barnes, Fred, 52
Baron, Alan, 48
Barr, Burton, 28
Bell, Jeffrey, 41, 42
Bell, Terrel H., 248
Bennett, William J., 248
Bentsen, Lloyd, 59
Biaggi, Mario, 73
Biden, Joseph R. Jr., 7, 119, 122, 152, 258
Black, Merle, 158
Black vote, Jackson and, 210-213, 259
Bolin, Wesley, 27-28
Bolles, Don, 27
Bolling, Richard, 142
Boren, David L., 165
Bork, Bill, 92
Bradley, Bill
  background, 9, 35-42
  interest group ratings, 43
  policy stands, 45-48
  previous elections results, 267
  Senate career, 42-45
  tax reform issues, 37-38, 44, 143
Brock, Bill, 102
Brock, David A., 83
Broder, David, 189
Brown, Harold, 181
Buchanan, Mary Estill, 191-192
Buchanan, Patrick, 180
Buckley, William F. Jr., 65
Bumpers, Dale, 6, 152, 258
Burke, Adrian, 72

273

Index

Burris, Roland W., 256
Bush, George
  background, 52, 58-59
  campaign of 1980, 51, 61-63
  campaign of 1988, 12, 63-65, 238
  civil rights issues, 54-56
  congressional career, 53-58
  Dole, 64
  heir to Reagan, 3
  Iran-contra affair, 8, 51, 63-64
  policy stands, 64-65
  political appointments held, 60-61
  previous elections results, 267
  vice presidential campaign of 1984, 51-52
  Watergate affair, 60
Bush, Prescott, 58
Buzick, Lon, 94
Byrd, Robert C., 101, 165
Byrd, Robert L., 126

Caddell, Pat, 157
Califano, Joseph A. Jr., 175, 206
Campaign contributions, 12, 13
Campaign organization, 12
Candidates' previous elections results, 267-271
Carey, Hugh L., 74, 75, 230
Carlson, Frank, 92
Carr, Howie, 116, 117
Carrick, William, 148
Carswell, G. Harrold, 95
Carter, Jimmy, 11, 102, 158, 240
Castro, Raul, 27
Cavanaugh, Thomas E., 210, 211
Challenger crash, 165
Champion, C. Hale, 118
Christian Broadcasting Network, 233, 236
Church, Frank, 61
Civil rights, 54-56, 92, 202-207
Clark, James B. "Champ," 151
Clark, Jimmy, 169
Clark, William, 182
Clinton, Bill, 6, 113, 152
Coelho, Tony, 146
Colby, William E., 61

Conable, Barber B. Jr., 225
Corcoran, Tom, 256
Cordrey, Richard, 126
Cox, Jack, 59
Cramer, William C., 56
Crash of 1929, 10
Crash of October 1987, 10
Cuomo, Mario
  background, 68, 71-74
  governor, 76-78, 80
  gubernatorial campaign, 74-76, 78-80
  involvement in 1984 presidential campaign, 69-70
  political philosophy, 70
  previous elections results, 268
  question regarding candidacy, 6, 9, 67-68, 83
  style and views, 81-82
Cuomo, Matilda, 72

Daley, Richard J., 207
Danforth, John C., 92
Darden, Claibourne, 168
Daschle, Thomas A., 113
Deaver, Michael, 182
Defense policy
  Haig, 173
  Hart, 193-194
Del Belo, Alfred B., 79
Delegate selection, "Super Tuesday," 13
Democratic Governors' Association (DGA), 19
Democratic Leadership Council, 19, 147
Democratic National Convention of 1984, 69-70
Democratic Party, pre-nominating season, 6-8
Democratic presidential candidates, 10, 11
Dewey, Thomas E., 254
Dicks, Norman D., 164
Dixon, Julian C., 221
Doak, David, 148
Dole, Bina, 87-88
Dole, Doran Ray, 87
Dole, Elizabeth Hanford, 98
Dole, Robert J.

Index

background, 86-87
Bush, 64
campaign of 1988, 3, 53, 85, 102-103, 133
campaign for vice presidency, 97-98
civil rights, 92
congressional career, 92-102
deficit, 101
interest group ratings, 94-95
Kemp, 226
military experience, 88-90
previous elections results, 268
taxes, 87, 99-100
Dominick, Peter H., 190-191
Donatiello, Nick, 46
Douglas, Paul H., 245
Dukakis, Euterpe, 113
Dukakis, Katharine "Kitty," 107
Dukakis, Michael S.
  accusations, 11
  agricultural issues, 112-113
  background, 106, 113-114
  Biden pull-out, 7, 119
  campaign of 1988, 12, 116-119, 153
  energy policy, 112
  governor, 105-113, 119
  gubernatorial campaign, 106-108, 114-118
  media coverage, 116-117
  political ideology, 110-111
  previous elections results, 269
  taxes, 112
  television skills, 117-118
Dukakis, Panos, 113
Du Pont, Eleuthère Iréné
Du Pont, Elise, 124
Du Pont, Pierre S., 123
Du Pont, Pierre S. "Pete," IV
  agricultural policy, 131-132
  background, 122-124
  campaign, 6, 9, 14, 52, 121, 128-131
  congressional career, 124-125
  drug policy, 122-124
  employment policy, 123-124
  governorship, 126-128
  interest group ratings, 130

policy, 122-123, 131-135
previous elections results, 269
tax policy, 135

Eagleton, Tom, 145
Eckstein, Paul, 22, 25, 26
Education policy
  Babbitt, 32
  Bush, 64-65
  Simon, 246-248
Eisenhower, Dwight D., 14-15
Employment and Training Choices, 111
Energy policy, 112
Environmental policy, 194-196
Epps, Garrett, 155
Estes, Billy Sol, 91
Evans, Rowland, 181
Evans, Timothy, 207
Evins, Joe, 161
Exon, J. James, 193

Fahrenkoph, Frank, 82
Falwell, Jerry, 240
Farrakhan, Louis, 209
Federal budget deficit, 8-9
Ferraro, Geraldine A., 51
Fink, Stanley M., 77
Fitzwater, Sidney A., 253
Fletcher, James C., 166
Ford, Gerald R., 61, 86, 97-98, 179-180
Foreign policy
  Bush, 64
  Haig, 173
Freedom Council, 240
Fulbright, J. William, 177

Gaines, Richard M., 117
Galbraith, John Kenneth, 59
Garcia, Robert, 221
Garfield, James A., 231
Gephardt, Jane, 137, 142
Gephardt, Loreen, 139, 142
Gephardt, Louis, 139
Gephardt, Richard A.
  abortion stand, 149
  agricultural regulation, 150-151

275

Index

background, 138-142
campaign of 1988, 138-139, 146, 151-153
campaign funding sources, 11
congressional career, 142-151
Dukakis, 112
Gore, 153, 168
interest group ratings, 145
policy stands, 139, 148-150
previous elections results, 269
Simon, 33, 153
tax reform, 37, 147
Gilligan, Robert, 128
Gingrich, Newt, 100
Ginsburg, Douglas H., 167
Glenn, John, 158
Goldwater, Barry, 123, 192
Goodman, Robert O., 209
Goodpaster, Andrew, 180
Gorbachev, Mikhail S., 209
Gordy, William J., 127
Gore, Albert Jr.
　arms control expertise, 162-165
　background, 156, 158-161
　campaign of 1988, 7-8, 155, 167-169
　congressional career, 161-167
　defense issues, 168
　interest group ratings, 163
　previous elections results, 270
　Senate campaign, 164
　"Super Tuesday" strategy, 155-158
Gore, Albert Sr., 158-160
Gore, Tipper, 160, 166-167
Gralike, Donald J., 142
Gray, Kenneth, 255
Greenfield, Jeff, 33
Greenstein, Robert, 246
Groundwater Management Act, 28-29
Gruening, Ernest, 59

Haig, Alexander M. Jr.
　background, 171-172
　campaign of 1988, 6, 8, 133, 173
　NATO commander, 180-181
　policy stands, 173-174
　political and military career, 173-179
　secretary of state, 181-184

Haig, Patricia, 174
Hamel, Chris, 17-18, 32
Harkin, Tom, 150-151
Harrell, David Edwin Jr., 241
Hart, Gary
　arms control expertise, 193-194
　background, 187-190
　campaign of 1984, 11, 151, 153, 196-198
　campaign of 1988, 6-7, 187-188, 198-199
　congressional career, 192-196
　environmental policy, 194-196
　interest group ratings, 195
　personal problems, 45, 198-199
　political philosophy, 193
　previous elections results, 270
　Senate campaign, 190-192
Hatch, Francis W. Jr., 107
Hatch, Orrin G., 220
Hawkins, Augustus, 249
Haynsworth, Clement F. Jr., 95
Helms, Jesse, 46, 100
Hersh, Seymour, 176
Hertzberg, Hendrik, 166
Hirschfeld, Abraham, 79
Hogan, Mark, 190
Hollings, Ernest F., 158
Holman, Phyllis E., 90, 91, 93-94
Huetig, Roger, 130
Humphrey, Hubert H., 12, 140, 245, 249
Hunt, Albert, 48
Hurwitz, Andrew, 22, 30
Hyatt, Gregory S., 115

Iowa caucus, 11-12, 151, 157
Iran-contra affair
　Bush's role, 8, 51, 173
　Dole, 101
　impact on Republican candidates, 10
　Traficant, 264

Jackson, Jesse L.
　background, 202-203
　black vote, 210-213, 259
　campaign of 1984, 158, 201, 209-211
　campaign of 1988, 7, 10, 208, 211-213, 239
　civil rights activity, 202-207

Jewish vote, 208-209, 212
  policy stands, 208-209
  previous elections results, 270
  role in Chicago politics, 207-208
Jamieson, Bill, 30
Javits, Jacob K., 230
Jewish vote, 208-209, 212
Johnson, Lyndon B., 59
Jones, James R., 253
Jordan, Hamilton, 146

Kariotis, George S., 115
Keane, James P., 230-231
Kemp, Jack
  abortion issue, 220
  background, 216, 227-229, 231
  campaign of 1988, 3, 215-216, 231
  congressional career, 217-227
  economic philosophy, 221-222, 227
  interest group ratings, 225
  policy stands, 219
  on social issues, 220-221
  support for supply-side economics, 221
  taxes, 99, 224-227
Kennedy, Edward M., 6, 248, 256
Kennedy, John F., 15
Kenton, Glenn C., 129
Kilpatrick, James J., 230
King, Edward J., 106-108, 115-116
King, Martin Luther Jr., 203
Kinnock, Neil, 119
Kirk, Paul, 19
Kirkpatrick, Jeane, 183
Kissinger, Henry, 176, 177
Kleckner, Dean, 132
Koch, Edward I., 74-76
Krupsak, Mary Anne, 73-74
Kull, Jane, 21

Laird, Melvin, 177
Lambrecht, Bill, 153
Lamm, Dick, 23-24
Lance, Bert, 212
LaRouche, Lyndon H. Jr., 261-262
Latham, Tom, 130
Laxalt, Paul, 226

Leach, Jim, 131
Lebanon, Israeli invasion, 184
Lehrman, Lew, 76
Leone, Richard, 41
Lindsay, John V., 73
Loeb, Nackey, 6
Long, Gillis, 143
Long, Russell, 43
Lucas, Peter, 116
Lundine, Stan, 79

McAteer, Ed, 165
McCarrick, Ed, 72
McCarthy, Richard "Max," 229
McCloskey, Pete, 235
McGovern, George, 11, 96, 189-190
McHale, Kevin, 117
Media coverage
  early campaign mechanics, 11-12
  Dukakis, 116-117
  impact, 12
  nominating season, 1-2
  Robertson, 239
Meese, Ed, 182
Military Reform Caucus, 193
Miller, Mel, 80
Mochary, Mary, 42
Moe, Richard, 148
Mondale, Walter F., 18, 69, 97, 158, 187, 197-198, 210, 257
Moose, Richard, 176-177
Mora, Jim, 228
Murphy, Evelyn, 118
MX missiles, 144, 164, 194

Nader, Ralph, 179
National Aeronautics and Space Administration (NASA), 165-166
National Security Council, 176-177
Negative advertisements, 11
New England, political independence, 115-116
New Hampshire primary, 11-12, 151, 157
Niskanen, William A., 131
Nixon, Richard, 15, 59, 60, 93, 177
North Atlantic Treaty Organization

Index

(NATO), 180-181
Nunn, Sam, 6

Obey, David R., 144, 253
O'Neill, Thomas P. Jr., 114-115, 144, 145
Operation Breadbasket, 203, 204, 206
Operation PUSH, 204-206
Ornstein, Norman, 83
O'Rourke, Andrew, 79-80
Oshel, Val, 255
Outierrez, Alfred, 21

Packwood, Robert, 38
Parent's Music Resource Center, 166
Pell, Claiborne, 182
People United to Save Humanity (PUSH), 204-206
Pepper, Claude, 137
Percy, Charles H., 243, 256, 257
Pines, Burton Yale, 131
Political magnetism, 9
Prayer in school, 233
Presidential campaign of 1960, 14-15
Presidential campaign of 1992, 14
Presidential nominating process changes, 12-13, 231
Primaries, 231
"PTL Club," 239
PUSH for excellence (PUSH-EXCEL), 206-207

Quinn, Robert, 114

Rath, Tom, 53
Rather, Dan, 51, 52
Reagan, Ronald
 election as referendum on terms in office, 2
 impact on Republican candidates, 10, 14, 233
 impact on Republican Party, 3
Reilly, Edward, 111
Religion in politics, 6, 209, 212, 239-240
Religious broadcasting, 233, 236, 239
Republican Party, 2-3
Republican presidential candidates, 9-10

Revenue and Enforcement and Protection (REAP), 112
Rice, Donna, 198
Richardson, Elliot, 179
Robertson, A. Willis, 234
Robertson, Adelia "Dede," 234, 236
Robertson, Marion G. "Pat"
 background, 234
 campaign, 3, 6, 233-241
 "invisible army," 240
 Jackson, 239
 military service controversy, 235
 policy stands, 239
 religious conversion, 236
Robinson, William I., 92
Rock, Philip J., 256
Rockefeller, Nelson A., 83
Rogers, Stanley, 161
Rogers, William, 177
Roosevelt, Franklin D., 14
Rostenkowski, Dan, 37, 38, 147
Roth, Herrick S., 190
Roy, William R., 96

Sarbanes, Paul, 182
Sargent, Francis W., 114
Sasso, John, 118-119
Sawyer, Eugene, 207
Saxbe, William, 93
Schlant, Ernestine, 41, 47
Schrum, Robert, 148
Seabrook nuclear power plant, 112
Sears, John W., 108
Seith, Alex, 257
"700 Club," 236
Shapiro, Irving S., 131
Shlaudeman, Harry, 184
Shultz, George, 184
Siegel, Mark, 259
Simon, Paul
 background, 244, 253-258
 campaign of 1988, 8, 152-153, 258-259
 congressional career, 247-253, 257-258
 federal budget, 250
 Gephardt, 33, 153
 interest group ratings, 252

278

Index

policy stands, 245-246
political ideology, 245-246
previous elections results, 271
Senate campaign, 256
Simpson, Alan K., 192
Smoot-Hawley Act, 150
Social Security, 9
Southern Baptist Church, 233-234
Southern candidates, "Super Tuesday," 13, 235-236
Southern Christian Leadership Conference (SCLC), 203, 204
Specter, Arlen, 88
Stassen, Harold, 262-263
Stephens, Bill, 29
Stevenson, Adlai E., 83
Stock market crash of 1929, 10
Stock market crash of October 1987, 10
Stockman, David, 143, 225
Strategic defense initiative (SDI), 134, 165, 218-219
Strauss, Robert, 201
Sullivan, Leonor K., 142
"Super Tuesday"
  Gephardt, 152
  Gore, 155-158
  impact, 2, 13
  Jackson, 212
  Robertson, 235-236
"Superdelegates," 152, 211
Supply-side economics, 221-222
Switzler, Royall H., 115
Symington, Stuart, 179
Synar, Mike, 144

Tax policy, 17-19, 112, 135, 246
Tax Reform Act of 1986, 37, 38
Thompson, Gordon, 160
Thurmond, Strom, 250

Traficant, James A. Jr., 263-265
Trippett, Sherman W., 126
Trippi, Joe, 148
Troy, Matthew, 73
Truman, Harry S, 83, 254
Tsongas, Paul, 182
Tully, Paul, 119

Udall, Stewart L., 189
Underwood, James, 82
U. S. Labor Party, 261

Van Buren, Martin, 53
Vance, Cyrus, 175
Veliotes, Nick, 46
Verenes, Chris, 157
Vietnam War, 175-177
Viguerie, Richard, 222

Walker, Daniel, 255
Wallace, George C., 158
Wanniski, Jude, 224
Warnicke, Ron, 25
Washington, Harold, 207
Watergate affair, 60, 96, 177-179, 182
Weicker, Lowell Jr., 96
White, Kevin H., 114
White, Robert, 182
Will, George, 60
Williams, Harrison A. Jr., 47
Wirth, Timothy E., 35, 36
Wolpe, Howard, 251
Woods, Harriett, 144-145

Yarborough, Ralph, 59
Young, Andrew, 203, 210
Young, Coleman, 210

Zappa, Frank, 166

E 880 .C365 1988

DATE DUE